If you ask what is the good in general of paideia [education],
the answer is easy. Paideia makes good men, and good men act nobly.
—Socrates, quoted by Plato

Fathers, do not exasperate your children; instead, bring them up in
the training [paideia] and instruction [nouthesia] of the Lord.
—St. Paul

To be a schoolmaster is next to being a king. Do you count it lowly employment
to imbue the minds of the young with the things of Christ and the best of
literature and return them to their homes honest and virtuous persons? In the
opinion of fools, it is a humble task; but in fact, it is the noblest of occupations.
—Desiderius Erasmus

All studies, philosophy, rhetoric, are followed for this one purpose,
that we may know Christ and honor Him. This is the
end of all learning and eloquence.
—Desiderius Erasmus

Moral education is impossible apart from the habitual vision of greatness.
—Alfred North Whitehead

The solution of a geometry problem does not in itself constitute a
precious gift, but the same law applies to it because it is the image of
something precious. Being a little fragment of particular truth, it is a pure
image of the unique, eternal, and living Truth, the very Truth that
once in a human voice declared: "I am the Truth."
—Simone Weil

We do indeed give the primacy to that spiritual truth revealed in the Bible
and incarnate in Christ. That does not mean, however, that those aspects of
truth discoverable by man in the realm of mathematics ~~chemistry~~
are any whit less God's truth than the truth as
the time there is the unity of all truth under God
in education at the peril of habituating ourselves
of learning found on some avowedly Christi
—Frank E. Gaebelein

D1516607

A CHRISTIAN
PAIDEIA

A CHRISTIAN
PAIDEIA

THE HABITUAL VISION
OF GREATNESS

D. BRUCE LOCKERBIE

purposeful design®
PUBLICATIONS
A Division of ACSI

Books, Textbooks, and Educational Resources
for Christian Educators and Schools Worldwide

Purposeful Design Publications is the publishing division of ACSI and is committed to the ministry of Christian school education, to enable Christian educators and schools worldwide to effectively prepare students for life. As the publisher of books, textbooks, and other educational resources within ACSI, Purposeful Design Publications strives to produce biblically sound materials that reflect Christian scholarship and stewardship and that address the identified needs of Christian schools around the world.

A Christian Paideia: The Habitual Vision of Greatness

ISBN 978-1-58331-064-9   Catalog #6527

Purposeful Design Publications
A Division of ACSI
PO Box 65130 • Colorado Springs, CO 80962-5130
www.acsi.org

Once more, to Lory:

by calling, a Christian who teaches;

by profession, a teacher of young children;

by her loving patience, a wife from whom I continue to learn.

CONTENTS

EDITOR'S NOTE

All the essays in this collection were first written and presented as addresses to a variety of audiences in a range of settings over a span of twenty-five years. Given the occasional nature of the original texts, which included introductory remarks, words of welcome, and incidental phrases, I have purposed to draw out the integrity and value of each piece apart from any reference to a particular gathering, event, or time and thereby make possible their reading for years to come.

One of the challenges, as I have seen it, has been to discriminate among the contingent elements, such as references to certain contemporaneous events and figures, in order to focus on the timeless principles of Christian schooling. Thus, I have seen fit at times to remove references to specific news headlines or popular culture icons where their impact and influence have diminished with time in favor of focusing on the enduring ideas and ideals of Christian schooling.

The collection divides into three parts, yet there remains an inherent, organic interconnectedness between them. Indeed, the philosophical and theological underpinnings of Christian schooling must inform both one's calling to it and the carrying out of that vocational mission in the best possible way. The integrated nature of the principles presented here, therefore, naturally calls for some overlap from chapter to chapter and from section to section. While I have aimed to reduce as much as possible any unnecessary redundancy, I have also allowed for the important reiteration of essential principles.

Finally, I would like to express my gratitude and appreciation to the author for the opportunity through his words to become better acquainted with and more greatly enriched by the history, ideas, and ideals of Christian schooling so clearly articulated here. It has been my privilege to know Christian schooling first as a daughter, then a student, and later a professor. In contributing to these pages, I am honored to come alongside my father in his calling to Christian schooling, to which he has dedicated his life's work.

Ellyn Lockerbie Grosh, PhD
Wilmette, Illinois
Winter 2005

Bruce Lockerbie had just turned thirty when he taught my senior English class at The Stony Brook School. He was a formidable teacher, highly entertaining and provocative in class, a relentless interlocutor, and very fond of his red pen when grading the weekly composition. I have a vivid memory of reading, nay, relishing *The Scarlet Letter, Hamlet, The Great Gatsby,* and above all *Moby-Dick,* thanks to him. For most of us seventeen-year-old boys he was, in roughly equal measure, both intimidating and inspiring.

What made him so? The obvious answer would seem to be that he possessed those gifts in effortless abundance that we sought or dreamed hopelessly of attaining: superb conditioning and speed afoot; a beautiful baritone voice that, unlike us, he was not ashamed to use; eloquence and wit coming out of every pore; smiling faith without doubts; and dashing self-assurance bordering on the boldness of a pirate. Being boys, we envied, admired, and resented him all at the same time; and he, bless him, seemed not to notice or care. He just charged on, never failing to supply rivers of red ink in the margins of our weekly compositions.

Later, as I came to know Lockerbie as a man, I began to appreciate the more significant reasons for our boyish ambivalence toward him. There was in our teacher a kind of integrity that we would not often encounter in this life, and it was that integrity, not his manifold gifts, that threatened and challenged us. He brought to everything he did the intensity of his faith, his convictions, his desire for excellence, his will to win, his uncompromising standard. Even his humor and friendships were tinged with the high seriousness of a disciplined and well-ordered life.

This book ostensibly celebrates the speaking gifts of my old teacher, but his eloquence is not in rhetorical flourishes. It is in his integrity and in his persistent call for integrity. In these speeches I encountered not only my old English teacher but a God-serving man tempered by a life spent largely in the service of schools, many of which call themselves "Christian." He is orthodox enough in his beliefs not to be surprised at living in a godless and iniquitous age, yet he is scandalized, as he ought to be, by the shameless hypocrisy and duplicity of believers who appear unwilling or unable to act in accordance with their words and beliefs, especially in their institutional lives.

The speech "Postmodernism, Cosmology, and Christian Schools" provides the context for this critique. Ironically, in this speech Lockerbie implicitly demonstrates the integrity of nonbelievers, whose postmodernist contempt for revealed religion, utter rejection of the existence of or necessity for absolute truth, and reliance on opinion rather than evidence make their assault on the Christian foundations of our society and its schools and colleges, although not commendable, at least consistent. The same, alas, cannot be said for many believers, who refuse to defend and live by the tenets of their faith, to be witnesses (martyrs) in a godless age, to teach and learn as though "all truth is God's truth," to be contemporaneous with Christ, and to live in the moment between His judgment and His mercy.

In speech after speech, Lockerbie sounds this theme. Whether speaking of the Christian school's fear of an inductive and objective search for truth, its use of secular models of pedagogy and curriculum, its neglect of rigorous Bible study at every grade level, its exclusion of non-Christian students and families, its submission to the state's dumbed-down teacher certification requirements and school accreditation standards, its refusal to deal fairly and charitably with headmasters, or its unwillingness to *value* Christian *paideia* as evidenced by what it pays teachers and charges parents who are capable of paying what a Christian *paideia* is worth—Lockerbie is calling into question the integrity of the Christian school movement and of those who govern and lead these schools. It's a stunning and disheartening indictment. The wonder—and the saving grace—is that so many Christians are willing to listen to it.

Lockerbie's discipleship to Christ as Lord makes him critical of the lack of integrity in both increasingly incompatible traditions in which he lives, works, and worships: the evangelical and the Episcopal. In both traditions, he is, like one of his heroes, Socrates, a gadfly—tolerated by Episcopalians, who exalt tolerance over obedience to the Word of God (now largely discredited in their worldly minds by modern science and reason), and by evangelicals, for whom self-flagellation can be a substitute for obedience. In this book, Lockerbie's audience is primarily the evangelical who, in spite of all his claims of biblical belief, is unwilling to "renew his mind" in conformity with the precepts of Scripture, or perhaps to have a mind at all, preferring to find his *paideia* within a mindless, meretricious American culture.

I have had some experience working within or near these two traditions myself, heading what one might call the "missing links," namely, schools having Christian foundations or affirming Christian traditions that have drifted along with society into a secular intolerance of the very Christian teachings that motivated their founders. In one of these schools, named for a saint with unequivocal teachings on the rules of life and sexual morality, we were never to refer to "rules" since doing so was said to violate a canon of contemporary adolescent psychology, and students were encouraged *from the pulpit* to "share [their] sexual gifts" with one another, albeit through the "safe" medium of a condom. (That priest is now a bishop.) At another school the controversy over the teaching of the

Bible *as literature* was so great that it could be done only in the primary school, and even then only Old Testament stories could be taught. Where is the integrity in that? Should those schools not change their names, rewrite their charters, and adopt new mission statements?

Probably not. Words are changing their meanings. Soon their new meanings will obviate the need to make these revisions, either because the old charters will interest only antiquarians or because their words will mean whatever the powers that be *now* choose to have them mean. As we have seen repeatedly in our public life, we can lie with impunity simply by claiming a different, more personal meaning for our words. Whereas once it was assumed that I was wrong if I failed in my arbitrary use of language to make my meaning clear, it is now, in our solipsistic age, others who are wrong if they fail to hear what I mean. This subversion of language is profound and broad and devastating in its consequences, especially to our sense of integrity, a high-sounding word that now means whatever one wants it to mean. We can all have integrity simply by defining it to fit our own sorry behavior.

My old English teacher surely understands this. That is why he labored many years ago over those barely literate compositions, insisting that we use the right words rightly, his contribution to our *paideia*, our civilization, our integrity. Yet when words no longer preserve or protect a meaning, how is it possible for there to be a correspondence between words and deeds? And then what becomes of integrity itself? Thus Lockerbie's case for an authentic Christian *paideia* and his unmasking of our postmodern age's hidden (and not so hidden) agenda become all the more urgent. As the French philosopher and theologian Jacques Ellul recognized after World War II, the Christian faith may have to invent another language (or resurrect a dead one) if it is to convey the meaning (and power) of its original message.

Lockerbie's speeches demonstrate that the degradation of modern language's meaning and usage is not an esoteric or irrelevant observation. It lies at the heart of the Christian's ability to hand on his *paideia* to his children, as well as at the heart of our civilization's ability to connect with its own past and of its people's ability to sustain a purposeful and meaningful dialogue with one another.

David V. Hicks
Harrison, Montana

PREFACE

The chapters in this book represent the texts of some of my speeches delivered over a half century and spanning my vocation as a Christian school educator.

This calling did not start with a Damascus road epiphany, nor even with God's voice in the night calling the boy Samuel or the young man Isaiah. In fact, it happened slowly, over time. Beginning in the fall of 1956, after my graduation from New York University, I arrived at Wheaton College in Illinois to teach English, assist in coaching track with Gil Dodds, and take graduate courses in theology. I remember well my own surprise when I discovered that, far above those courses in theology and even more than the coaching duties, I enjoyed preparing for and teaching my English students.

In the spring of 1957, Frank E. Gaebelein, founding headmaster at The Stony Brook School on Long Island, New York, invited my wife, Lory, and me to join the work there. Over the next thirty-four years, that work included teaching English and Bible, coaching track and cross-country, supervising a boarding-student residence hall, directing choral and instrumental music, coaching the debate team, and editing the alumni quarterly—the full array of duties common to a boarding-school faculty member. After serving as dean of faculty, I was honored to be named the Thomas F. Staley Foundation Scholar-in-Residence, a position that allowed me to represent the school around the world.

Rather early in my vocation, I began to speak and write about Christian schooling as I understood it and as it was practiced at The Stony Brook School. Frank Gaebelein had recently published *The Pattern of God's Truth*, making the case that "all truth is God's truth." The now-familiar call for "the integration of faith and learning" was not yet a cliché of Christian education. Some of my early bookings, therefore, asked specifically for me to address the implications of *integration* for the classroom teacher. I delivered these addresses—among other places—at the Park Street Church in Boston, at Calvary Baptist Church in New York City, and at the annual convention of the Christian Businessmen's Committee in Bal Harbour, Florida.

In 1962, I returned to Wheaton College to address the Conference on Writing and Literature; so began my interest in framing some of my talks around literary topics. Eventually, these grew into a series of lectures, often sponsored by the Staley Foundation, published in book form as *The Liberating Word: Art and the Mystery of the Gospel, The Timeless Moment: Creativity and the Christian Faith,* and *Dismissing God: Modern Writers' Struggle Against Religion.*

By 1970, I had been commissioned to write a history of The Stony Brook School's first fifty years, entitled *The Way They Should Go*. For this task I needed to acquire a bootstrap knowledge of the history of education and the several philosophies that had dominated Western and especially American schooling. Published in 1972 by Oxford University Press, that book, by its wide reception, gave me credibility as an observer of and commentator on Christian schooling and led me to present a broader historical overview in *A Passion for Learning: A History of Christian Thought on Education*, published by Moody Press in 1994.

As my teaching and administrative experience grew, I developed a fuller grasp of the scope of Christian schooling. Now my interest extended beyond philosophy and curriculum to the operational details, including marketing and financial concerns. I discovered that, although my assignment may have been to speak about how a teacher might integrate his Christian faith with Shakespeare's sonnets or challenge students to adopt a biblical worldview in their academic studies, I was also being asked to have lunch with the admissions committee or the development officer. I realized that I was being asked for advice over a wide range of institutional issues. All I needed to qualify as a consultant was to charge a fee for my wisdom!

Through my association with the National Council of Teachers of English, the College Board, the Educational Testing Service, the National Assessment of Educational Progress, and other agencies came opportunities to expand my professional experience. In 1964, the College Board appointed me its first educational consultant for the Advanced Placement Program, later also for International Baccalaureate. In 1973, Vernon Grounds of Denver Seminary invited me to be among the leaders of the inaugural Summer Institute on Faith and Learning, sponsored by what has become the Council of Christian Colleges and Universities. Thereafter, my consulting included institutions of Christian higher education.

In 1984, James A. Adare, then my colleague at Stony Brook, joined me in founding PAIDEIA Inc., using the Greek word for *education*, a word familiar to Socrates, Plato, Aristotle, and Paul of Tarsus. By 1991, burgeoning consulting obligations had overtaken my commitment to The Stony Brook School, so I resigned to take up the duties of PAIDEIA Inc. full-time. In God's providence, our work has grown, and PAIDEIA Inc. now serves institutions and agencies across the spectrum of worthy causes. A grant from the Lilly Endowment Inc. led to my writing *From Candy Sales to Committed Donors: A Guide to Financing Christian Schools* (1996), which appears to have influenced Christian schooling to strengthen its financial base in support of the mission to educate.

Many of these addresses were prepared expressly for events sponsored by the Association of Christian Schools International, whose Purposeful Design Publications has produced this book. I am grateful to friends at ACSI who have sponsored my opportunities to prepare and deliver these remarks: Alan Graustein, Jerry Haddock, Derek Keenan, Mark Kennedy, Bob Miller, Roger Norrie, Rohn Ritzema, David Rhodes, Randy Ross, John Schimmer, Ken Smitherman, and John Storey. I thank Steve Babbitt, director of publishing services, for his help in seeing this book into print and Mary A. Endres for her thoughtful editorial assistance.

I am also grateful to my daughter, Ellyn Lockerbie Grosh, who brought her keen eyes and her gift for language to the task of compiling, editing, and adapting these oral addresses for reading.

In publishing this collection, I hope to encourage other Christian educators, as I myself have been encouraged.

D. Bruce Lockerbie
Stony Brook, New York
Winter 2005

ACKNOWLEDGMENTS

Throughout these texts I have taken ample opportunity to credit Frank E. Gaebelein with much of my early thinking about what it means to be a Christian who teaches and leads a school.

I wish also to acknowledge others who influenced my developing vocation. Donn M. Gaebelein and Karl E. Soderstrom, who followed as headmasters of The Stony Brook School, provided me freedom to grow. Older and admired colleagues at Stony Brook set a high standard of Christian example: Pierson Curtis, Marvin W. Goldberg, John Warren Hershey, O. Floyd Johnson, and Donald W. Marshall.

Several persons on the margins of my life exerted influence greater than they will ever know: Kenneth O. Gangel, Vernon C. Grounds, Mark O. Hatfield, Gerald F. Hawthorne, Carl F. H. Henry, J. Wesley Ingles, Clyde S. Kilby, D. Elton Trueblood, Stanley M. Wiersma, and Sherwood Wirt.

My profound thanks to all who engaged with me in serious debate and challenged my yet unformed and fragmentary understanding of the vocation of a Christian-who-teaches, thereby helping me eventually to set down on paper my philosophy, principles, and practices for attaining a Christian *paideia*.

D.B.L.

ONE

WISDOM AND WORLDVIEW,
KNOWLEDGE AND EPISTEMOLOGY,
UNDERSTANDING AND INTEGRATION

INTRODUCTION TO PART 1

Christian schooling is an organized, institutional effort to educate the young. In particular, it is a cooperative alliance among parents in the home and spiritual mentors in the church and school. Because it purports to be "Christian," it is grounded in the precepts of Holy Scripture. It finds its mandate in the language of God's message through Moses to the people of Israel:

> Hear, O Israel: The Lord our God, the Lord is one. Love the Lord your God with all your heart and with all your soul and with all your strength. These commandments that I give you today are to be upon your hearts. Impress them on your children. Talk about them when you sit at home and when you walk along the road, when you lie down and when you get up. Tie them as symbols on your hands and bind them on your foreheads. Write them on the doorframes of your houses and on your gates. (Deuteronomy 6:4–9)

This command of God through Moses calls upon parents to claim for themselves, then convey to their children, a recognition of God's *wisdom* and His delight in human *knowledge*, but also His insistence upon *understanding* as essential to living according to His standards. These parents were to imbue their offspring with a clear sense of who the God of Abraham, Isaac, and Jacob really is and what He demands of those who claim to follow His law and precepts.

To obey this command fully would require a new methodology, a new pedagogy, based on an all-encompassing, all-pervading relationship with "the Lord our God." The command charges God's people to "impress ...

on your children" the character of God and the mandate to love Him completely—every day from dawn to dusk and in every aspect of life.

Only so could the children of former slaves in Egypt be prevented from acquiring by default an idolatrous worldview through an education such as Moses himself must have had to overcome. Only so could God's people begin to possess an epistemology—a system of knowing—rooted in their confidence in God's attributes. Only so could they learn to appreciate the *wholeness* of an integrated life of faith and obedience.

Two thousand years later, the same sort of instruction came to godly parents in a different cultural context. The Greco-Roman world espoused an education, or *paideia*, that was founded on principles of civic responsibility and character development. In *The Republic*, Plato quotes Socrates as follows: "If you ask what is the good in general of *paideia*, the answer is easy. *Paideia* produces good men, and good men act nobly." So Greek families sent their sons to teachers like Socrates, Plato, and Aristotle to learn the arts and sciences of *paideia* and to learn how to "act nobly."

But Paul of Tarsus—trained in Jewish theology and Greek philosophy and Roman law—knew that mere *paideia* was not sufficient to overcome the ignoble fetters of sin. For that, a child must be taught something different, something more. So St. Paul urges the parents in Ephesus to "bring up your children in the *paideia* ... of the Lord" (Ephesians 6:4).

Today's Christian school participates in the heritage of the Israelites on their pilgrimage to the Promised Land and in the legacy of the Early Church in its departure from the customs and philosophy of education in the pagan Mediterranean world. Just as God summons Moses to institute a new system of educating children, so the apostle Paul differentiates between the *paideia* of Socrates' academy and "the *paideia* ... of the Lord."

What is that difference? What are the marks of a Christian *paideia*?

1

A BIBLICAL SYSTEM OF KNOWING

This address was first presented to the administration and faculty of Green Valley Christian School in Watsonville, California, on October 8, 1999.

What are the distinctives of a Christian school? What are your school's distinctives? If, as happens regularly, my office telephone were to ring and someone asked me to recommend a worthy school somewhere in your community, why would your school come to mind? What is it about your school's vision, mission, and plan that sets it apart from other schools? How is your school's philosophy different? Please, don't say merely that you have a caring and dedicated faculty, as if that were somehow unique to your institution. Please, don't suggest that you have involved parents or supportive boosters. None of these is a distinctive that sets your Christian school apart.

What, then, can you offer? To begin—and sadly so!—your school might stand out in many people's estimate if only because it takes more seriously than most Christian schools its mission—rather, its obligation— to be utterly and entirely committed to being a *school!* My contention is this: the primary and only legitimate purpose for our school's existence *as a school* is to be a place of academic teaching and learning where Jesus Christ is honored as Lord. Note the absolute phrase *as a school.* We who have been called by God to serve Him might have chosen to do so in any of at least a hundred different ways. We might have founded a yearlong youth retreat; we might have begun a drug counseling center or a hospice for unwed mothers or a senior citizens' community. Instead, we chose to found or join a *school*, which by its very name conveys certain expectations among those who choose to enroll and send their children to us.

What, then, are the essentials of a genuinely *Christian* education in a Christian school? I believe there are several we can list:

1. A founding vision to be an educational institution that honors Jesus Christ
2. A mission to educate students and point them toward becoming disciples of Jesus Christ
3. A commitment to hire and retain only adults whose Christian faith is manifest in their vocation

These three elements are fundamental to the founding and sustaining of a Christian school.

School means teaching and learning in a formal manner and setting to fulfill its mission. Even those who oppose institutionalized schooling and prefer home schooling recognize the necessity of setting aside a time and a designated location in the home for the formalities of teaching and learning. But teaching and learning alone are no guarantee of Christian schooling. Not even teaching by and learning from godly teachers guarantees the fullness of Christian schooling that produces mature and maturing Christian disciples, although that's certainly a start. In fact, it's more than a start; it's what Frank E. Gaebelein called "the *sine qua non* of Christian schooling: no Christian education without Christian teachers."

Now to some educators who call themselves Christian, such a statement as Gaebelein's is unacceptable. It's far too narrow, provincial, and restrictive. It hinders the kind of open dialogue they favor among persons of diverse religious faiths—or even no religious faith. It presupposes that a benign secular humanist or professed agnostic or earnest Muslim has nothing to contribute to our students' learning. And if we go so far as to insist on appointing Christian believers rather than unbelievers to the faculty of our school, we find ourselves accused of educational quackery and—far worse, in these days of political correctness—a lack of sensitivity regarding issues of diversity and multiculturalism.

We all know about such schools. In Atlanta, after forty years of requiring that all board and faculty members profess Christian faith, an eminent school changed its policy, eliminating those restrictive clauses. The new head-of-school was pandering to an emotional appeal by Jewish civic leaders who used the threat of a potential charge of anti-Semitism to gain their ends. With astonishing speed, the board acted to do the expedient thing: they voted to welcome non-Christians to the board and to the classroom. The case became another instance in the tragedy of American education: the collapse of an educational institution's heritage of Christian faith. Even so remote an observer as Ed Koch, the former mayor of New York City, commented on the folly of the board: "If this school calls itself a Christian school, then they ought to hire Christian teachers. Does a yeshiva hire non-Jews to teach how to be a better Jew?"

Here's where the governing board in Atlanta failed the test: in addition to its failure to recognize the inherent relationship between institutional purpose and the personnel who carry out that purpose—"the *sine qua non* of Christian schooling"—the school board in Atlanta suffered from another defect. They didn't know or comprehend the significance of a distinctly Christian way of acquiring wisdom, knowledge, and understanding, the importance of advancing a biblical recognition of wholeness. Yes, it's essential to the mission of Christian schooling that we enlist committed disciples of Jesus Christ to do the work of Christian schooling. Yes, it's important that we set as our goal certain desired outcomes for our graduates. But even then—even with earnest believers on the board, in administrative offices, and in our classrooms—we haven't guaranteed that our school will be a place where teachers and students together are increasing in the knowledge of God.

There's something more to be attained before we can be sure of reaching that goal—three more objectives our school must reach:

4. A thoroughly developed biblical world-and-life view that permeates the curriculum
5. A commitment to a biblical epistemology, or system of knowing
6. A rigorous effort to seek and present the integration of biblical truth

In short, that "something more" is a philosophy of education whose approach to teaching commends to both teachers and students a way of learning entirely different from a secular methodology: teaching and learning from the vantage of a Christian world-and-life view, with a biblical epistemology and a conscious effort to discover the wholeness of biblical integration—truth in whole rather than in fragments.

What, then, do I mean by this fancy phrase "Christian world-and-life view"? Its origin is the German word *weltanschauung*, and it presumes a metaphor or analogy for *point-of-view, vantage point,* or *perspective.* For instance, some people exist as if all of life were lived in a cell behind bars. Prince Hamlet speaks of his dead father's kingdom, now under his uncle's usurping rule, and says, "Denmark's a prison." So too, your less eager students may see their schooling from the point of view of unwilling subjects sent to a destination not of their choosing for a term of twelve or fifteen years. Sounds like a prison sentence, doesn't it? The worldview of those students is going to be shaped by every connection they can make to incarceration and confinement. The attitudes they project will help to form the platform on which they stand and from which they look out on the world.

That's how I choose to define *worldview* for you, as "a place to stand." By this I mean that every human being finds a figurative platform or vantage from which to take his or her moral bearings and find a moral outlook on life. We talk about worldviews informally whenever we compare life to a voyage or a game or a race. In fact, our schools use a Latin word meaning "race course" or "the track inside the stadium"—the word *curriculum*. Some time ago, I was a middle-distance runner, competing in major races against world-class competition. As my career as a runner was winding down, I turned to a novel event called the steeplechase—a race almost two miles long with thirty-five barriers to leap, including a water jump three feet deep and twelve feet long.

Your school's curriculum, the course your students must pursue from start to finish, is like a steeplechase in that it demands stamina. Along the way, there will be numerous hurdles for students to negotiate without stumbling. You may well ask them, Did you get off to a good start? Are you keeping up with the leaders? Have you set a goal for yourself? Are you aiming for one of our school's highest academic distinctions, or will you be content to be among the also-rans who get a diploma just for finishing the course?

For Christians, there is also a world-and-life view to inform our lives. The Christian perspective derives from biblical assertions declaring the existence of God, His work in creation, humankind's sinful nature, God's plan in history to redeem humans through the incarnation and atonement of Jesus Christ, God's sustaining work through the Holy Spirit's presence in each believer and in the church, and the consummation of history in the disclosure of the Lordship of Jesus Christ and God's ultimate judgment. These are the basic planks in the platform that supports a biblical world-and-life view. And what is that platform, that place to stand? The Christian worldview finds its platform at the foot of the cross and at the door of the empty tomb. From that vantage, the Christian looks out and sees a world that is in need of redemption. The Christian also sees a world that has been redeemed from the emptiness and moral bankruptcy of death.

We cannot overemphasize the importance of acquiring and representing a Christian worldview. We cannot overstress the need to determine our place to stand and to use that vantage to influence and reflect every private thought and every public act. Representing a Christian worldview ought to be the hallmark of any mature experience with Jesus Christ in the life of a believer, whatever his or her calling or occupation. But for us as Christian school educators, understanding the significance of a worldview is a matter of the greatest urgency and therefore ought to be the primary focus of our profession.

But beyond a place to stand, every Christian school needs the structure of a thinking process, or an epistemology. *Webster's New Collegiate Dictionary*, Eleventh Edition, defines *epistemology* as "the study or a theory of the nature and grounds of knowledge, especially with reference to its limits and validity." Thus *epistemology* is simply the technical word for answering these questions:

1. How do we know what we know?
2. How do we know that what we know is true?

Let's begin with the first question, *How do we know what we know?* Or, on a larger scale, we might ask, *How do we know anything at all?* Sometimes—but only rarely—we know by experience or, as scientists might say, by empirical evidence, but mostly we know what we know by faith. That is, we take the word of somebody else—a sports play-by-play announcer or a political reporter or a doctor offering his diagnosis or a stockbroker reading the Wall Street ticker or a salesperson saying how elegant that new dress looks. Even the least religious person cannot live much of a life except by faith.

In the spiritual realm—the metaphysical rather than the physical—we may still rely upon tangible, tactile, physical evidence. The empty tomb is one such piece of evidence. But while we rejoice in the facts of our reasonable hope, we who are believers in God the Father Almighty, maker of heaven and earth, and in Jesus Christ, His only Son our Lord, must also accept a great deal of what we believe by faith, without the blessing of tangible evidence. Our starting point must be the conviction that God *is*, God exists. The writer of the letter to the Hebrews states it this way: "[A]nyone who comes to [God] must believe that he exists and that he rewards those who earnestly seek him" (Hebrews 11:6). The reward of believing that God exists is the growing realization that God will not make fools of us for so believing. God will affirm His existence in our very lives, blessing us with the assurance of His presence among us.

The next stage in our faith is acknowledging that God is personal, possessing the characteristics we call attributes, the foremost of which is *truth*. The particular attributes are apportioned among the Persons of the Trinity: thus, God the Father reveals the attribute we call *volition*, or divine will; He wills the world into being. God the Son—the Eternal Word—possesses the attribute we know as *communication*, or divine reason; He speaks the world into existence. God the Holy Spirit has the attribute we know as *illumination*, or divine light; He enlightens the darkened cosmos and the mind of every human being.

Fearfully and wonderfully as we are made—*in imago dei*, in the image of God—we human beings, uniquely among all creatures, possess these same divine attributes. We can will, we can speak, we can illumine our world with the light of reason. Like the Trinity—although with manifestly limited powers—we are able to summon miniature universes into being. We call it our creativity—our *poiesis*—though in reality we create nothing in the way God does—*ex nihilo*, or out of nothing. We have merely engaged in the art of *mimesis*, the art of imitating the Creator.

Furthermore, we can engage with the Trinity in the threefold aspects of *wisdom*, *knowledge*, and *understanding*. How do these terms differ from each other? By definition, we hold that God's divine wisdom exceeds our comprehension. God's wisdom is enveloped in mystery and is disclosed to us only as God chooses. Thus there are some things that God withholds from our grasp, including many of the answers to our question, *Why?*

Next, God is concerned that we human beings exercise the gift of knowledge that He has given specifically to us. Other creatures possess instincts, including sexual urges, reactions to fear or hunger, and predatory impulses, and other creatures can be trained to react or respond to repeated stimuli. Only human beings can use the powers of will, expression, and illumined reason to acquire a knowledge of nature and human nature. Furthermore, by what reformed theologians call "the cultural mandate" of Genesis 1 and 2, God summons His human creatures to learn all that can be known about our environment and our role as its stewards. We are commissioned to be bearers of the image of God as artists, keepers of the historical tradition, and perpetuators of the glory of God.

But God is also concerned that human beings learn spiritual understanding, or discernment. Since the wisdom of God is dispensed to us solely at His discretion, and since the totality of human knowledge is beyond the scope of any one of us, it behooves us to treat with great care and discretion whatever wisdom and knowledge we are granted. Such discretion is available to us as a gift of the Holy Spirit, who offers understanding, or discernment, as a means of guiding us into all truth. For it is *truth*—the end result of coming to perceive God's wisdom through human knowledge and with the benefit of discernment—that we must seek.

When we begin to comprehend the meaning and significance of a biblical epistemology, we will hold two seemingly opposite tenets in dynamic tension: First, we will boldly assert the existence of truth and the importance of making truth the goal of learning. Second, we will humbly acknowledge a need for balance between recognizing our inadequate human condition and affirming that God encourages the quest for wisdom, knowledge, and understanding.

Without apology, we will assert the fact that absolute, objective truth exists. Furthermore, we will assert that objective truth, rooted in the eternal and lasting verities of the character of God, is *true* because it *is*. So we will have no need for shame when we maintain that *life* begins when sperm and egg fuse to form an embryo; no need to look askance when we insist that *marriage* implicitly refers to a relationship between a man and a woman; no need to be embarrassed when we hold that there is no such thing as moral neutrality or benign unbelief that has no effect on the way we teach or coach or otherwise influence our students.

At the same time, we will not hesitate to admit that the quest for knowledge is always incomplete without a complementary quest for wisdom and understanding. We will have no hesitancy about acknowledging how past errors—such as justifying slavery or the three-tiered universe—have been exacerbated by finite yet doctrinaire pronouncements lacking verifiability. We must all be willing to say that we see through a glass darkly. We never have the last word on truth, but we must act by whatever light we are given. So on moral issues we accept God's promise or declaration; on nonmoral issues we rely on evidence that conforms to principles of reason; on all doubtful matters we retain a humble attitude.

We are called to be a teacher or an administrator or a board member, and in that high calling we are required to know what we know. Furthermore, it helps if what we know we know is true! But beyond our scholarship—which we must never denigrate or treat cheaply—beyond our grasp of God's wisdom and the scope of our human knowledge, lies the gift of discernment, the gift of understanding. It isn't always how intellectual we are that touches a child. What matters most is the grace with which we teach. For, as the great Moravian pastor John Amos Comenius, the "father of modern education," once said, "God does not call us to heaven asking us smart questions. It is more profitable to know things humbly than to know them proudly" (Simon S. Laurie, *John Amos*

Comenius, His Life and Educational Works [Cambridge: Pitt Press Series, 1895]).

Finding our place to stand, asserting the validity of our biblical world-view, and recognizing a distinctively biblical system of knowing—all these lead to the possibility of *integration*, redeeming the brokenness and fragmentation around us and finding wholeness. For some time now, Christian higher education, in colleges and seminaries, has been talking about "the integration of faith and learning." Much of this emphasis stems from a book written not by a college professor or seminary president but by a schoolman, my headmaster and mentor Frank E. Gaebelein. That book is *The Pattern of God's Truth*, which is still in print, thanks to ACSI. Gaebelein argues two points: first, that "all truth is God's truth." In so bold a declaration, Gaebelein was not uttering anything new; in fact, he was citing the early church fathers Justin Martyr and Augustine of Hippo.

The early fathers and Frank Gaebelein span almost 2,000 years, yet the message is the same. The God we worship is both holy and wholly integrated; it is we who by our sinful nature are broken and disintegrated. But this concept had almost been forgotten when the young Frank Gaebelein, barely twenty-three years old, was asked to found a boarding school for boys. He had a vision—well beyond his time—of a school where the Lordship of Jesus Christ and the authority of the Bible were at the center to provide an education that could be whole. So in his inaugural address in 1922, he called for such a school. Thirty years later, in 1952 at Dallas Theological Seminary, he gave a set of lectures that became *The Pattern of God's Truth*. Again, his theme was integration.

I worked in that school, which was Frank Gaebelein's only model for biblical integration. In fact, he hired me to teach English and direct music and coach track and live with my wife in a boys' dormitory when we were only four years older than our charges. Let me confess to you that I did not arrive at The Stony Brook School already knowing the slogans of integration or practicing it in my classroom. In fact, I will tell you that I was well along in my career and priding myself on my rising status in the National Council of Teachers of English and other professional groups, while at the same time glorying in the self-assurance that nobody visiting my Advanced Placement English class would mistake me for a Christian teacher. I was chairman of the English department at The Stony Brook School, and I didn't know the meaning of "the integration of faith and learning."

Why was I so ignorant and hostile toward appearing to be a Christian teacher? Because even though Frank Gaebelein was my headmaster, even though I had read his book, even though I was receiving the benefits of his editorial critique of my early attempts at writing for publication—I had formed a poor impression of what it means to infuse my teaching of language and literature with the verities of Scripture. I didn't know the difference between *integration* and sermonizing or preaching platitudes to my students. Because I didn't know the difference, I avoided as much as possible tacking a moral lesson onto a poem, as in the children's party game "Pin the Tail on the Donkey."

My ignorance kept me from integration. But my ignorance extended beyond mere philosophy or pedagogical method. I was also fundamentally ignorant of the Bible—*me*, a Baptist preacher's kid who had memorized Bible verses, who had a university major in religion and graduate courses in theology from a leading evangelical institution! But I didn't really know the text of Scripture until a colleague became ill and I was asked to substitute for him over several weeks in an eleventh-grade Bible class. Preparing lessons for the inductive study of Matthew's Gospel was what introduced me to the realities of integration through an intimate acquaintance with the Word of God.

Yes, I came to know the significance of the axiom "All truth is God's truth." But for me an often overlooked second phrase is even more compelling: Gaebelein speaks of "the unity of all truth under God." What does this mean? It means that nothing is outside the warp and woof of the Almighty's great tapestry. Even the tiniest thread, seemingly unrelated to the central image, has its place in the great pattern of things. The starting point, as always, is the individual teacher's personal relationship with God-in-Christ and the Christian worldview that presupposes the sovereignty of God and the authority of Scripture. Once we begin to think in such terms, we'll begin to experience what Gaebelein calls "the unity of all truth under God"—the realization that everything is connected to everything else.

But as with all such realizations, when once they become our passion, it's easy to assume that they ought to be everyone else's passion as well. Thus is born ideology and cant and the language of propaganda. Once I became convinced of the importance of integrating the truth of Scripture with my course work in reading and writing, I expected everyone to be just as excited and to do the same! Here's when I began to learn a useful lesson, which I'd like to illustrate with an account of a different kind of integration.

In the winter of 1947, the chief executive officer of a major corporation made a stunning decision to promote an employee. That CEO was Branch Rickey; that corporation was the Brooklyn Dodgers baseball club; that employee was an infielder named Jack Roosevelt Robinson, then assigned to the Montreal Royals in the International League. So the first African-American player was introduced to major league baseball. And was baseball thereafter integrated? Did white players welcome black players into their homes and communities and churches and schools? Did white fans accept and cheer loudly for Jackie Robinson and Larry Doby and Roy Campanella and Don Newcombe and Satchell Paige? And now, decades later, how integrated is America as a result of the national pastime's eliminating the color barrier? Ask the same questions of America's schools: Since the 1954 Supreme Court decision, *Brown v. Board of Education*, are Topeka's schools fully blended so that race is no longer an issue? Is your Christian school entirely representative of the racial population of your community?

What's my point? Simply this: *integration* cannot be achieved by legislating from on high. Thirty years of court-ordered busing has proved that. The same is true for intellectual and spiritual integration. As head-of-school or curriculum coordinator or chairman of the school board's educational policy committee—whatever your role—you cannot draft a memo that declares, "Starting Monday, all teachers will integrate their lessons with their faith." It just won't work. Rather, we must encourage every Christian school teacher, administrator, and board member to seek integration as an *individual*. One must find its application to one's own *vocation* before it can become *institutional* and a distinctive of the school.

Worldview, epistemology, integration—it all begins with finding a biblical place to stand—not an easy task. One reason for the difficulty is that modern society knows nothing of—indeed, appears to want nothing to do with—a whole vision of life, especially when that vision is based on claims of authority revealed from a divine source. At the same time, many evangelical Christians are just as lacking in their ability to grasp what wholeness might represent. They have adopted a dualism that partitions life into categories called "sacred" and "secular." Their spiritual immaturity results in a lack of discernment, in teaching that fails to perceive instances of grace in common life. Instead, they package their spirituality in specifically pious acts reserved for appointed times and places, regarding as neutral or even suspect their presumably less spiritual acts. So attending chapel or studying the Bible is *spiritual*, whereas attending a lecture or studying history is *secular*. Says who? Some of our students are unprepared to recognize in their academic studies the same efficacy of grace they expect from a missions trip. It is this very contradiction that our schools must seek to replace with a perspective of biblical reality, a biblical worldview.

Developing a Christian worldview means more than merely adopting a philosophical perspective. It also means what St. Paul urges, to "take captive every thought to make it obedient to Christ" (2 Corinthians 10:5). It means thinking-and-acting like a Christian. Those of us in Christian schooling claim a very specific calling, primarily of helping young people in their preparation for a lifetime of learning and of joyful and willing service to Jesus Christ. As an administrator or teacher or board member, your calling is to assist these young people—and where necessary their teachers—in acquiring a solid world-and-life view, finding a place to stand that will give a true and balanced vision of reality through the lens of Scripture.

Let us be convinced of what we believe to be true; let us live in the light of that conviction. But let us also remember what the pastor of the Pilgrim voyagers told them just before they sailed aboard the *Mayflower.* Pastor John Robinson, too ill to make the voyage himself, preached their farewell sermon and said, "I am verily persuaded the Lord hath more truth and light yet to break forth out of His holy Word." Let us therefore live and teach and learn in the glow of that promise.

2

INTEGRATION AND THE LIFE WORTH LIVING

The year 1994 marked the fortieth anniversary of the publishing of The Pattern of God's Truth, *the groundbreaking book on Christian education by Frank E. Gaebelein. Because the book had originated as the W. H. Griffith Thomas Lectures at Dallas Theological Seminary, PAIDEIA Inc. collaborated with the seminary in sponsoring the Frank E. Gaebelein Memorial Colloquium on September 23–24, 1994. Speakers included Gretchen Gaebelein Hull, daughter of Frank E. Gaebelein; Kenneth O. Gangel, then academic dean of the seminary; Vernon C. Grounds, chancellor of Denver Seminary; and the late James Montgomery Boice, alumnus of* The Stony Brook School *and then pastor of Tenth Presbyterian Church in Philadelphia, Pennsylvania. This was the closing address at the Gaebelein Memorial Colloquium.*

I last saw Frank E. Gaebelein in October 1982. The occasion was alumni weekend at The Stony Brook School on Long Island, sixty miles east of New York City. As headmaster emeritus, retired for nineteen years, Dr. Gaebelein was present with his friend, the Honorable Mark O. Hatfield, United States Senator from Oregon, for the dedication of Gaebelein Hall, a spacious library and classroom building.

A crowd of some two thousand had assembled for the occasion—the current student body and faculty, trustees and their friends, graduates of the school, members of the community. An amphitheater of folding chairs faced the handsome new Georgian building with its white pillars. But as the band played a processional hymn and the platform party began to make its way toward the site, the crowd broke from their seats to line the walk as a guard of honor in tribute to the one for whom the building was to be named.

For the last time, Frank Gaebelein walked up Chapman Parkway, a boulevard lined with Japanese elms and named for the Presbyterian pastor J.Wilbur Chapman, whose songs "Our Great Savior" and "One Day When Heaven Was Filled with His Praises" had first been sung in the tabernacle at the top of the hill. As a younger man, the athletic headmaster had often raced students up the length of that campus drive. Now he came haltingly, steadied by those walking with him.

It was a moment not to be forgotten—a vignette worthy of photographic recall—not merely because of the sentimental history of a small school on Long Island but for the sake of the Kingdom of our Lord and of His Christ. For that procession to the podium may well have represented the true passing of one era and the inception of another.

Not that Frank Gaebelein and Mark Hatfield were in any respect subject to the hierarchies of generational separation by chronological age; but they were different in vocation and sphere of service. Gaebelein had never quite been for Hatfield the mentor he was for Carl F. H. Henry, who—as a young and newly converted newspaper editor on Long Island—sought Gaebelein's counsel for his own calling. Instead, Gaebelein and Hatfield, so alike in their prayerful bond of friendship, were very different in their public ministries. One represented the academy, the other, the political arena; one, the pulpit, the other, the stump; one, the realm of theological argument, the other, the art of political consensus.

Here, then, came the pedagogue and scholar, accompanied by the former college professor, sometime governor and now senator; here came the biblical expositor and his weekly Bible study colleague; here came the civil rights proponent and the civil rights legislator; here came the philosopher of Christian integration and with him the practicing politician of evangelical purpose and principles.

Recalling that day in October 1982, I suggest its parallel with an earlier event, exactly sixty years before. For in the fall of 1922, in the tabernacle just beyond where Gaebelein Hall now stands, another crowd had gathered, this time for the inaugural ceremonies that would commence the work of The Stony Brook School. On that occasion, Frank E. Gaebelein— all of twenty-three years old and fresh from graduate studies at Harvard University—had just concluded a year of planning curriculum and recruiting both students and faculty for the new school. His youthful horizons had seemed unrestricted by the realities of other people's decision making. He had anticipated opening a school with 150 or more boys who would come for university preparation in a context of biblical precept and godly example. To that end, he had crisscrossed the country in search of the finest teachers and the ablest students.

The result of his labors sat before him on that inaugural day: nine men and women appointed to teach a total of 27 boys, ranging in age and ability from very young children of mixed scholastic gifts to young men of promise—including one student who, after only a year, would become Stony Brook's first graduate and first one to be admitted to Princeton University.

To have worked so hard for a year with such high expectations and hopes; to have hired away from their secure positions at stable schools experienced and equally hopeful teachers; to have made his case before countless audiences of interested parents, and then to find only a few more than two dozen students—how could anyone not feel disappointed?

But both the address he gave that day in 1922 and the remarks he made at the dedication of Gaebelein Hall in 1982 reveal the sort of man that was Frank E. Gaebelein. In short, his speeches were focused not on human endeavor and accomplishment but on the truth and reliability of the Holy Scriptures. He was not a man easily discouraged or readily rebuffed by adversity. After all, he was an accomplished pianist who had mastered the intricacies of a Bach two-part invention; he was a technical mountaineer who had learned to overcome both the rock face and the fear it produced. In those experiences, he had found grace to help in time of other kinds of need. He had put his faith to the test and found it sufficient.

And what does the example of such faith-in-action mean to us today? Much has happened in the years since Frank Gaebelein last walked the Stony Brook campus. We have witnessed astonishing changes in the world at large, in this nation's government, in our political and social standards, in attitudes toward education, in the challenges facing our schools—most particularly, in the conflicts between secular values and spiritual virtues.

Thank God for the few evangelical voices in positions of national leadership calling not for a return to mere "traditional family values" but for a revival of truly *biblical* virtues. But what about the rest of us? Where is the political will of the far-fabled evangelical majority that every Gallup Poll announces as "born again" and trusting in Jesus for personal salvation? Where is the evidence of spiritual wholeness or biblical integrity derived from living our lives in a harmony of faith and action? Where can we find the example of integrated and balanced Christian experience? How can we learn by analogy what the architects of a suspension bridge must know: how to maintain the flexibility, adaptability, imagination, and creative capacity we need to fulfill our responsibilities while at the same time losing none of our strength or purpose?

As Christians, we are called to examine ourselves and renew our serious commitment to achieving harmony in faith and life. But we are also called to critique our culture, to note how and why we are less effective witnesses for Jesus Christ than those who, two thousand years ago, "turned the world upside down" (Acts 17:6, KJV). We need to anticipate the future, to think ahead and project what options might be available to Christians wishing to live integrated lives; to seek the guidance of God in weighing how best to live out our faith in a manner that seems most reasonable, practicable, workable, and potentially effective for witness.

There is no single *Christian* philosophy of witness; however, there are varieties of ways of making known the mystery that is "Christ in you, the hope of glory" (Colossians 1:27). Some resolves may lend themselves more readily than others to exemplifying biblical virtues while examining and evaluating secular values to discover what compatibility there may be with Scripture's teaching, if any. The philosophy to which Frank Gaebelein subscribed might be summed up as the quest for a biblically integrated life—the life worth living, a life with a purpose fulfilling itself day by day.

And what is that high purpose? For us as for him, that purpose is nothing else than to teach and remind each other that "the fear of the Lord" (Psalm 111:10) is the starting point for the pursuit of wisdom, knowledge, and understanding. Equally, the fear of the Lord is the final goal. For as Desiderius Erasmus wrote, "All studies, rhetoric, philosophy are followed for this one object, that we may know Christ and honor him. This is the end of all learning and eloquence" (*The Collected Works of Erasmus*, J. K. Sowards, ed. [Toronto: University of Toronto, 1985]).

To achieve such a high purpose—to fulfill such a grand mission— requires a strategy that will help our feeble human intellect to grasp and retain its glorious calling. This strategy has been known since the beginning of the church, when St. Paul wrote to the Roman and Corinthian and Colossian believers, as well as to Timothy and Titus, about their need to infuse their minds with truth. To the Romans, Paul spoke of a process of mental transformation and renewal; to the Corinthians, of possessing and becoming possessed by "the mind of Christ" (1 Corinthians 2:16), taking captive every thought and making it subject to His Lordship; to the Colossians, of entering into the treasury of wisdom and knowledge that is hidden in Christ; to Timothy and Titus, of making sanctified use of the academic skills of argument and persuasion learned in their pagan academies.

Clearly, the apostle Paul was urging his converts to recognize the presence of God's truth in all of wisdom, knowledge, and understanding. Surely, he would affirm, there are categories and levels of truth. There is *salvific* truth—that is, truth about how to be saved. But there is also truth about the rainbow, truth about volcanoes, truth about Neil Armstrong's 1969 walk on the moon; truth about a child's growing up in a secure home with loving parents; truth about the basic reasons for economic cycles as well as the rise and fall of nations. The learned Paul of Tarsus wanted his converts to perceive the truth of God in all of these spheres.

Following his example, most of the church fathers taught the same doctrine. Justin Martyr told the Senate of Rome, "Whatever has been uttered aright by any man at any time belongs to us Christians" ("The Second Apology," *The Fathers of the Church*, Thomas B. Falls, ed. [New York: Christian Heritage, 1948]). Augustine of Hippo wrote that "every good and true Christian must recognize that wherever he may find truth, it is his Lord's" (*On Christian Doctrine*, D. W. Robertson Jr., trans. [Indianapolis, IN: Bobbs-Merrill, 1958]). Some, like Tertullian, opposed any broad acceptance of human knowledge as a reservoir for divine truth. But over the intervening centuries—with only exceptional periods of anti-intellectualism—orthodox Christianity has come to believe that, if Jesus Christ is "the way, the truth, and the life," then truth has no other origin than in Him.

For most of his years as head of a college-preparatory school, Gaebelein doubled as a writer and editor, producing books of his own, editing a monthly magazine called *Our Hope*, serving on the board and editorial committees for the American Tract Society and for such works as the Scofield Reference Bible. His book *Christian Education in a Democracy*, published in 1951, was commissioned by the National Association of Evangelicals as an answer to the Harvard report *General Education in a Free Society*.

Ever since those inaugural ceremonies at Stony Brook in 1922, Frank Gaebelein had been reiterating the teaching of the church fathers about the need to find intimations of wholeness in the revelation of God, and looking for a means to correlate human knowledge and understanding with the wisdom of God. In that early speech, Gaebelein spoke of the word *correlate* as "happily chosen because it summarizes the essentials of the Stony Brook plan.... The central aim of this school is to correlate Christian principles, the great and eternal verities, with education of a type high enough to merit intimacy with such exalted ideals."

Three decades later, when invited to deliver the W. H. Griffith Thomas Lectures at Dallas Theological Seminary, Gaebelein prepared a series of addresses that would spell out the case for understanding God's truth as a whole more succinctly than anyone else had attempted in the last 1,500 years since the Bishop of Hippo had written his treatise *On Christian*

Doctrine. But Gaebelein chose a new image for these lectures. Instead of using the term *correlate*, he now spoke of a need to *integrate*, a term both more dramatic and more demanding. While his case for integration is rigorous, Gaebelein succeeded in paring away layers of theory and theological obfuscation by condensing his argument to a single sentence of just five words: "All truth is God's truth."

These lectures, repeated the following year at Denver's Conservative Baptist Seminary, were prepared for publication by Oxford University Press in 1954 under the title *The Pattern of God's Truth: Problems of Integration in Christian Education*. In an early passage, Gaebelein stated his thesis: "All truth is God's truth." The thesis wasn't new, but the succinctness of his phrase made it a maxim. In a short time, *The Pattern of God's Truth* became the single most influential book on the reading lists and in the libraries of Christian school educators. In its forty years, the book has never been out of print. Some leaders I know tell me that they reread *The Pattern of God's Truth* every single year.

What are the deep implications of Gaebelein's words "All truth is God's truth"? Of course, to speak in terms of *truth* and of *God's truth* is to identify oneself as someone convinced that truth is more than a relative, subjective human perception. Such terms indicate that we have taken a stance, adopting a world-and-life view that sees reality in terms of divine transcendence belonging to a personal God who is the very source and fountainhead of truth. Beyond this assertion, to speak of *God's truth* is to affirm that God has wonderfully chosen to communicate His truth to us— *and that we can know it*.

None of these presuppositions comes easily; nor does what follows. We are on a journey toward full apprehension of God's truth. None of us has yet arrived at that destination, which is only to be reached when we fall prostrate in the very presence of God. Until then, we must be willing to grapple with the meaning of *truth* and its counterfeits. We must study the mediation of truth to us in wisdom, knowledge, and understanding. We must also be prepared to wrestle with the complexities of *epistemology*, the study not only of how we know what we know but also—and more importantly—how we know that what we know is true. Then we must immerse ourselves in truth, infusing what we know and understand with truth about God's interest in such knowledge and understanding. And we must transmit to others, by precept and example, our sense of wholeness as we speak about nature and human nature in relation to God's truth.

We call this phenomenon *integration* because it has to do with our perception of the integrity or wholeness of truth, including the question that is generally ignored by the secular scholar: *What is God's interest in this matter?* This is the paramount question. To help in finding its answer, integration means drawing many fragmented parts into a whole; integration means finding that the whole thereby obtained is indeed greater than the sum of its many parts. Integration sees not merely the multiplicity of threads that make up the warp and woof but also the pattern in the tapestry. Integration understands that no filament of knowledge, no aspect of human endeavor, no gift or talent or skill or craft exists in a vacuum apart from anything else.

Those of us who are called Christians find the call to integration spelled out clearly in Holy Scripture. We are summoned to wholeness, first, by knowing who God is and loving Him as Lord. We are commanded to love with our whole being: heart, soul, strength, and mind. In doing so, we learn both how to appreciate our own gift of life and also what it means to love others as ourselves. The same principle holds for the educational principle called integration. It must begin within. Thus, integration must first be *personal*, then *vocational*, and only afterward *institutional*.

To desire personal integration means that one aspires to have not only an integrated intellect but an integrated life. In this world of broken promises and broken spirits, broken hearts and broken homes, a working model of integration is hard to find. For the Christian, however, that model comes to us from St. Paul's challenge to adopt "the mind of Christ."

Unlike a Supreme Court justice, God doesn't compel us to act in obedience to His will. He intends, rather, to win our willingness through a process of transformation and renewal: as Ben Haden puts it, changed lives signified by a changed way of thinking and acting. But we aren't to be left in a vacuum of transformation and renewal, devoid of guidance and instruction. We have—by God's grace—the apostolic teaching, the Gospel narratives, the history of God's dealings with His people in the Law and the Prophets. In short, we have the Bible and its claim to be not only God's written revelation but also the normative standard for Christian behavior.

We need Christian leaders willing to stand firm on both the biblical criteria for faith and the objective truth of the Bible. This is a broad and bold subject, but here let me merely point out that the necessity of affirming objective truth has never been more urgent. Objective truth is true because it *is*. Just as the first step in knowing God is to "believe that He exists" (Hebrews 11:6), so the first step in knowing objective truth is to believe that it exists and is true. With all due respect to the late astronaut Jim Irwin and his search for Noah's ark, archaeology doesn't prove the Bible to be true; archaeology *confirms* the accuracy of the Bible's account. But if Noah's ark can never be found, is the Bible less true? If a grave were to be discovered with the remains of a man crucified two thousand years ago, would that invalidate the Resurrection?

To be an integrated person—of one mind intellectually—one needs to be a whole person in all four dimensions of one's being and experience: mentally, physically, emotionally, and socially. So having "the mind of Christ" demonstrates itself beyond formal worship through service to others. Since Jesus Christ is Lord, we honor Him by humbly and consistently making ourselves the servant of others. Here again, compulsion will never achieve the desired end. We cannot force someone to demonstrate brotherly love or to use her gifts for the sake of someone else. Such acts come only from within.

But there is more to being a whole person than simply taking all knowledge to be your province. In fact, in order to become a whole person—in biblical terms—one needs to come to terms with the differences among divine *wisdom*, human *knowledge*, and spiritual *understanding*. In short, to become a whole person in biblical terms means coming to recognize how God's epistemology works.

The first premise of a Christian epistemology is this: God knows more than we know. God's wisdom exceeds human knowledge. Divine wisdom is both ineffable and incarnate; it is both mystery and revelation. But this does not discredit human knowledge or make it of no importance. Some careless readers of Genesis 3 assume that the sin of Adam and Eve was to eat the fruit of the tree of knowledge, as if God would have preferred to keep them innocent and ignorant. Not so. The tree from which they ate the fruit was the tree of *the knowledge of good and evil*. It was the same tree whose fruit hangs on display for young children whose parents are indiscriminate about the television viewed and the music played in their homes. Suddenly a child's naïveté is shocked into knowledge in advance of his years, and he knows what he need not have known—what God in fact would have preserved him from ever knowing if only Eve and Adam had not yielded to disobedience, vanity, and deception.

Nonetheless, God encourages human knowledge. Indeed, the cultural mandate under which every human being lives as a caretaker of God's creation—including the other creatures ordained by God—demands that we come to know and understand nature and human nature. We are to study this planet and its place in the cosmos, the atoms of which we are made, and our own place in the cosmic scheme of things. And with that instrument of human knowledge, we may also approach the outer ranges of God's wisdom.

To that end we have been given the capacity to appreciate beauty, to marvel at magnificence, to weep over human tragedy, to aspire to a greatness of which we perceive only a shadow, to overcome certain limitations inherent in our mortality, such as disease and its causes. So we study physics, we learn the mechanics of architecture, we remember and organize the events of the past, we travel by ever-faster conveyances to distant points, we celebrate new discoveries, we acquire information, we express ourselves in prose and poetry, and we adorn our lives with art.

But as biblical Christians, we never assume that human knowing inevitably leads to the heart of divine wisdom. We believe that the heart of divine wisdom is ultimate truth, but experience teaches us that far too often human knowledge leads not to truth but to error. Therefore, we need to temper our quest for human knowledge with a gift called *understanding*.

Understanding empowers us with the ability to use our human knowledge in such a way that it connects with and complements divine wisdom. Understanding is the grace that enables us to appropriate what we know and implement that knowledge with tact and sensitivity and humility. To sum it up, understanding means *discernment*. We often hear references to "the wisdom of Solomon," but it seems more accurate to refer specifically to what Solomon asked of God and received, "a discerning heart" (1 Kings 3:9).

The gift of discernment—understanding—is what marks the potential of human intellect as exceeding the powers of artificial intelligence. The gift of discernment spells the difference between an effective use of one's intellect and mere genius. For without discernment, none of us is more than an idiot savant, able to retrieve useless data like a computer run amok.

Wisdom and knowledge demand discernment. American poet Emily Dickinson illustrates our need for discernment in this poem (*The Complete Poems of Emily Dickinson*, Thomas H. Johnson, ed. [Boston: Little, Brown, 1960]):

> Tell all the Truth but tell it slant—
> Success in Circuit lies
> Too bright for our infirm Delight
> The Truth's superb surprise—
>
> As lightning to the Children eased
> With explanation kind
> The Truth must dazzle gradually
> Or every man be blind—

What is the poet's message? It's not sufficient to dazzle someone with an undeflected bolt of God's wisdom; that's too much for anyone to bear. It's not even sufficient to convey our vast knowledge to someone who is terrified by the thunder and lightning. What frightened child wants to hear a lecture on the properties of electricity and their phenomenal appearance in thunderstorms whenever meteorological conditions combine to form a collision of frontal systems? What that child needs is an "explanation kind"—a story about how, whenever God goes bowling, all the angels clap every time He gets a strike. Yes, we need the gift of understanding—the gift of entering empathetically into someone else's condition, feeling what she or he is feeling, and using God's wisdom and our knowledge to find a different means of telling all the Truth we know.

But like all other good and perfect gifts, such a gift of understanding comes only from the Father. Understanding comes as a result of faith and hope and obedience. Understanding comes in relation to the development of a biblical understanding of reality, a biblical epistemology, a biblical world-and-life view. And, frankly, it comes more slowly to some than to others. That's why integration at the institutional level is hardest of all.

Some of us in the Christian community—but by no means all—have been trained to think in such terms. We need more such Christians who think: mature persons who see reality through the lens of biblical reason; reasoning persons who think in Christian categories about their art or science, about their marketing strategy or human resources decisions, about current events and history, about entertainment and creature comforts, about personal and interpersonal relations. Such thinking is the core of what it means to achieve harmony in faith and action, to live an integrated life: one that begins from within and extends outward, one that encompasses our whole being—heart, soul, mind, and strength—as individual believers and inspires the whole being of those with whom we have to do.

An integrated life acknowledges what Frank Gaebelein named "the unity of all truth under God." And to encourage such a realization, we need able and godly spouses and friends, pastors and administrators, executives and encouragers, who also think in Christian categories and who also perceive the unity of all truth under God. Only so can we hope to lead the church of Jesus Christ toward a renewal of what it means to live each day in such a manner as to reflect the wholeness of God's truth.

If we are to redeem "the integration of faith and learning" and "all truth is God's truth" from devaluation as evangelical clichés; if we are to imbue ourselves, our families and friends, our congregations and colleagues and students, with insight that opens us all to "the unity of all truth under God"; if we are to achieve these ends, we must avoid three dangers inherent in our work.

The first danger is that of ignoring any need to integrate. This is the folly of a thoroughly secularized mind that denies the obvious: that the *dis*-integration we see all around us suggests a need for *re*-integration. Such a mind has been desensitized to any recognition that faith and work stand on common ground. This mentality is represented in the error of public education with its impossible fiats against incorporating instruction even in social values—never mind moral virtues—for fear of offending someone.

This is also the worldview that defends political scalawags on the grounds that either their personal wretchedness or their Bible toting on Sunday mornings has nothing to do with the way they fulfill the public trust. In the midst of President Clinton's publicized personal scandal, I recall hearing one state's governor declare, "Who cares? I just want to know if he punches in on time the next morning." What better definition of secularized disintegration could we seek?

But the tendency to ignore any need to integrate is also the perspective of some professing Christians who also see themselves as somehow bifurcated into sanctified churchgoers on Sunday and secular professionals the rest of the week. Do we not see such people in Christian homes and churches and schools?

The second danger is that of taking integration for granted. Here we confront several false assumptions. Too often we assume that personal faith in Jesus Christ qualifies someone to teach or administer in a Christian school or college or seminary in a manner that promotes the integration of faith and learning. This fallacy suggests that example alone conveys an understanding of integration. It doesn't. Example is priceless, but example needs explanation and expression, an explicit articulation of *who* and *what* are being exemplified, and *why*.

A second way of taking integration for granted is assuming that being a Christian automatically leads to living that is Christian. It doesn't. The Christian who teaches or preaches or sells or drives a truck needs preparation and method and strategies and alternatives to doing that work, plus an openness to the spontaneous illumination of the Holy Spirit. But I recall, from thirty-five years of classroom teaching, that the Holy Spirit blessed me with spontaneous illumination in direct proportion to the degree of labor I put into my lesson plans and lectures. This rule reminds me of what the South African pro golfer Gary Player says, "The harder you work, the luckier you get" (http://en.thinkexist.com/quotations/golf/). If students in Christian schools, colleges, and seminaries—and Christians in the pews—are to learn to recognize what Gaebelein calls "the unity of all truth under God," it won't happen through luck or magic. It begins in prayer at the outset of one's preparation and continues to the end of the lesson or sermon or sale or eighteen-wheeler's haul.

The third assumption in taking integration for granted is that integrated living happens apart from the close study of God's Word. It doesn't. No one can bring the light of Scripture's truth to shine upon our work without really knowing what Scripture says. To put it bluntly, you can't integrate out of ignorance. Thus, our Christian teachers and administrators, pastors and physicians, salesmen and truck drivers need formal and informal Bible study on a continuing basis as a means of sharpening their integrative skills.

But if the second danger is taking integration for granted, the third lies in overdoing and thereby trivializing any attempt at integration. I'm thinking of those few schools that teach arithmetic based on biblical numerology or botany derived from a study of all the plants in the Bible. Here the intentions are earnest, the motivation is high, the conscientiousness unimpeachable. But the method is too pretentious or too picayune. It lends itself to that worst of all examples of Christian pedagogy so rife in pious textbooks—what Edgar Allan Poe called "the didactic moral lesson"—tacking on a homily at the end of a poem. If integration doesn't apply to the real world, it doesn't apply at all.

What we need is balance. Integration fuses two objective realities into one truth. But we must first recognize the existence of each seemingly separated reality and deal with each on its own terms before we can achieve such balance. Taking integration for granted is one form of imbalance; overdoing an attempt at integrating is another. The Swiss theologian Emil Brunner offered this constructive analysis of the task facing us: "The nearer anything lies to that center of existence where we are concerned with the whole, that is, with man's relation to God and the being of the person, the greater the disturbance of rational knowledge by sin" (*Man in Revolt: A Christian Anthology*, Olive Wyon, trans. [Philadelphia: Westminster Press, 1947]).

Our challenge is to recognize this reality and adapt our living accordingly. To paraphrase Socrates, the disintegrated life is not worth living; and to quote one greater than Socrates, "I have come that they may have life, and have it to the full" (John 10:10).

So this process of integration grows as we mature spiritually and intellectually. I am convinced that integration cannot be taught primarily as a course in anybody's education department. It must be taught and learned through personal, vocational, and then institutional example.

And it must be learned anew every day.

3

POSTMODERNISM, COSMOLOGY, AND CHRISTIAN SCHOOLS

This address was prepared as a white paper for the Middle Atlantic Christian School Association and was delivered on February 26, 1999, at Eastern University in St. Davids, Pennsylvania. It was later presented at various ACSI events from Anchorage, Alaska, to Columbia, South Carolina.

> The only remaining "ism" is postmodernism, which is not an ideology but a repudiation of ideologies. Its relativism is the admission that every attempt to construct a comprehensive, utopian world-view has failed. It is a formalized expression of despair.
>
> —Charles Colson ("The Sky Isn't Falling," *Christianity Today*, January 11, 1999)

One of the most overworked terms in popular use among the self-proclaimed intellectual elite is *postmodern* or *postmodernism*. Hardly anyone knows what it means if, indeed, it has any valid meaning! But used repeatedly, the term takes on a life and influence far exceeding its denotation. In fact, its connotations help to define the prevailing attitudes of secular-minded men and women at the beginning of a new millennium.

In choosing to discuss "Postmodernism, Cosmology, and Christian Schools," I am undertaking to deal with a topic about which I do not consider myself an expert, merely an observer of the phenomenon. In fact, *postmodernism* is a word I try to avoid using because I consider the very term suspect—an invention, an inflated neologism concocted for the purpose of sounding erudite and profound when speaking of something essentially as shallow and corrupt as is much of current culture and the attitudes it engenders. Yet, for all its meretricious mystery and sham sophistication, postmodernism is too influential a concept to be ignored. Furthermore, in its disdain for a sovereign and transcendent God, postmodernism is too pervasive an attitude for Christians—in particular, those of us who are educators—to ignore.

For these and other reasons, I am eager to grapple with postmodernism and its manifestations in our society. Charles Colson calls postmodernism "the only remaining 'ism' ... which is not an ideology but a repudiation of all ideologies" and "a formalized expression of despair." This is a helpful beginning; but let me choose not to begin in the conventional manner, by defining postmodernism and assuming that I have thereby boxed it in for subsequent dissection and analysis. Instead of nailing down a definition of postmodernism, I'd like to do a typically postmodernist thing and allow the definition to arise from my observation of the movement in actual life, beginning with a few stories.

My book *Dismissing God: Modern Writers' Struggle Against Religion* is about exactly that: reducing God as a factor in anyone's life. The book presents the life and work of two dozen American, British, and European writers. In most cases, it traces their spiritual pilgrimage from a religious—sometimes, indeed, godly—upbringing to skepticism, agnosticism, unbelief, militant disbelief, and finally cold contempt for the very notion of faith. One of those authors is the poet Emily Dickinson. Among her nearly eighteen hundred poems is this gem (*The Complete Poems of Emily Dickinson*, Thomas H. Johnson, ed. [Boston: Little, Brown, 1960]):

> Those—dying then—
> Knew where they went—
> They went to God's Right Hand—
> That Hand is amputated now
> And God cannot be found—
>
> The abdication of Belief
> Makes the behavior small—
> Better an ignis fatuus
> Than no illume at all—

Dickinson expresses at once both orthodoxy's certainty and apostasy's uncertainty. In only nine lines, she moves us from the limitless expanse of being in the presence of God to a confining existence marked by discarded faith; from the sure light of hope in the promises of God to the false light of despair. Her poem reminds me of a contemporary figure, not a world-class man of letters, yet certainly a well-known American. As a young man, he was student chaplain at his boarding school and leader of the foreign missions prayer group. Sounds like everybody's ideal teenager. His name is Ted Turner, and he has since described the Christianity of his youth as "a religion for losers" (*Dallas Morning News*, June 14, 1990).

Another story: In my final year of teaching at The Stony Brook School, I assigned—as always—a passage from St. Paul's letter to the Romans to be recited from memory. On the appointed day, I was standing at the classroom door and welcoming my students, one at a time, to step into the corridor and recite from chapter 8, beginning at the familiar 28th verse, "And we know that in all things God works for the good of those who love him," and ending with its transcendent climax in verse 39, "neither height nor depth, nor anything else in all creation, will be able to separate us from the love of God that is in Christ Jesus our Lord."

I called on a young woman, a brilliant student already accepted for admission to one of the most selective colleges. She came to the corridor and began to recite flawlessly; then she hesitated and stopped. I assumed that she had suffered a lapse of memory and began feeding her the next line. She waved me off, assuring me that she had learned the text. Then she began to cry. I tried to console her, and again she protested. "I can't say these words anymore. I no longer believe them," she told me. I asked her if she cared to explain. Through her tears and sobs she told me, "I used to consider myself a believer." "Why *used to?*" I inquired. "It wasn't intellectually respectable anymore to be a believer," she replied. "There were just too many things I couldn't explain."

Here's another story: On December 18, 1998, *The New York Times* carried on its front page news of an international scandal. An anthropologist named David Stoll has been studying the life and work of Rigoberta Menchu, an indigenous Guatemalan woman whose account of human rights abuses among Central American native peoples won her the Nobel Peace Prize. Now Stoll finds that much of her autobiography cannot be substantiated. For instance, her claim never to have received any formal education is contradicted by a group of Roman Catholic nuns who taught her in their school. So, what have we here? The letters to the editor, published two days later, defend the woman and attack the investigator. One letter excuses her excesses by asking, "Where are the rules for autobiography written down anyway?"

Similarly, an eminent American historian, Daniel Horowitz, published a book about a woman who also reinvented her life story, omitting all her experiences—from before World War II—as a Marxist sympathizer, a left-wing activist, and a labor union agitator, organizer, and journalist. Instead, in 1963, she presented herself as just a typical suburban housewife seeking to escape what she called "the feminine mystique." Her name, of course, is Betty Friedan. Curiously, Ms. Friedan and her cohorts on the radical fringe of feminism are displeased that anyone should have bothered to correct a record she had so carefully altered.

In these seemingly unrelated incidents, we have some of the effects of postmodernism in microscopic proportions: contempt for God, disdain for truth as an absolute, intellectual arrogance, *ends* to justify whatever *means*, and above all, self-determined ethical and moral standards subject to no higher authority. For unlike modernism—which asserts itself to be in rebellion, takes on a convention of its own, and becomes as dogmatic as what it overthrew—postmodernism insists upon the vacating of any standards, any precedents, any criteria, anything that might be classified as judgmental or value-based—anything beyond one's own private code. By the standards of postmodernism, any claim that truth exists as an objective reality, that it can be known and communicated as such to others, must be regarded as an ethical flaw, a character defect that makes one, at the very least, an unacceptable dinner guest. Thus postmodernism restores the ancient maxim of Protagoras: "Man is the measure of all things." This mandate applies most particularly to religious standards, as illustrated in the following story.

One of New York City's most popular morning broadcasters is a woman named Joan Hamburg, whose program is generally geared to helping women obtain bargains. But sometimes she alters her program with a topical discussion, as she did on one pre-Christmas occasion. Her studio guests were women of various religious persuasions married to men of every other possible religious preference: something like a Lutheran married to a Buddhist, a Reform Jew married to a Moonie, a Quaker married to a Hindu—you get the idea. They were all talking in terribly pleasant terms about how they celebrate the religious holidays so that nobody gets offended, and the telephone calls were coming in from listeners simply delighted to learn how this was possible. Then came a call from someone who said, "You can only be holding this discussion because your particular religious convictions are of no consequence to you."

The air went dead. Joan Hamburg was speechless, her guests dumbstruck. Then they retaliated, and you would have thought that this caller had declared World War III. The host castigated him as someone of mean spirit and ill will, a bigot and a grinch. The guests expressed their outrage that anyone could accuse them of being insincere about their respective religious traditions. You see, in the middle of a postmodernist dialogue, he had uttered a truth, a statement so stark in its reality that it cut through all the falsity of polite speech by daring to declare what polite speech sought to obscure: if we believe that religion matters at all, it matters precisely because it is of ultimate significance and cannot be compromised into a *mélange* of comfortable doctrines, whereby I'll give up the Trinity if you drop the notion of reincarnation.

But postmodernism has never been able to extirpate religion from real life. As every reasonable person knows, politics and religion are the obverse and reverse of the same coin; they join the material and the spiritual sides of human experience, things earthly to things heavenly. Politics and religion are economically and psychologically inseparable. Tragically, they are also linked militarily, as the ongoing strife in the Middle East and elsewhere reminds us.

To be sure, our society has crossed over the border from what I describe in *Dismissing God* as the collapse of conventional piety into unbelief, militant disbelief, and on to postmodernism's contempt for the very notion of truth as it is revealed in Scripture and in the Person of Jesus Christ. At the highest levels of our most sophisticated and intellectual classes, a person cannot be granted credentials of scholarly attainment, rational action, or even simple good sense if at the same time he or she professes religious faith in and commitment to the supernatural mystery of a transcendent God. The reason, I suggest, is that postmodernism's moral base in self-centeredness is characterized by a universal vertigo and the sense of cosmological abandonment.

Rejection of any claim for God derives from postmodernism's cosmology. Both astronomically and philosophically, cosmology is the human effort at locating us and our environment in relation to all the other environments and their possible inhabitants. Whether or not we are astrophysicists by training, each of us defines or accepts someone else's definition of the shape of the universe as a necessary step toward finding our place in it. For the traditional Hindu, the universe is a tray set on the backs of a series of animals. For the Greeks of the heroic age, the universe found its acme at Olympus, its center at Delphi. In time, and with the help of Galileo and Copernicus, human beings reached beyond such limited heights and found their center in the sun, and from there they reached toward the nebulae. But with the advent of modernism, humans shifted their center from nature to the machine, to technology.

In the industrial revolution of the nineteenth century, humanity feared being replaced by a machine at the center of meaning. Next came the socialist revolution and the fear that we were little more than a mass-produced form on which are written the words "Do not fold, spindle, or mutilate." Then followed the cybernetic revolution and modern technology's threat to replace human intellect and imagination with artificial intelligence. In the crisis of modernism's mechanized existence and human depersonalization, humanity found no comfort in the notion of a transcendent God who is interested in us.

But the cosmology of postmodernism has restored the individual—*me*—to the forefront of all meaning, dismissing God altogether as mere fantasy. Postmodernism has declared any religious faith and commitment to be obsolete and irrelevant folly, a quaint absurdity. Instead, an *a priori* assumption holds that to admit to such beliefs presupposes a defective mind, shallow at best, deranged at worst.

Of course, none of this is original to postmodernism. Paul of Tarsus was accused of madness for claiming that Jesus of Nazareth had been raised from the dead. During the ensuing centuries, members of the academic class dared to place before their own culture the claims on behalf of Jesus of Nazareth to be Lord of the universe and Savior of the world. Such names as Justin, Clement, Origen, Tertullian, and Augustine of Hippo come to mind. Later came the great names in the historic development we call Christian humanism—names such as Erasmus, Luther, Calvin, Knox, Melanchthon, Zwingli—some of the most brilliant minds of their time. Here, for instance, is Erasmus: "All studies ... are followed for this one object, that we may know Christ and honor him. This is the end of all learning and eloquence" (*The Collected Works of Erasmus*, J. K. Sowards, ed., 1958). Surely, this is the grandest declaration of purpose in all the literature of Christian schooling and the very reason for the founding of most of the historic schools and colleges in our land.

Yet today, on campus after campus—including many founded to the glory of God and the testimony of Jesus Christ—a long-latent hostility against Christian thought has broken from below the surface. No longer content merely to rebel against conventional religion or orthodox Christianity, an illiberal stance now takes for granted the patent folly of holding to any orthodox Christian faith.

After sowing the seeds of theological modernism, we have reaped a whirlwind of postmodernist contempt. We have grown accustomed to the infidelity of churches and denominational leaders, school trustees, university presidents, seminary deans, division and department chairs who scoff at the faith and vision of institutional founders. We have witnessed the spiritual demise of institutions that have abandoned the mission entrusted to them, turning into scandalous embarrassment cornerstone inscriptions and dedicatory plaques. For them, religion is the ultimate irrelevance. As a former president of an East Coast university has said, "The university has become godless."

At most secular educational institutions, the only bond that holds the curriculum together is its obsession with the postmodernist triad of *race, class,* and *gender,* replacing the grand and classical tradition of *truth, beauty,* and *goodness.* Thus the decline of the North American curriculum to trashy and trivial courses, for as John Leo wrote in the August 30, 1999, issue of *US News and World Report,* "The professoriate now believes nothing can truly be known, so nothing truly matters."

What, then, of postmodernism? What is its cosmological center? Nothing. Beyond a geocentric universe, beyond a heliocentric cosmos, beyond nebulous reality, beyond a mechanistic design lies the black hole of nothingness, a maelstrom that sucks everything into itself. We can see its effects in some of my illustrations presented earlier. Let me offer this outline:

1. Contempt for revealed and supernatural religion, especially biblical Christianity in its evangelical proclamation of the gospel—generally attributed to "fundamentalism"—and its summons to submission under the authority of a holy God and of Scripture
2. Reliance on generalization and labeled opinion rather than on specific evidence, especially if that evidence undermines one's preferred position
3. Disdain for logic or formulations of argument, particularly cause and effect, and a perverse pleasure in inconsistency "A foolish consistency is the hobgoblin of little minds," wrote Emerson in his essay "Self-Reliance" (*Self-Reliance and Other Essays* [New York: Dover, 1993]).
4. Subjectivity to the extreme of solipsism, whereby one's own attitudes have a validity quite apart from fact, experience, maturity, superior reason, or any other attribute of one's opponent
5. An utter rejection of the existence of or necessity for absolute truth and an utter reliance on truth's subordination to relativism
6. A willingness to deceive—whether by word or act—to achieve whatever end one determines is politically expedient, economically beneficial, or experientially gratifying
7. As a corollary to relativism, the utter dependence on an inversion of truth that makes falsehood appear true and truth false; or the inveterate refusal to acknowledge truth in preference for falsehood
8. An attitude toward language that eliminates the possibility of finding common ground in either denotation or connotation, since words mean only what the speaker eventually decides they

mean, subject to convenient editorial review, depending on circumstances and self-serving purposes

9. The refusal, therefore, to judge anyone else by standards tied to moral absolutes, including even the rule of law, since the language of the law or of common experience can no longer be construed as having either precedent or current meaning

These several observations concerning postmodernism don't begin to exhaust its implications. But in looking at these or any other aspects, we see that one overarching reality about postmodernism is that it both creates and depends upon an environment of despair in which *chaos* is not only the theme but the emotional commitment of its proponents. Chaos is ultimate disorder, ultimate negativity, ultimate void, ultimate disorientation, ultimate emptiness, ultimate confusion. Chaos represents a state of being profoundly contemptuous of and therefore lacking in structure and form, so that it is the description of God's creation after Lucifer's rebellion in heaven: "formless and empty, darkness ... over the surface of the deep" (Genesis 1:2).

This darkness is all-pervasive, all-encompassing. More than the mere absence of light, it is the presence of evil. Wherever disorder reigns, the possibility of evil is present. So the darkness of chaos signifies and contributes to a quenching of illumination, a stifling of insight, and the ruination of any potential for logical progression toward enlightenment. It is this state of human rebelliousness that St. Paul describes in his letter to the Romans: "Their thinking became futile and their foolish hearts were darkened" (Romans 1:21).

In my book *Dismissing God*, I devote several pages to an explication of the towering poem that best captures the consequences of chaos, the product of postmodern despair. That poem is "The Second Coming" by William Butler Yeats (*Selected Poems and Four Plays* [New York: Scribner, 1996]). Here is its first stanza:

> Turning and turning in the widening gyre
> The falcon cannot hear the falconer;
> Things fall apart; the centre cannot hold;
> Mere anarchy is loosed upon the world,
> The blood-dimmed tide is loosed, and everywhere
> The ceremony of innocence is drowned;
> The best lack all conviction, while the worst
> Are full of passionate intensity.

What evidence can be summoned that Yeats' vision is accurate? None more compelling than the confusion permeating much of current thinking. I cite several areas but will develop only one that confusion infects: (1) the dysfunction of discourse, (2) the missing relationship between cause and effect, (3) refusal to commit to anything higher than oneself, (4) studied negligence or nonchalance toward serious issues, (5) inordinate pleasure at daring in the face of potentially calamitous danger, and (6) an absence of wholeness.

Look at this latter point, the absence of wholeness. In his book *The Death of Outrage: Bill Clinton and the Assault on American Ideals* (New York: Simon & Schuster, 1999), William J. Bennett writes about the former president's character: "The leader must be whole; he cannot have his public character be honest and his private character be deceitful."

We who work in Christian schools and colleges have become familiar with the concept of wholeness, which we call *integration*. We use the concept frequently in speaking of "the integration of faith and learning," by which we mean the wholeness between what we believe to be true about God and His revelation in Jesus Christ and in the Scriptures, and what we understand about our academic discipline and its truths. We ask that our teachers and coaches exemplify how their Christian faith influences their thought, affects their intellect, shapes their world-and-life view, and impinges on their professional endeavors. Thus we seek to bring together in wholeness the wisdom of God and our own aspiration after human knowledge, discovered and appreciated through the discernment that comes to us through the Holy Spirit—and manifest in action that comports with both our professed faith and our calling. Our growth toward spiritual maturity is measured by the consistency with which we think and act in concord with these principles.

The tenets of postmodernism, however, refute any claim that a consistent worldview should permeate a person's thought. Such would be the "foolish consistency" of which Emerson wrote; such is the chief symptom of fanaticism. But we in Christian education also know—and insist on— another form of integration that postmodernism denies. Beyond academic integration, we insist that our board members, administrators, faculty, and to some degree our students exemplify the principles of scriptural morality and behavior on which our school is founded. We expect wholeness in living as well as in thinking.

We would not tolerate—as do some schools—our faculty living together in a sexual relationship without benefit of marriage. We would not tolerate a coach's adjusting an athlete's transcript so that she or he can be admitted to a more competitive university. We do not tolerate—or we should not—a pious fraud who prays profoundly in public but in private gossips about a colleague or belittles the head of school or trashes a board member. We ask for—and we expect—a life that is consistent with the precepts of Scripture.

Postmodernism will have little or nothing to do with such calls for consistency of behavior, especially if that behavior appears to be imposed on the social order. Rather, postmodernism has agreed to celebrate individualism and an anomaly it calls "diversity." Thus *relativism* rules, and *tolerance* becomes the highest good.

In his book *The Closing of the American Mind* (New York: Simon & Schuster, 1988) the late Allan Bloom examined the degree to which American higher education has been taken over by relativism rather than the unfettered search for truth, by political correctness and the necessity for tolerance rather than a discriminating and balanced critique of reality. Bloom's much-heralded and much-maligned book opens with this sentence: "There is one thing a professor can be absolutely certain of: almost every student entering the university believes, or says he believes, that truth is relative." Bloom continues: "Openness—and the relativism that makes it the only plausible stance in the face of various claims to truth and various ways of life and kinds of human beings—is the great insight of our times."

Some years ago, when I was serving as consultant to the College Board and Educational Testing Service, we devised a writing assignment for the English Composition Achievement Test whose stimulus read, "The trouble with being open-minded is that your brains might fall out." Clearly, such is the danger facing postmodernism: it represents the moral impoverishment of a studied emptiness of intellect, of spirit, of soul. Postmodernism—we can now deduce—is the vacuous consequence of the absence of truth and the devaluation of moral criteria into a vast, indiscriminate stew of relativism. Furthermore, as the Old Testament prophet discovered, there is death in the pot, a botulism of political expediency and solipsism.

What, then, is the antidote to such a toxic environment? I believe it is to be found in the gospel of Jesus Christ. The gospel also is a cosmology, for it offers a definition of the shape of the universe. But beyond philosophy, beyond the metaphor of world-and-life view, the gospel provides literally a physical—indeed a personal—explanation of why things need not fall apart and how the center, in fact, can once again hold. For the cosmology of the gospel is centered not in nature nor in man nor in machine, but in Christ. Hear once more the compelling words of St. Paul to the new Christians in a city called Colossae:

> He is the image of the invisible God, the firstborn over all
> creation. For by him all things were created: things in heaven

and on earth, visible and invisible, whether thrones or powers
or rulers or authorities; all things were created by him and for
him. He is before all things, and in him all things hold together.
(Colossians 1:15–17)

Jesus of Nazareth, God with us, is the very *eikon* of who God is. He is
the creating and sustaining Lord of the universe; He is the very center of
being and meaning; He is the cosmic center. Beyond all the sophistry of
postmodernism lie only the wretchedness and nausea of a life spinning
away and apart from God. In Christian schools such as yours, you know
how to find and restore peace at the center, peace where the Lord of the
universe is in control and calms the soul's vertigo and the mind's fear.
Christian schooling knows the cosmology that restores the Creator to His
rightful place at the center of His handiwork.

The late Lebanese statesman Charles Habib Malik said that "responsible Christians face two tasks—that of saving the soul and that of saving the
mind" (*The Two Tasks*, Cornerstone Books, 1980). A Christian school exists
to redeem, as Malik argued, the souls and minds of all who study there.
But, as Malik warned, if we do not redeem the mind—if we do not teach
our students by example what it means to think and act as Christians—we
will have no reason to rejoice in merely having saved their souls.

4

VERITAS: THE INTEGRATED CURRICULUM

Since 1984, PAIDEIA Inc. has sponsored a summer conference to bring together Christian school leaders—board members, heads-of-schools, their key administrators and faculty—for the purpose of inspiring each delegate to a higher standard of excellence. For some years, PAIDEIA Inc. has been advancing the cause of VERITAS: The Integrated Curriculum, not as a commercial product but as a principle. This address was delivered at the conference on June 19, 1997.

A Christian school has—or ought to have—certain distinctives that set it apart from secular or merely church-related schools. Among the most self-evident of these obligatory distinctives are (1) a mission to educate so that Jesus Christ is honored by what is offered in His name, (2) a believing governing body, administration, and faculty who are united in their faith and in their commitment to fulfilling the school's mission, and (3) a set of common expectations as desired outcomes for students, including academic, social, and behavioral outcomes leading to a hoped-for spiritual outcome: namely, a relationship with God by faith in Jesus Christ.

An increasing number of Christian schools can now point to a mission statement, an articulated reason-for-being, a purpose. In fact, increasing numbers of teachers, administrators, and board members in such schools can actually recite their school's mission statement from memory. I encourage you to do more than memorize your school's mission statement; I urge you to make it your own. By making your mission statement a part of your active mental life, you are committing yourself to living out its implications personally as well as vocationally and institutionally.

To fulfill that mission effectively, however, a Christian school must be governed and administered by godly men and women who, in turn, appoint only similarly dedicated men and women, united in faith, to teach and coach and counsel students. This is what Frank Gaebelein calls for in *The Pattern of God's Truth* (New York: Oxford University Press, 1954) when he writes about "The Teacher and the Truth," insisting that "the school ... that would develop a Christ-centered and biblically grounded program must have fly from its masthead this standard, 'No Christian education without Christian teachers,' and must never, under any condition, pull its colors down."

How tenuous such a principle can be! How many are the schools and colleges and seminaries that once held fast to the biblical faith but are now derelict! Indeed, our own ACSI schools are not immune to the lures and temptations that would compromise and eventually destroy our founders' vision. We know how hard we must work, one day at a time, to establish a school with a standard that can be called "Christian."

The first two distinctives of such a school are its mission and the Christian educators who commit themselves to that mission. The third distinctive is common expectations. Every Christian school would claim to know what sort of behavioral outcomes it expects of students. Yes, a Christian school is definitely concerned about outcomes. Indeed, a Christian school ought to be a paragon of "outcomes-based education," even if that phrase has been debased in current educational jargon by its association with advocates of so-called "cultural diversity" and other forms of political correctness! As Christian educators, let's not be afraid to assert that we have always stood for moral and spiritual corollaries to what we teach.

In this regard, every Christian school can open its parent or student handbook and point to its rules and regulations and its graduation requirements regarding decorum, specifying what will and will not be tolerated before the ax drops and the student is expelled. But sometimes a Christian school has the wrong expectations or fortifies a child's rebellion by accentuating guilt over grace.

I can hardly erase from memory my encounter a few years ago with a school where the student newspaper's headlines were almost nauseatingly pious: "Sophomore Class Delights in Bible Study," "Juniors Learn Humility as Volunteers," "Missions Trip Evangelizes Haiti," and so on. There was much about being spiritual, little about being teenagers, suggesting that a lot of parents and some teachers were being fooled.

I'd been invited to deliver the commencement address, then stay over for end-of-year meetings. At the commencement exercises, my remarks were superfluous because a half-dozen seniors gave their own speeches, all of which sounded like sermons. But the next morning, the first thing the administrators did was hold a prayer meeting to intercede with God on behalf of the senior class, most of whom had gone off for a weeklong unchaperoned binge at one of the notorious Gulf Coast resorts and gambling dens.

Here's a happier story: For most of its history, one school had set a standard among a certain group of schools for the docility and legalism it demanded. Then the pastor of the sponsoring church determined that it was time to, as he said, "open the windows and let the fresh air in." As a graduate of the school himself, he remembered well the conniving ways in which he and his classmates had evaded the school rules, compounding any act of disobedience with lies to cover it up. What a difference today! A new level of expectations has resulted in a new respect for honesty over mere conformity and a new understanding that students must be given the dignity of dissent if they are ultimately to stand for themselves on the foundations of faith.

These, then, are the three distinctives of Christian schooling: a clearly defined mission, educators unified in their Christian commitment, and wise disciplinary expectations. But these three aren't sufficient to satisfy the obligations of a Christian school. There is another distinctive that I consider to be equally obligatory, and unhappily, it is far too often missing, nonexistent, and unheard of among Christian school teachers and other leaders. I believe these three attributes are incomplete without the fourth, an *integrated curriculum*.

How, then, might a school transform its course of study from that of a Christian school with a serious interest in solid academic learning to a Christian school with an outright commitment to teaching a course of study that would support the mission and enhance the likelihood of achieving its desired outcomes? Certainly, if you read the professional journals such as *Education Week*, you'll find lots of display ads from publishers and conference planners promoting changes in curriculum, even something called an "integrated curriculum." What's generally meant by that description is an *informed* curriculum, designed around the idea that teachers in all classes are teaching what their successors will expect students to know when they reach the next level. It's a variation on what used to be called "scope-and-sequence."

But it isn't real *integration*, is it? It's more like an assembly line or the job of laying bricks or any other task that requires a base and a continuum of related activity to complete it. As I've already suggested above, integration is something else. Real integration achieves such a degree of wholeness that even the blending of parts can scarcely be perceived, for there are no cracks or lines denoting overlap; the fusion is total.

The difficulty facing us is that of comprehending what we have almost never experienced. We've seen little or no instances of total integration; rather, we've seen appalling evidence of its opposite, which is *fragmentation*. For instance, almost any orchestral or choral conductor will tell you that he or she wishes to become integrated with the music being performed and the musicians performing it. But how often have we sat in the audience or stood on the choir risers and been aware—too much aware—that the person of the conductor has become an impediment to fully appreciating the music? His wild gesticulations or her rapturous idiosyncrasies are simply a distraction.

Or consider this: A distinguished panel of men sits in an imposing room questioning the moral probity of a man, and then a woman, before them. This is the United States Senate Judiciary Committee, whose chairman is a confessed law school plagiarist; whose ranking majority member cheated in law school and is a notorious womanizer, one of whose episodes led to the death by drowning of a victim. Others on the committee have their stories, but the point is this: none of them indicates the slightest degree of awkwardness or chagrin or irony of displacement at fulfilling his office. There is no integration of a recognition of personal failure with a respect for the law and its high demands. As a result, the public looks on with cynicism at such a blatant display of hypocrisy.

Integration as an ideal is not, humanly speaking, simply a near impossibility; it's a distant dream. Furthermore, integration is a necessity only because of the Fall. If Adam and Eve had not sinned, nothing broken would have needed repair; wholeness would have been the rule. And so, as Christian school leaders, we ought to approach the concept of an integrated curriculum humbly, in full recognition that we are attempting to do the work of God in education. As John Milton wrote, in 1644, "The end ... of learning is to repair the ruins of our first parents by regaining to know God aright" (*The Portable Milton*, Douglas Bush, ed. [New York: Viking, 1955]).

In no way, however, does the concept of integration belong exclusively to evangelical and Reformed Christian thinkers. An integrated and blended curriculum is an employment of an ancient method of instructing the whole person so that the mind, the body, and the spirit might learn together. It is what the Greeks knew as *paideia*. In some form, it became the model for the University of Chicago's Robert M. Hutchins, Clifton Fadiman, and others who popularized the *Great Books* idea, which was later advocated by Mortimer Adler and *The Paideia Proposal*.

But the idea of a Christian *paideia*, while seemingly borrowed, has a uniqueness all its own, and that uniqueness derives from a Christian recognition of the source of truth and its unity in God's revelation of wisdom, knowledge, and understanding.

Why then have Christian educators been so lax, so indifferent, so aimless in our curriculum planning and delivery? Why have we waited so long to develop some means of conveying to children and adults alike what Frank Gaebelein calls, in *The Pattern of God's Truth*, "the unity of all truth under God"? Why have we allowed, as Gaebelein again asserts, "the fragmentary kind of learning found on some avowedly Christian campuses"? Why have we trailed along behind even those secular educational reformers who point out that all too often areas of knowledge and experience are divided artificially into "subjects" meeting in isolated classrooms and taught without communication or reference by specialists to whom it never seems to occur that their field of knowledge may have some connection to another sphere of knowledge? For instance, might not an American Civil War novel somehow relate to the historical study of that war or the geographic study of Virginia's terrain or the study of American government or the biblical study of the causes of war or a student's independent study of any number of matters concerning nineteenth-century economics, social behavior, artistic development, or personal family history?

Here's a practical example from my own teaching experience. Years ago, I was English department chairman and teacher of twelfth-grade boys at The Stony Brook School. I'd been newly granted a master's degree in American studies, for which I'd written a two-hundred-page opus on "Christian Orthodoxy in *Moby-Dick*," a surefire antidote to insomnia, I assure you. Like all energetic and ambitious young scholars, I was eager to transmit to my students everything I'd learned en route to that master's degree by way of my dissertation. So I assigned *Moby-Dick*—all nine hundred pages of it—to all sections of senior English class, along with multiple additional readings for the Advanced Placement section, which I also taught.

But while only the AP class had the burden of polishing my pride by also reading some of the books in my bibliography, all four sections had the responsibility of adding to their reading of *Moby-Dick* the voluminous number of passages I'd assigned from the Bible. Genesis, Job, Ecclesiastes, the book of Jonah, and other selections filled my students' every idle hour—when they weren't already dazed by reading Herman Melville's saga of Ahab and Ishmael on the whaling vessel.

Now, you need to know that, while I was relatively new to teaching twelfth-grade English, I had a colleague who was brand-new at teaching twelfth-grade Bible, a course of equal academic standing with my English class. He was teaching Paul's letter to the Romans and the Gospel of John and having a wonderful time assigning such supplementary texts as Camus's *The Stranger* and *The Fall,* Dostoevsky's *Crime and Punishment,* and Stevenson's *Dr. Jekyll and Mr. Hyde,* all intended to parallel and illustrate the biblical texts that were under close scrutiny in his classroom.

Well, you can guess what happened. The same twelfth-grade boys came to both of us and said, with respect but also exasperation in their voices, "May we ask why you two gentlemen don't confer with each other? One of you is teaching Bible in the guise of an American literature course; the other is teaching world lit while pretending to teach Bible. Give us a break!"

Of course, they were perfectly within their rights to call us to account for the fact that neither the Bible teacher nor the English teacher had bothered to find out what the other guy was doing. In a couple of instances, we discovered that our assignments had actually overlapped. Quite unconsciously, we'd assigned the same material to be read by the same students in two distinctly different classes and never bothered to try making any connection between them.

Thus it was our students who pointed out to us the folly of our artificial and essentially foolish representation of education as a set of unrelated beads with no string to hold them together in a beautiful and unified necklace of knowledge. After we recovered from our chagrin, my colleague and I set about to mend our ways.

We designed courses which, for reasons of school records and transcripts, we named Bible-English 12 or 11 or 10. In some instances, we incorporated history as well. These courses never pretended to "cover" (what a dreadful word for any professional educator to use!) anything. Rather, they were intended to teach our students the art of close and critical reading, powerful and effective rhetoric in argument and persuasion, and—most of all—what our own founding headmaster espoused as "the unity of all truth under God."

We continued teaching *Moby-Dick,* but now our parallel readings of Scripture weren't merely tacked on but were blended into the very fiber of our lesson plans and expected outcomes. We continued reading Romans and John's Gospel, but now our parallel readings of Camus or Dostoevsky or Stevenson had conscious, intentional purpose and design; we knew what we were about. We were looking to string together our otherwise isolated pearls of wisdom. We were consciously seeking to integrate the otherwise fragmented bits and pieces of knowledge into a whole marked by divine wisdom and Spirit-imbued discernment.

This is the theory behind what I present to you as *VERITAS*: The Integrated Curriculum. But know that I am not trying to market a line of textbooks. I'm not dispensing packaged lesson plans. Instead, I'm attempting to convey a concept. I want to motivate and encourage teachers and administrators and curriculum planners who are already doing their own imaginative and creative thinking to consider ways by which they might better present truth as a unified whole. I know that if a few strategically influential people are inspired, the whole Christian school community will follow.

In that student body at Stony Brook was a young man named David Hicks, who went on to Princeton and from there to Oxford as a Rhodes Scholar. In time, he became head of St. Andrew's Episcopal School in Jackson, Mississippi, where he took some of the principles he'd learned over the years and developed a curriculum based on the reading of ancient texts along with modern history and literature and the Bible. By means of his influential book *Norms and Nobility*, he has continued to advocate such an integrated course of study in other schools.

In Dallas, where he was head of St. Mark's School of Texas, David Hicks began to influence administrators at Trinity Christian Academy in Addison to consider their own version of an integrated curriculum. Over a period of two or three years, Mike Beidel—then headmaster at Trinity—led his faculty to adopt an integrated curriculum, designed by Beidel's successor, Dan Russ, and drawing all the reading courses together at one grade level into a single block of time as one course taught by one teacher. This is the curriculum praised by Ronald Nash in his book *The Closing of the American Heart* (Probe Books, 1990).

In an era when "school reform" is a necessary reality as well as a political slogan, our Christian schools can excel in the future simply by recognizing what the fragmented secular mind seems never to be able to grasp, which is this: the unity of all truth under God allows for the unity of all learning because of its common origin in the mind of God. But this concept of unified curriculum and the unity of truth must also stem from a unified world-and-life view: a Christian *paideia* born out of a Christian *worldview*, a vantage utterly real yet utterly full of hope, without pie-in-the-sky blandishments yet possessed by grace. It is a view of life that asserts the fact of evil along with the fact of redemption available through Jesus Christ. Our world-and-life view, therefore, is in balance, accounting for both paradise lost and paradise regained.

The sources of a Christian world-and-life view manifest in a Christian *paideia* will always be the same as those experienced by Paul's young friend Timothy, whose formal education in Lystra's school consisted of the same elements as that of any other Greek youth. We know by inference from Paul's letters and their several references to rhetoric and athletics that Timothy had received just such a typical education. But what marks Timothy's experience are two additional elements: first, the godly instruction in the Scriptures given to him by his mother and grandmother; and second, the godly example of their lives and the life of his surrogate father, Paul of Tarsus. So, in 2 Timothy 3:14, we read, "But as for you, continue in what you have learned and have become convinced of, because you know those from whom you learned it."

The future of Christian schooling depends entirely on the example of those who teach with rigorous demands a curriculum aimed at excellence from a Christian world-and-life view. Only such a curriculum will result in a Christian understanding of the arts and sciences, a Christian *paideia*. But this Christian *paideia* cannot be taught out of a vacuum; it must be taught in the context of biblical study and knowledge.

In 1956, when I began teaching English at Wheaton College, every undergraduate student—no matter what the academic major—enrolled every semester in a two-hour Bible course. Today throughout the membership of the Council of Christian Colleges and Universities, such requirements have all but disappeared. Even the traditional Bible college now demands less in the way of formal Bible study.

Over and over again, in my opportunities to address the leaders of Christian higher education, I ask the same questions: Why have you chosen to diminish your diploma requirements in biblical studies? Why have you relegated your courses in Bible to a couple of surveys? Why are you contributing to the biblical illiteracy now epidemic throughout evangelicalism? Why are you kowtowing to the professional societies and graduate schools, which demand more and more course time in their particular areas? Why is evangelical higher education so preoccupied with gaining academic respectability at the expense of biblical knowledge, a choice that James Davison Hunter calls "cognitive bargaining"? I'm still waiting for a reply.

With the appalling default of most evangelical colleges on thorough, comprehensive undergraduate teaching of the Bible, our schools must do even more in our Bible teaching to challenge our students, to stimulate our best thinkers, to heighten their imagination, and to evoke their best questions. Nothing is too sacred to be questioned by a sincerely inquiring mind. For us who teach, the answer may be difficult or incomplete or otherwise unsatisfactory, but while there may be such inadequate responses, there is never such a thing as a stupid question.

Only in such a context of biblical understanding can the fruit of a Christian *paideia* grow to harvest. That fruit will be evident in thought and action pleasing to Jesus Christ, in young people who think and act as Christians. But to achieve this goal, we first need to learn, and then teach our young people, how to absorb the living truths of Scripture into the very fiber of our thought and action. This we can do only as we steep our minds in the Word of God, then discipline ourselves to think with the mind of Christ. Indeed, "the integrated curriculum" will be *integrated* only to the extent that it is integrated from within so as to achieve unity among the many parts. This kind of unity means *personal* and *vocational* and *institutional* integration.

If institutional integration is to work, we need to begin with a personal commitment to wholeness, for personal and vocational integration must come before we can make any attempt at institutional integration. Personal integration calls for a consistency of temperament and manner to assure one's integrity as a professional teacher. To me this means learning to love the Lord with all four aspects of our being—heart, soul, strength, and mind: with our heart as the seat of emotions and affection, with our soul as the seat of worship and devotion, with our strength as needed for physical endeavor, and with our mind as the place of illumination, expression, and will. Such integration ought also to be a vocational objective of our daily lesson plan, for only if our own lives give witness to the wholeness of truth will this concept begin to make any sense to the students we teach.

But, as important as is our own spiritual and vocational academic integrity, we must do more. We must also struggle to achieve institutional integration as an academic goal at every grade level and within every sphere of knowledge. The pursuit of academic integration is not just for secondary students; it should also apply from prekindergarten and the primary grades through graduate school. In fact, to the degree that children are being offered all or most of their instruction from a single teacher, the ideal of academic integration is enhanced—if the teacher is consciously working toward that end.

For make no mistake, the youngest child may not be able to pronounce or spell "integration," but she knows when it's missing. And often it's not just our departmentalized middle and junior high or senior high classrooms that are cut off from each other in the manner described above. Is it just possible that even in the self-contained elementary classroom, something less than integrated teaching may be happening? Perhaps it's not so in your school, but I imagine there are some elementary classes in which children have the math lesson, followed by the reading lesson, then recess, then the geography lesson, followed by the Bible lesson—and at the end of the day, they have no awareness of having been exposed to the unity of truth.

But let us also remember that integration in and of itself is not our ultimate goal. Integration is only a means to the highest end, which is *self-application*. We want every believing student in the Christian school to come to the point of maturity that asks, What does this lesson say to me? What is its truth as applied to my life? If the lesson is about the environment, the teaching is not successful unless a student is willing to stoop over and pick up a piece of litter—even someone else's trash. Merely to know that God has mandated the care of His creation isn't enough. Just to know that pollution of any kind is bad for the natural and human environment isn't enough. We need to understand and apply that knowledge as action. So then, the integration of faith and learning must become the integration of faith and action: thinking-and-acting like a Christian must become the primary outcome toward which our schools are aimed.

The word we have adopted to describe a school's academic program, its offerings year by year, its course of study, is *curriculum*, the Latin word for "race course." The track inside a stadium is a curriculum that every athlete traverses. Our use of the word in education is fitting, for each of us teachers—at whatever level we teach—is a mentor, a coach of young athletes. Along with them we must ask and answer the same questions the athlete asks: Where do we begin? How far are we going? Where do we end? Who else is in the race? What's the best pace to assure completion without exhaustion or cutting corners?

As believing Christians-who-teach, we know the truth of St. Paul's several analogies to the race of life. One of the most humbling is his admission to the Philippians: "Not that I have already obtained all this, or have already been made perfect, but I press on.... One thing I do: Forgetting what is behind and straining toward what is ahead, I press on toward the goal to win the prize for which God has called me heavenward" (3:12–14). And as teachers conscious of how little we know and how much remains to be learned, perhaps we will ask an additional question: not, Will the prize match the quality of my effort? but, Will my effort be worthy of the prize?

Here, then, is *VERITAS*: The Integrated Curriculum as a concept for Christian schools. If you are willing to accept the premises I've attempted to construct, I invite you to consider the implications of this curriculum for your school. It is not a prepackaged curriculum based on Christianized textbooks filled with pretty stories and pristine prose—and sometimes laughable misrepresentations of history, science, and the arts. Rather, it is a whole and holistic course of study informed by "the unity of all truth under God."

5

THE CHRISTIAN SCHOLAR

For many years, Dr. Roy W. Lowrie Jr., cofounder of ACSI, served as headmaster of Delaware County Christian School, Newtown Square, Pennsylvania. One of his protégés and successors as headmaster, Dr. Stephen Dill, organized an event for October 7–8, 2004, intended to emphasize the school's historic and ongoing commitment to providing an education in the framework of "thinking-and-acting like a Christian." This was the keynote address for that conference on "Renewing the Mind."

In August 1837, a former pastor-turned-lecturer rose to address the Phi Beta Kappa Society at his alma mater Harvard College. His name was Ralph Waldo Emerson, and his speech was entitled "The American Scholar." It remains a notable address because Emerson used that occasion to summon teachers and students to free themselves from bondage to traditional European ways of teaching and learning—conventional systems of knowing—and seek instead a uniquely American standard for education.

In this era of so-called "globalization," "multinationalism," and "cultural diversity," it may seem an exercise in chauvinism and provincialism to talk about "the American scholar" or "a uniquely American standard for education"—but not to Emerson, whether in the fourth decade of the nineteenth century or in the first decade of the twenty-first century. After all, this was the same Emerson who, for the dedication of a monument in his hometown of Concord, Massachusetts, just one year earlier, had written the most famous occasional poem in American literature. His "Concord Hymn," composed to mark the sixtieth anniversary of

American independence, used to be memorized by every schoolchild. Remember these lines?

> By the rude bridge that arch'd the flood,
> Their flag to April's breeze unfurl'd,
> Here once th' embattl'd farmers stood,
> And fired the shot heard 'round the world.

It was no embarrassment, therefore, for Emerson to stand before an audience of professors and their students and lay before them the claims of a new worldview. According to his understanding, Americans were different from Europeans. As citizens of the New World, Americans ought to see through new lenses a perspective different from that of a myopic Old World; Americans ought to think differently than Old World citizens. And so, without hesitancy or chagrin, Emerson issued his challenges to an audience whom he considered to be still locked into ways of thinking-and-acting that were unrepresentative of the American character and prospects but that Emerson called "the sluggard intellect of this continent."

Perhaps someone in this audience is already wondering if I've wandered into the wrong meeting, intending to address a graduate seminar on American literature at the University of Pennsylvania. Or maybe you're thinking you're in the right place but at the wrong event. Let me comfort you by assuring you of the method in my indirection.

At the ingenuity and invitation of the administration of Delaware County Christian School, we have come together to consider a proposition implicit in the title of this gathering: "Renewing the Mind Conference." Underlying this title is a presupposition derived from a primary text and an assessment of its contemporary application. That text, familiar to biblical Christians, is the passage found in St. Paul's letter to the Romans, chapter 12, verses 1 and 2, which I first memorized in the King James Version: "I beseech you therefore, brethren, by the mercies of God, that ye present your bodies a living sacrifice, holy, acceptable unto God, which is your reasonable service. And be not conformed to this world: but be ye transformed by the renewing of your mind, that ye may prove what is that good, and acceptable, and perfect will of God."

What is the apostle declaring to his readers? He is asserting his inspired judgment that the Roman reader who professes to believe the earliest Christian creed, that "Jesus Christ is Lord," needs to behave accordingly. The clear inference is that the professing Christian is *not* so behaving and must necessarily alter his behavior to reflect the reality of his faith. In short, St. Paul is calling for a total transformation in the life of each believer.

But to acquire the transformed life of which the apostle speaks, that same Roman Christian, before addressing the way she or he acts, must first undergo a renewing of the way she or he thinks. A new worldview is called for, a new perspective on reality seen through the lens of the gospel. Even before a complete canon of Scripture is in place, St. Paul is promoting the essential mandate of a biblical world-and-life view. This first-century scholar—trained in Jewish theology and Greek philosophy and Roman law—is saying, "Prove the authenticity of your faith and your redemption through Jesus Christ by living a changed life derived from your changed mind."

Transformation and renewal based on a recognition of who we are—that's the theme of our time together, and it grows out of St. Paul's message to the Roman believers. It's also the theme of Emerson's "American Scholar," an essay based on his assessment of the state and condition of American education in his time. As a graduate of both Harvard College and the Harvard Divinity School, Emerson was familiar with the curriculum and methods by which professors of that day transmitted their knowledge to their students. He knew the irony that "meek young men grow up in libraries, believing it their duty to accept the views which Cicero, which Locke, which Bacon, have given; forgetful that Cicero, Locke, and Bacon were only young men in libraries when they wrote these books."

Emerson pointed to the role and character of the American scholar: "The office of the scholar is to cheer, to raise, and to guide men by showing them facts amidst appearances." And he declared rhapsodically, "Free should the scholar be, free and brave" (*Selections from Ralph Waldo Emerson*, Stephen E. Whicher, ed. [Boston: Houghton Mifflin, 1957]). Emerson understood the traditional reliance of scholars upon their forebears rather than upon current observation and empirical evidence. He sensed the frozen rigidity and reluctance to break out of the tried-and-true, what someone has called the seven most deadly words to impede progress: "We've never done it that way before."

And so, to paraphrase Emerson's message to the men of Harvard College and to all his subsequent readers, "If you are truly Americans, residents of this vast new territory of untrammeled opportunity, stop thinking-and-acting like transplanted Europeans. Start thinking-and-acting like new human beings, new creatures, new citizens of the New World. Stop imitating the conventions of a decadent class-conscious society; stop pandering to the expectations of a royal aristocracy. Instead, begin thinking-and-acting on the principles of a democratic society, where both uninhabited land and fresh ideas are in rich abundance."

Like Emerson, Paul of Tarsus has also made his assessment. He has checked out Roman behavior and lifestyle. He has examined and differentiated among the godless secularism of hedonistic immorality, the emptiness of idolatrous pagan religion, the legalistic insufficiency of Jewish ritual, and the dynamite promise of justification with God through faith in Jesus Christ. But he calls for more than mere affirmation of "the power of God unto salvation" (Romans 1:16). Faith-as-words-only is not enough. St. Paul calls for a daily demonstration of commitment by means of "a living sacrifice"—that is, our offering up to God lives that are dead to ourselves and our own desires, yet fully alive to doing God's good and acceptable and perfect will.

Apparently, this kind of commitment is a Christian virtue that Paul finds lacking not only in Rome but also in Corinth and Ephesus and Philippi and Colossae and everywhere else in the new realm of faith. So he challenges his Roman readers to do whatever is necessary to fulfill this challenge; to prove their faith by their works, yes; but also to make as their starting point whatever change is needed in how they think, how they reason, how they prioritize, how they speak, and then how they act and do and perform and live. In other words, he calls the Romans to a test of how well each of them is thinking-and-acting like a Christian.

As twenty-first-century Christians, we need to be equally honest in our self-examination. We can be grateful whenever someone helps us toward such honesty by inviting us to participate in a group activity like this one. My wife attends a twice-weekly physical exercise class. In doing so, she is much more faithful about keeping herself fit than am I, in my lonely and all-too-occasional trip to our basement treadmill. I need a group activity like hers to make me more consistent and dedicated to my own well-being.

But the leadership of Delaware County Christian School isn't just performing a community service to evangelicals throughout the City of Brotherly Love and its environs. This school has had the courage to take a long and serious look inward. After more than fifty years of seeking to fulfill the vision of Joe Bayly and other parents, and also of Roy Lowrie and of Ken Tanis, the current leaders of Delaware County Christian School have wisely determined that renewing the mind to attain "the mind of Christ" (1 Corinthians 2:16) is not a one-time thing, not a historic legacy to be passed on automatically from generation to generation, not a casual component of the mission statement or a footnote in every employee's contract and every board member's agreement to serve and every parent's application for a child's enrollment. This school—to its everlasting credit—has determined that thinking-and-acting like a

Christian must be intentional, pervasive, comprehensive, daily, hourly, momentary, and sincere—thus this evening's and tomorow's emphasis on "renewing the mind."

It is my privilege to serve as a facilitator—or perhaps more accurately a gadfly—to this process. In this role, I have the opportunity to address this general audience tonight and a more particularly academic audience tomorrow. I am speaking this evening to teenagers and their parents, to faculty and administrators and their spouses from this school and from others, to board members and their spouses, to grandparents and perhaps to pastors and others who care about Christian schooling without the same level of professional involvement in this or any other Christian school. In addressing all of you, what should my message be?

Simply this: Like Emerson and Paul of Tarsus, I call upon each of us to know who we are and to do whatever it takes to live according to that distinctive. First, we must know who we are, and who we are—or who we ought to be—is a disciple of Jesus Christ. Any disciple is a pupil sitting at the feet of the teacher, or an athlete subject to the rigors of training and competition determined by the coach. But if we are disciples, we must do whatever it takes to adhere to the discipline of our master. For instance, that's what it means to be a disciple of Mortimer Adler or Elton Trueblood or Frank Gaebelein or Howard Hendricks; that's what it means to be a disciple of Vince Lombardi or John Chaney or Joe Paterno; that's what it means to be a disciple of the late Robert Atkins or Richard Simmons or Dr. Phil or Dr. Laura or Rush Limbaugh or Bill O'Reilly or Sean Hannity or Michael Moore or Adam Smith or John Maynard Keynes or Rick Warren or Henri Nouwen or Chuck Swindoll or whoever else you submit to as pupil-to-teacher.

If we claim to be disciples of Jesus Christ, we too ought to know who we are, then do what our discipleship demands. If we are to be disciples of Jesus Christ, we must be willing to subject ourselves to a certain discipline; otherwise, our claim to be disciples is fraudulent. And if we make such a profession, our daily lives must be characterized by earnest adherence to the discipline that Jesus Christ demands.

And what is the discipline that Jesus Christ demands of us? To be like Him. To be like Him in thought and word and deed. To love the Lord our God with all our heart and soul and mind, and to love our neighbor as ourselves (Matthew 22:37–39). To acknowledge that in ourselves dwells no good thing except by the forgiving grace of God. To recognize our responsibility to witness to others through the integrity of our lives, using words only when necessary.

As educators or as parents of students in a Christian school, we need to accept the discipline that sets our learning-and-teaching apart from godless and utterly secular learning-and-teaching. We must perceive the differences among wisdom and knowledge and understanding: Wisdom is a divine attribute, possessed only by God unless and until He chooses to dispense that wisdom by revelation. Knowledge is also God's gift to us—the summons to know all that we can about nature and human nature. Understanding, or discernment, is the special gift of the Holy Spirit, whose enlightenment leads us into all truth. So, while there may be elements of God's wisdom disclosed to me and vast ranges of knowledge acquired through my studies, the key to any effectiveness as a learner-and-teacher will be my grasp of understanding, my power to discern how best to use what I have learned and what I wish to teach to others.

But all of this—however earnestly desired by Steve Dill and his administrative team, by the board and its members, by every parent who has committed a child to this or any other school for the purpose of educating that child "in the nurture and admonition of the Lord" (Ephesians 6:4)—all of this will be thwarted, or sterile at best, if it is imposed by administrative fiat or board policy. One thing I can assure you about this evening and tomorrow: there will be no memo to the faculty stating that, effective on Monday, October 11, all teachers and coaches at Delaware County Christian School will integrate faith and learning in each lesson and workout according to this-and-this formula. The reason that won't happen is that it can't happen that way, except as an empty and essentially meaningless dictum from an ineffectual leadership.

No, true discipleship demonstrated by thinking-and-acting like a Christian and implemented by the fusing of biblical faith and truth into every aspect of wisdom, knowledge, and understanding can occur only when it is first personal, then vocational, and finally institutional.

Each of us must have an encounter with the risen Christ and—like Cleopas and his companion at the inn of Emmaus—we must have our eyes opened and our heart burning within us at the recognition of who Jesus Christ really is. Until the individual teacher—like the individual accountant, banker, chef, doctor, engineer, farmer, grocery clerk, homemaker, and so on—takes on "the mind of Christ" and begins thinking new thoughts with new insights based on biblical precepts and principles; until the individual educator applies personally what it means to be a disciple of Jesus Christ, there can be no transformed life, no renewed mind, no thinking-and-acting like a Christian visible to others.

Second, once each of us as an individual believer has begun to see through the lens of Scripture, has begun to think-and-act like Jesus Christ, the application to our vocation must soon follow. One can hardly think-and-act like a Christian husband or wife, parent or friend, without also thinking-and-acting like Jesus Christ as a professional, whatever the field of employment.

We have a belated but nonetheless timely instance of such a logical expectation from some members of the hierarchy of the Roman Catholic Church in regard to supposedly Roman Catholic politicians who have set aside their professed commitment to the faith for the sake of politics. These are the demagogues whose highest creed is to "give the people what they want" rather than to stand fast for the doctrines of their own church. Most of them hide behind a curtain of private conviction vs. public policy. They can't bring themselves to impose upon a diverse populace their own private beliefs, yet they whine and assume a martyr's complex when the church warns them about their public disavowal of its teaching.

You are blessed, I believe, to have an exception to that sorry example in the person of your junior United States Senator, the Honorable—and I stress that title!—Rick Santorum. We have all been blessed—I believe—to have as president of the United States of America a man who may very well lose his office in a few weeks—not primarily because he found no weapons of mass destruction or failed to capture Osama bin Laden but because of his willingness to speak forthrightly about his evangelical principles and act accordingly. Would that every professing Christian in the legislative and executive and judicial branches were as daring!

Third, only after individuals begin to apply their personal commitment to a transformed life and a renewed mind to their vocational life and work can thinking-and-acting like a Christian become an institutional reality. Even then, what happens institutionally will be a direct result of individuals who make their personal integration a function of their vocational integration. Colleagues at the same grade level and colleagues in the same department will share their joy at finding a new motivation for learning-and-teaching like a Christian. They'll tell each other about the newest discovery, the latest insight, the exciting coherence just uncovered, the astonishing moment of a student's probing remark. They'll decide to collaborate on some project to bring to concrete reality the inferences they sense by intuition. They'll ask the headmaster to approve some extraordinary funding. And thus a curriculum will be developed.

The purpose of such a curriculum will be to fulfill the goal set by a relatively new Christian believer named T. S. Eliot more than sixty years ago. Just before the outbreak of World War II, Eliot was musing over what he called *The Idea of a Christian Society*—a sort of heaven-on-earth utopia. Of course, there would an educational system with schools. But what sort of schools? Eliot wrote, "The purpose of a Christian education would not be merely to make men and women pious Christians.... A Christian education would primarily train people to be able to think in Christian categories" (New York: Harcourt, Brace, 1940).

What a concept! Imagine! Christians who "think in Christian categories"! Whatever might that imply? What could be the consequences of such thinking? Could it possibly lead to *acting* in Christian categories?

But let's not leap too far ahead of Eliot. He isn't calling for mature Christian thinking; he's only proposing that a Christian education would "train people to be able to think in Christian categories." Perhaps you find that deflating, anticlimactic, even disheartening. I don't. I find it totally realistic, given the generally anemic condition of the evangelical church today. We are ignorant of what the Scriptures say, what the Scriptures mean, and how the Scriptures apply—although we're quite familiar with the latest pop evangelical author's ideas—because most of our pastors have long since given up expository preaching that opens the text line-upon-line, precept-upon-precept.

And what about many of our Christian schools, where a so-called course in Bible has as its textbook not the Word of God itself but a manual on various worldviews or a handbook on teenage moral dilemmas? What about schools in which adults who were hired explicitly to be models to the young cannot give a well-reasoned expression of how their art or their science—their academic discipline—reflects and is imbued with God's truth?

So I say, let's begin where people are rather than where we wish they were. First, one must be able to think in Christian categories before such thinking will become action. And perhaps, for some here, this conference is such a beginning.

What might be the results, the consequences, of our beginning to think-and-act like Christian scholars and students? In 1855, a somewhat scruffy vagabond—a newspaper editor and notorious carouser—published a volume of jottings unlike anything ever seen before. His name was Walt Whitman, and he called his book *Leaves of Grass* and its central poem "Song of Myself" (John Townsend Trowbridge, "Reminiscences of Walt Whitman," *The Atlantic Monthly*, Feb. 1902). When asked about the genesis of his verse, Whitman replied, "I was simmering, simmering, simmering, and Emerson brought me to a boil." In other words, the challenge offered eighteen years before by the philosopher resulted in the product of the poet almost two decades later.

Who knows what might develop as a result of the Delaware County Christian School faculty's challenging your students to think in Christian categories? Who knows which of those students—responding to that challenge and witnessing how the challenger lives out his or her own call for thinking-and-acting like a Christian—who knows what God will do with that young life? It could well be that he or she, motivated by you and your colleagues, will be the next Jim Elliot, the next Franklin Graham, the next Condoleezza Rice, the next Janet Parschall, the next Rick Santorum, the next believer to stand the world on its head for the gospel of Jesus Christ.

Who knows what might happen—under God—if every one of us began by renewing the mind and transforming the life so that we are thinking-and-acting like a Christian!

TWO

GOD'S CALL TO JOYFUL SERVICE

INTRODUCTION TO PART 2

For every Christian adult, the call of God to some form of creative and productive industry is—or ought to be—a call to joyful service. Whether the call is to drive a truck or work on an assembly line, to plead a case in court or manage the affairs of a modern home, to teach a class or administer a school—a Christian believer is urged by Scripture to understand it in terms of *vocation*, a sacred calling.

Like the child Samuel and the young man Isaiah, some of us have heard a voice in the night calling us by name. Like them, we have responded, "Here am I. Send me!" But one way or another, each of us has answered God's divine want ad and accepted His summons to joyful service.

What is it that makes our service joyful? It is the fact that, in God's grace, we are able to make full use of our gifts. We recognize some of those gifts early on, while we discover others some time later as they are nurtured and developed.

"Consider it pure joy," says the apostle James, "whenever you face trials of many kinds" (James 1:2). Those of us who head schools know that the essence of our joyful service is rarely found in the day-by-day operational details. Rather, we discern our joy in the long pull toward a distant goal—in the slow growth of a maturing student, in a struggling young teacher's eventual mastery, in the blessed news of a graduate's spiritual renewal, in the thrill of a generous donor's financial contribution. These are usually sufficient to overcome the less joyful aspects of our work: a board member's caustic criticism, a self-absorbed parent's obsession with her own child's demands, a trusted teacher's moral failure, a potential donor's disappointing rejection of an appeal.

So too with those of us who administer certain areas of responsibility, who teach or coach or direct students. Our joyful service is experienced in the whole tapestry, not merely in the tiny knots and threads that make up the warp and woof of our lives.

One thing more: God never calls us to serve without equipping us for that service. When God called Moses from the burning bush to demand that the Egyptian ruler release the Israelite slaves, He empowered Moses beyond his speech limitations and made him strong for the task. So too with each of us: the God who calls us is able to prepare us, sustain us, and reward our faithfulness with His commendation "Well done!"

God's call to joyful service—it's the reason for our vocation in Christian schooling.

6

COMMITTED TO CHRISTLIKE COMPASSION

Christian Educators Association is a regional affiliate of Christian Schools International. For the annual convention in Chicago, Illinois, on November 5, 1981, I had the honor of presenting this keynote address.

I always feel at home in the company of other Christians who are called to be teachers and administrators of schools—Christian educators in the best sense of that phrase.

It's not just what we have in common—the educational lingo we use as our native tongue, that bane and blessing known as the PTA, those schoolboy howlers we never tire of telling. Here's an example of the latter: The Thomas F. Staley Foundation designates its lecturers as "Distinguished Christian Scholars." A student, learning that I was to leave our campus to spend some time on the college lecture circuit, asked me in all seriousness, "Dr. Lockerbie, how did you get to be an *Extinguished* Christian Scholar?" It's not the similarities in any of our job descriptions that bind us together. It's not the terms of our employment, or the occupational hazards of burnout and middle-age malaise, or the fear of mid-career identity crisis. It has nothing at all to do with what the American Federation of Teachers refers to as "the professional relationship between change agent and client."

What unites us is neither our job, nor our employment, nor our career or profession. What unifies us as Christian educators is our *vocation*—our calling—to do the work of Jesus Christ Himself to the glory of God the Father.

To be a Christian educator is a high calling. Indeed, we stand in a grand tradition: Paul the rhetorician and philosopher; his pupil Timothy, whom Paul commissioned to make good use of all that Timothy had learned in his classical schooling; Justin Martyr, at whose school in Rome students learned that "Whatever has been uttered aright by any man at any time belongs to us Christians" ("The Second Apology," *The Fathers of the Church*, Thomas B. Falls, ed. [New York: Christian Heritage, 1948]). The list goes on: Clement of Alexandria, Origen, and Augustine of Hippo, who declared, "Every good and true Christian must recognize that wherever he may find truth, it is his Lord's" (*On Christian Doctrine*, D. W. Robertson Jr., trans. [Indianapolis, IN: Bobbs-Merrill, 1958]).

Over the centuries, wherever the Cross has been planted, the school and university have soon followed. Christian schooling is no mere alternative to public education; it is the very wellspring and mainstream of education in Western civilization. Public schooling is the new kid on the block, with heroes no grander than Horace Mann and John Dewey. I'll stack my saints up against the National Education Association's any day! For above and beyond the church fathers and the apostles stands an even greater model for the Christian educator to emulate.

Throughout the Gospels, Jesus of Nazareth presents Himself as a teacher. The word translated in the King James Version as *master* is better rendered by modern translations as *teacher*. So in Luke's accounts of the parables, the point of departure is often a question or statement addressed to Jesus thus: "Teacher, what must I do to inherit eternal life?" "Teacher, tell my brother to divide our father's estate with me." So too, in John's Gospel we read that when the two disciples of John the Baptist hailed the young rabbi from Nazareth, when they offered themselves as candidates for His instruction, He welcomed them with the traditional phrase by which a rabbi accepted his pupils, "Come and see." Come and enter into a new world of intellectual and spiritual enlightenment. Come and have your eyes opened to the truth. *Come and see.*

For any who aspire to hear and follow the call of God to be a teacher, our model must be Jesus Christ, the Master Teacher. We must pattern our lives after Him in His unswerving allegiance to truth; in His fidelity to the truth about God the Father and His eternal Word; in His constancy to the truth that God's love is universal, extending to Jew and Samaritan and Syro-Phoenician and Roman and Greek alike. We can mold our lives to be like His, we can be imitators of His life, only if we begin to learn His character and share His attitudes, only if we clothe ourselves in those qualities that make for godly living.

The first of these qualities is compassion. As God's chosen people, holy and dearly loved, we are to express love to others in return. The particular kind of love the apostle Paul summons the Colossians and all of us to exhibit isn't gooey and syrupy, sentimental with *1-u-v,* or parasitical with hearts and flowers and *what's-in-it-for-me?* The love demanded of those who would follow Jesus is self-giving and unconditional love, or *agapé,* and it begins with compassion.

A sign that warns us just how decadent and corrupt our world has grown is the way good words have lost their primary meaning and have been debased by evil usage. Today it's almost impossible to use the joyous word *gay* without creating nervous smirks and intimations of perversion in an otherwise decent audience. Likewise the word *myth* has been tainted by abuse so that it carries with it connotations of deliberate falsehood instead of retaining its radiance of mystery and sublime story.

The same has happened to the word *compassion,* a word now associated all too often with weakness rather than strength, with maudlin pity rather than courage. For this, at its root, is what the word conveys: the strength and courage to take upon oneself the shame and scorn, the discouragement and failure, the broken hopes and shattered dreams of somebody else and, in love, to bear the other's pains as if they were your own—because they *are* your own! When Jesus encountered the leprous man, we read that "filled with compassion, Jesus reached out his hand and touched the man" (Mark 1:40–42). So far as that culture and its medical science were concerned, Jesus was taking on enormous risks in touching the leper. But how much did that deter Him?

Part of fulfilling our calling to be Christians in education depends on how much we are willing to take risks in expressing compassion for those with whom we serve—our colleagues and our students, our administrators (who, God knows, need all the help they can get!), and the parents who support our schools. I am a writer and an educator today because of the example of a man in London, Ontario, who knew how to reach out and touch with compassion a lonely, frustrated fifteen-year-old boy. For me, in my vocation, David Carr has been like a signpost pointing the way down a highway, showing me the right path. By his kindness, humility, gentleness, and patience, he provided me with a valuable example to emulate, a living milestone, a model of compassion patterned after the example of Jesus Christ Himself.

One of the most outwardly gruff men I used to know was John Quigley, a former elementary-school teacher near my home on Long Island. John Quigley was once a great 400-meter runner, a national record holder while still in high school. In fact, he was considered a leading candidate for the United States Olympic team in 1940 and 1944—except, of course, there were no Olympic Games in either 1940 or 1944. Instead, Quigley spent three years in George Patton's army and several months in a German prisoner-of-war camp. Years later, he kept his interest in track and field alive by serving as a starter at major meets in Madison Square Garden or at the Penn Relays. Many a sprinter was terrorized by the sound of Quigley's voice: "I'm gonna hold ya, ya know I'm gonna hold ya, so get your hands and feet behind the line...." Some would say that Quigley's tough tones were a reflection of his personal disappointment at not having had his hopes realized, but the people who said this didn't really know the man as I did.

For when my son Kevin was a junior at The Stony Brook School, he was one of the prerace favorites in the New York State indoor track championship meet. I was his coach, but because of a conflict in our schedules, I wasn't able to go with my son to the state meet at Cornell University. Later, he told me what happened. John Quigley was the starter, and at the line he did his usual thing: "Ya know I'm gonna hold ya...." The gun went off, and Kevin sprinted out of his block. But suddenly the searing hot iron of a muscle spasm gripped him, and he had to pull up lame. He limped to a corner of the arena, rage and tears mixing in him. As he stood there alone, crying, he felt a burly arm around his shoulders and that gruff voice said, "I know your dad isn't here, kid, so just pretend I'm your old man." John Quigley. Compassion. The two go together in my mind.

We are to bear one another's burdens, the Scriptures tell us, and so fulfill the law of Christ. And what is that law? Loving God and loving your neighbor as yourself. Feeling her pain, taking it upon yourself; letting him know some ease as you share his disappointment with him and for him.

It isn't always an athletic context. Children know disappointment in every area of their lives—at home when their parents announce an impending divorce, in their report cards, in their rejections from their chosen college, in their relationships with each other. We are called to clothe ourselves in compassion and spread that cloak of love and warmth around their shoulders.

Compassion also means putting ourselves into the other fellow's shoes, recognizing how easy it is for him to fail—not because of any special defect but because he's so much like me! We're summoned to show compassion by our forbearance and forgiveness because we so often need forbearance and forgiveness ourselves. Yet the hardest words for some of us to speak are "I'm truly sorry." I know this well myself, and although I say it to my shame, I also say it knowing the joy of forgiveness, for God saw fit to use an experience in our family to teach me the necessity of compassionate forgiveness and the value of learning to say, "I'm sorry. Please forgive me."

Years ago our family spent a summer in upstate New York, living in a rented house while my wife, Lory, took graduate courses at the state university there. We had taken Elsa, our highly independent cat, along for the summer. Several times she'd expressed her dissatisfaction with her temporary accommodations and had gone off for long periods. I was frankly concerned about getting her back home to Stony Brook. On the day that Lory's studies ended, we cleaned the house and packed our station wagon with the summer's luggage. Throughout that final morning, I kept sounding the warning about what would happen to anyone whose carelessness might let the cat get loose. I knew—as I somehow felt nobody else was capable of knowing—how inconvenienced we'd be if Elsa took off for the day. A couple of times, one or another of the children left the screen door ajar by mistake, and I pounced on the cat just before she made her getaway. Such evidence of everyone else's thoughtlessness confirmed my sense of personal superiority. I berated them all with increasingly horrible imaginings of the fate awaiting the culprit who might let the cat escape.

That culprit—as you've undoubtedly guessed—turned out to be me. When everyone was settled in the station wagon, I carried Elsa to the car and smugly placed her on the front seat, then slid in and slammed the door. Next stop Stony Brook. But the sound of the door scared the cat. She scrambled toward the back of the station wagon and sprang out the open tailgate window I'd neglected to close.

What happened over the next few minutes—which stretched into hours of diabolical anger—makes me ashamed even to speak about now. I'd been so sure of myself, so ugly in threatening reprisals against the person who might let the cat slip away. Now I had to face up to what my threats meant. Short of hara-kiri, I could think of no real punishment that would fit my crime. Not wishing to accept that sentence of death, I couldn't accept living with my own wretchedness either. In rage against myself, all perspective vanished, all focus became blurred. The only thing on my mind was how foolish I must appear to my wife and children. But instead of acknowledging that foolishness and asking forgiveness, I compounded my folly by indulging in recriminations against myself and everyone else. I'd tasted the bitterness of self-hatred; now I was spreading its poison around me.

Lory must have been praying for grace because we retrieved the cat almost right away, but it took me several hours to recover my senses. Just before reaching the George Washington Bridge, we pulled over at a hot dog stand. As we got out of the car—making very certain this time that

Elsa was safely stowed—I found the words to ask for pardon. Forgiveness washed by tears and blessed by laughter made those frankfurters the best I've ever eaten. When we got back into the car to continue our journey home, our ten-year-old daughter Ellyn said to me, "Elsa forgives you too, Daddy."

It's hard enough confessing our faults to members of our own family, yet sometimes the most difficult confession is the one we must make to our students. Here we are, in our exalted grandeur as omniscient purveyors of wisdom, who like Sir Francis Bacon have taken all knowledge to be our province—and we bungle the arithmetic in computing a student's grade. Or we correct what we think is a misspelled word, only to have the student show us a dictionary's confirmation that we're the one in error. Or perhaps our blunderings are far more serious than these. We select one student and dismiss another for a responsible part in the play, or a solo in the chorus, or an editorial position on the newspaper, and then we discover that our judgment has been faulty and the student we've chosen turns out to be irresponsible. Perhaps we jump to a wrong conclusion, basing it on a faulty assumption, and accuse an innocent student of perpetrating somebody else's infraction of the rules.

Does any of this sound familiar to you? It does to me. In my rookie year at The Stony Brook School, the boys in our residence hall and in my classes endured a great deal from this novice teacher. In fact, my gullibility and rashness were permanently recorded in a diary reference in the yearbook. On such-and-such a day, there had been a tremendous water fight on the third floor. The yearbook reads, "Mr. Lockerbie accused the wrong people, as usual." On another occasion, I arrived in the foyer of our residential building and was told by a notorious practical joker that the most rebellious boy in the senior class was in his room beating up his roommate. I barged through the door to his room, voice first: "Okay, break it up, you guys!" I shouted. There on the bed sat the boy and our saintly headmaster, Dr. Frank E. Gaebelein, both of them bowed in prayer.

But there are also times when we have all the facts and the guilty party stands before us. Our anger causes us to lose all sense of proportion, and so we mete out a punishment that far exceeds the crime. Here's when we must call upon our resources in common sense and adult responsibility, as well as spiritual maturity, to heal a broken relationship. The responsibility is ours. In my years of working with adolescents, I've seen proof over and over again that teenagers are far less petty and far less inclined to hold grudges than most adults. They do demand one thing, however, and that's the adult's honesty in looking them squarely in the eye and saying, "I have offended you, and I'm sorry. Please forgive me."

Again, I'm one who knows because I experienced just such an incident with a boy I encountered in an unpleasant manner on our school tennis courts. For a day or two I brooded over my affronted dignity. Then I decided to try to see the situation from his point of view. We met on neutral ground and talked quietly, assuring each other of our intended goodwill. But I could see that he was waiting for a final word that would convince him of my sincerity. When I apologized, he took my hand, visibly moved, and said, "Thanks, Dr. Lockerbie. This means a lot to me."

Note also that our Christlike compassion in forgiveness is to be unrestricted, complete, withholding nothing. We can't say to someone, "I'll forgive you, but I'll never forget what you've done." We are to forgive *as we have been forgiven*, which means the forgiveness that cancels out any debt, wipes the slate clean, buries the offense forever, and forgets. This is what our conference theme means when it summons us to exemplify Christlike compassion, living out in our lives the character traits we worship in Him.

One of these traits is personal concern for individuals. Jesus of Nazareth had time for children and their parents. He didn't seclude Himself behind an office door with a secretary to screen the calls and spare Him from intrusions on His time. Oh, there were volunteers willing to look out for His welfare—time-management specialists, no doubt!—front men who wanted to set up a strict schedule of appointments. But Jesus dismissed their offer to protect Him from the people. He welcomed the children; He took them in His arms and blessed them.

Furthermore, we read in the book of Matthew that Jesus gave stern warnings to those who would deter any child from finding his way to the arms of the Savior. For them, Jesus said, it would be better if a huge millstone were hung around their necks and they drowned in the depths of the sea (Matthew 18:6). Harsh words? No, words of dramatic power and judgment, for each of us knows the terrible responsibility we bear as teachers of children. It lies within our capacity as teachers to be either living milestones or damning millstones. Either we can direct our students by the example of our lives, or we can burden ourselves and them with the sham of our professed religion and thus drown in a sea of hypocrisy and religious pretense.

Let us remember—those of us who serve in so-called "Christian" schools—that what makes our schools *Christian* is not the charter or the cornerstone inscription or the founders' platform of principles. It is not the affirmation of faith we sign upon accepting our responsibilities, nor the chapel services, nor even the study of God's Word in our curriculum. Neither any one of these nor a hundred more ingredients can make a school *Christian.* What makes any school "as Christian as possible," as my former colleague and friend Peter Haile puts it, is the day-by-day decision on the part of Christians in the school—those who teach and administer, those who study and learn and play—to live and act this very day like Christians.

When we do so, the overriding principle of Christlike behavior manifests itself in love that leads to perfect unity. Such love permits no callous mockery of another's handicap, no jealousy over another's success, no gossip or slander, nothing that contributes to the fracturing of the unity Christ wants us to enjoy. But to achieve this desired and desirable end requires nothing less than total commitment to Christlike living.

There's a story told about a chicken and a pig who were walking past a church when they noticed the weekly message on the signboard: "WHAT HAVE YOU GIVEN TO GOD TODAY?" Well, the chicken looked at the pig, and the pig looked at the chicken, and both admitted it had been a long time since they had given God anything.

"Pig," said the chicken, "I think we ought to mend our ways."

"I agree," replied the pig. "What do you have in mind?"

The chicken thought for a while, then said, "Pig, I think we ought to present God with a plate of ham and eggs."

"You must be joking!" exclaimed the pig.

"What do you mean!" retorted the chicken, annoyed that his suggestion had been rebuffed. "Don't you think God would be pleased by our token offering?"

"That's just the point," said the pig. "What for you is a token offering for me is total commitment."

There seems to be a lot of poultry and pork in Christian schools these days—people who are well aware of how far short we fall of the ideal called Christlike compassion; people willing to go halfway and make God a token offering; people like the pig who are afraid of going any further because they realize that the cost of total commitment is nothing less than life itself.

Jesus Christ calls us to that total commitment. There can be no hedging, no equivocation, no looking back. He calls us with the same loving urgency with which He called Simon the fisherman and Levi the tax collector, Mary the prostitute and Saul the Pharisee. He called them, and He calls you and me today to serve Him wholeheartedly in a spirit of Christlike compassion that leads from kindness and humility, from gentleness and patience, through forgiveness and love into perfect unity.

7

TEACHING WHO WE ARE

Of all the speeches transcribed for this book, this address has been delivered more often and to more audiences than any other. Its first delivery was to a group of Christian school administrators and teachers meeting at Seattle Pacific University on November 12, 1982. The version that follows was presented on August 19, 1999, to the administration and faculty of St. David's School, an evangelical Episcopal school in Raleigh, North Carolina.

I first encountered a classroom teacher in 1941, in a tiny Canadian village on the Niagara Peninsula. On that first day of school, I raced home to the parsonage and burst in the door, shouting as loud as I could, "I love school! I can write my name, I can count to a hundred, I can draw a house. Do I have to go back?" My mother—wise woman that she was— kindly suggested that, inasmuch as I had not yet taken all knowledge as my province, I should return the next day and see if there was anything further to be learned. I did, and in a manner of speaking, I've been going back ever since.

I'm no longer a classroom teacher, and there are certain elements of school routine that I miss. For instance, I miss the pleasure of sharing great literature with students. I miss taking teenagers to their first Broadway production and seeing the awe and wonder in their eyes as a play they've read comes to life onstage before their eyes. I miss the delight of helping an aspiring writer see her first poem or story published. I miss the joy of mentoring a truly gifted public speaker. And, to tell the truth, what I miss most of all is the thrill of coaching a runner to his or her finest competitive achievement; at heart, I suppose, I'm more *jock* than *nerd*.

But there comes a point in every coach's or teacher's experience when it's time to pass the baton to someone else. I reached that point without regret because I knew I would be continuing to meet and work with teachers and administrators like you, to share my experience and, I hope, to encourage and inspire them and you in the calling to Christian schooling.

Yet to do so as more than just a cheerleader, let me dare to assume a prophetic role: not as seer or fortune-teller or predictor of the future but as spokesman for a vision, what the British philosopher and mathematician Alfred North Whitehead called "the habitual vision of greatness."

What a soaring phrase! What a challenge to anyone who hears it! Its context is found in a book called *The Aims of Education* (New York: Simon & Schuster, 1972), and the full statement reads as follows: "Moral education is impossible apart from the habitual vision of greatness." What is the goal? Not mere erudition but learning that exemplifies and instills a moral character. How can that goal be achieved? Not only by possessing and transmitting the asset called *vision*, nor even by ensuring that the *vision* is one of *greatness*, but by making that vision *habitual*—constant, unremitting, compelling—"the *habitual* vision of greatness."

In the days following the tragic Columbine school shootings, I had the opportunity to reflect on serious issues such as these. I found myself watching a good deal of C-SPAN, much of whose programming seemed focused on the return of students to school, and the moral and emotional climate there, especially in places where violence and tragedy had occurred in recent months.

I assume that the educational experts and psychological panelists and media pundits and even the politicians who appeared on C-SPAN's discussions were all well-meaning. None of them wanted to have any school, any community, any part of this nation savaged by yet another attack of child-upon-child, classmate-upon-classmate, student-upon-teacher. So know in advance that I assume for all of them the excellence of their intentions. But I must say—without apology for the seeming harshness of my judgment—that, almost without exception, the leaders of those schools were grossly limited in *vision*, devoid of almost any standard by which to measure *greatness*, and far too easily distracted by political considerations and labor union issues and misconstrued "rights" to be habitual about anything other than their insistence upon "tolerance" as the highest of all virtues.

Furthermore, as to why these well-intended educational leaders are weighed in the balances and found wanting, my opinion is this: their answers to the questions *Why did it happen?* and *How can we prevent a recur-*

rence? omit any reference to the biblical realities on which Christian schooling is founded. The sorry fact is that, in most of American education today, there is no sense of sin and separation from God, and consequently, there can be little need for the good news of "lost-and-found." For, as American short story writer Flannery O'Connor noted, unless there is a clear acknowledgment of the fact of *sin*, there can be no hope of *redemption.* Instead, the secular insistence on the fundamental goodness of all persons—the rejection of the doctrine of innate depravity in favor of a "feel-good" stroking of egos—leaves the public bemused by the facts. For instance, lacking the rigor and discipline and exclusive demands of a moral vision, what did these shallow idealists make of the fact that, upon entering Columbine High School on its second day in session, students and teachers were met by freshly painted swastikas on the lavatory walls? So much for "tolerance."

I remember when there was an alternative worldview to vapid idealism. The public schools I attended in Ontario, Michigan, and New York were very different from the public schools today. In every school I attended, including my high school in Brooklyn, New York, my Baptist-preacher father was welcome to speak at a schoolwide assembly, which for him became tantamount to a Youth for Christ rally.

I have kept several of my public elementary school reading texts published by secular publishing companies. Still affixed to pages of those old books from grades two and three and four are blue and silver and gold stars, pasted there by my teachers to show that I had acceptably memorized and recited the poems and other passages of literature on those pages. For the most part, the poems are childish rhymes, like this one from grade two (Author unknown, *The Man in the Moon As He Sails the Sky and Other Moon Verse*, Ann Schroeninger, ed. [New York: Dodd Mead, 1979]):

> The man in the moon, as he sails the sky,
> Is a very wonderful skipper;
> But he made a mistake when he went to take
> A drink of milk from the Dipper.
>
> He dipped right into the Milky Way
> And slowly and carefully filled it.
> The Big Bear growled, and the Little Bear howled,
> And scared him so he spilled it.

But also marked with stars are passages that I memorized, not for my Baptist Sunday school but for my public school, passages such as this:

And there were in the same country shepherds abiding in the
fields, keeping watch over their flock by night. And, lo, the
angel of the Lord came upon them, and the glory of the
Lord shone round about them: and they were sore afraid.
(Luke 2:8–9, KJV)

And this:

Though I speak with the tongues of men and of angels, and
have not charity, I am become as sounding brass, or a tinkling
cymbal. (1 Corinthians 13:1, KJV)

Today, the classroom literature textbooks used in most public
schools—and in many Christian schools as well—contain nothing of the
grandeur of Holy Scripture. The typical public school student is not
required to read texts from the Bible, and certainly does not memorize
them, or little if anything else. Indeed, the average public school teacher
knows even less about the Bible than did Tom Sawyer, who, when asked
to name two of the twelve apostles, came up with David and Goliath
(Mark Twain, *Tom Sawyer*, ch. 4).

The reasons for such ignorance are both complex and simple. They are
complex to the same degree that our social order, technology, and educational content have changed and become layered with intricate and often
contradictory demands. They are simple in that public schools—the mirror
of our society—are seldom any longer expected to provide their students
with educators able and willing to model mature and maturing citizens in
whom are evident what once were thought of as commonly accepted
virtues, such as decency, integrity, commitment, and loyalty, not to mention
a morality derived from religious faith.

Indeed, state-funded education in America has become godless,
reflecting our society's steady erosion from faith to skepticism to unbelief
to militant disbelief and on to cold contempt for the very notion of faith.
In strictly educational terms, this nation has gone from its earliest law
requiring compulsory schooling, the Massachusetts Act of 1647—
commonly known as the "ye old deluder Satan" law—to the Supreme
Court's decision three hundred years later, favoring Vashti McCollum and
her son in abolishing released-time religious instruction in schools.

And what has any of this to do with you who teach at a Christian
school? Very much, I believe. It behooves us to know why our school
exists: not just because public education has failed to maintain the Puritan
morality of New England in the seventeenth century or the Judeo-
Christian ethic of the earlier part of the twentieth century; not because

within the walls of our school parents can be assured that their children will be shielded from all manner of sinful behavior and attitudes; not because our curriculum is sanitized from reality. Our school exists because Jesus Christ is Lord.

Our earliest creed is this: *Jesus Christ is Lord.* This fact is what we affirm individually and corporately when we come together as a community to worship. Jesus Christ is Lord in spite of the world's rejection of His Lordship. As Christians who serve Him in Christian schools, our challenge is not to run away from the effects of the Fall and hide ourselves in churches and schools that are closed to unbelievers. Our challenge is to acknowledge the effects of the Fall by affirming a biblical world-and-life view, a worldview that sees our world in need of redemption but that also proclaims that very redemption to have been accomplished once and for all. Our challenge as teachers in such a school is to recognize the Lordship of Jesus Christ over every aspect of our calling. Thus we will become persons committed to teaching who we *are* instead of teaching only what we *know.*

Teaching who we are. So who are we? I assume that you are persons committed by personal faith in the Lordship of Jesus Christ. But I urge you also to make a total commitment to *the vocation of Christian schooling.* Whatever your role in education—administrator, classroom teacher, coach, or support staff—I urge you to think of your work not merely as a job but as a calling. The God who has made Himself known personally to Abraham, Isaac, and Jacob, to Moses, Ruth, David, and Esther, and preeminently through Jesus of Nazareth, calls us as well. No less than anyone else, we have been called to serve God as a teacher or administrator, a calling that makes us professional servants. Our service, therefore, is not first and foremost to students or their parents, to our governing board, or even to our donors. Rather, through our service to all of them we are, in fact, serving the God who calls us, because the way we serve others is the way we serve God.

Our calling as educators is hard work and as such deserves at least the same dignity afforded to other and often more visible jobs. But school administration is no mere job for wages, and classroom teaching is no mere occupation. Each of these is far more than a career, far more than a profession, even in the best sense of that word. Christian schooling is a calling, a high calling, and no one called to Christian schooling can ever heed that call without remaining—again, in the best sense of the word—an *amateur,* someone who does what she does not just for the money but for the love of it. Administering or teaching isn't just a skill to be mastered or a science to be reduced to a formula; it is an art to be loved.

"That's sheer idealism," someone may say, and be almost correct—only *almost*, however, because I prefer to identify the tone I'm advocating as the Christian virtue called hope. It's hope because all great teachers, including Jesus of Nazareth, hold up a model of hope for their students to emulate. Indeed, the very root of Western education is the quest for truth, beauty, and goodness, representing the highest ideals—the highest hopes—our society can promote.

But such ideals, such high hopes, can come only at the cost of our calling. Indeed, to be an educator costs time and energy and money. None of you punches a clock or even watches a clock, except to release a class to the next teacher. Our vocation demands as much time as is needed to complete our preparation for a board meeting, to review a committee proposal, to draft a budget, to grade our papers, to counsel our students, to plan a new strategy for enlisting donors, to pray for grace in meeting parents. Administering and teaching require time and energy, but our vocation also costs us money. Nobody accepts the call to teach expecting to strike it rich and retire to a luxurious lifestyle. There is a price to pay for the privilege of being a teacher, and only a sense of calling can justify that price.

Heading a school or teaching in it drains our physical energy and uses up our emotional resources. Only those of us who have spent our days in the presence of children fully understand the weariness of our work. At the end of a day, your arches sag, your spine slumps, your shoulder blades ache, your voice rasps, your brain throbs. All you want is a comfortable chair and a quiet hour to yourself, helped along by a cup of tea—or something stronger! Instead, you face a late afternoon of domestic chores—perhaps appearing at your youngest child's soccer match or preparing the family's evening meal or repairing a leaky faucet. Or there's a graduate course and its assignment looming, plus a stack of unread homework or student essays mounting like Everest. Meanwhile, some board member has left a voice-mail message on your home phone, calling for the appointment of yet another committee; and—of course—your current parent nemesis has made her daily call to remind you of your many imperfections. Then there are your church responsibilities and your ailing mother-in-law....

On top of any physical toll on your strength is an even greater emotional pressure. Because you have been made in the image of God and recognize that your colleagues and students are also beloved of God, you can't help noticing the weariness on the face of some faculty members, especially those who are holding second jobs in order to afford to teach at your school; or the anguish in the eyes of some of your students whose families may be on the verge of collapse and whose own lives are caught up in some personal vice or moral quandary. You care, and inwardly at least if not outwardly and visibly, you're involved; you suffer with them. This too is a price that all except the most hard-hearted in our schools have been called to pay. Sometimes it results in a negative dividend called "professional burnout."

But not necessarily. I believe it's possible to spend a long and productive lifetime in the classroom or office and its related tasks without experiencing the psychological starvation and neurotic despair of burnout. Let Doctor Lockerbie, if I may, prescribe a tonic against an epidemic in your Christian school:

Daily: Two healthy doses of mutual encouragement among colleagues

Daily: At least one positive comment about students

Daily: At least one positive comment about the board or pastor

Daily: Inveterate refusal to be corrupted by faculty gossip

Daily: One injection of imagination to suppose what would become of the world if your school and your role in it were to disappear forever

Daily: One moment of prayer that you will be a source of hope to somebody else

Daily: One moment of prayer that you will be an example of Jesus Christ for some teacher or student to emulate

There are too many cynics in our profession who would benefit from the perspective of Desiderius Erasmus: "To be a schoolmaster ... is the noblest of occupations" (*The Collected Works of Erasmus*, J. K. Sowards, ed., 1985). The truest sign of our calling to "the noblest of occupations" will be our godly influence on those we teach. But it takes time to acquire that confidence. To every beginning administrator, to those whose vocational ideals are still untarnished—as well as to every discouraged teacher—I offer this counsel: don't give up too soon. The personal sacrifice needed to turn your current job into a *vocation* is worth it all if, just once, you meet a former student, now an alumnus, who says, "You changed my life."

Paul tells Timothy to "continue in what you have learned and have become convinced of" (2 Timothy 3:14). Why? Because of the erudition of the man from Tarsus? Because of his golden oratory or his persuasive rhetoric? None of these. "Continue in what you have learned ...," he says, "because you know those from whom you learned it." In Timothy's case, the examples of his grandmother Lois and his mother Eunice began the godly influences on his life, and the apostle Paul carried them forward.

I know quite specifically who influenced me and my calling: They were a group of men—coaches and teachers who saw beyond my youthful inadequacies and found something promising to encourage. One recent summer, I returned to one of the cities where I had spent my early teens to address a meeting of Canadian Baptist men. I took that occasion to reflect on the way God had used a physical education teacher and coach to shape my life. Imagine my surprise and joy to learn that not only was he still alive but he was present in that very audience! What a blessing to be able to thank him, half a century later!

I encourage you to make *a total commitment to learning*—not just for learning's sake nor for a terminal degree in your field nor for promotion, but for your own sake and for the sake of those whom you presume to teach. As professional educators, we must give learning high priority in our lives.

Some years ago, one of the hi-tech industries pitched itself in television commercials as "the knowledge business." I suppose they meant well, promoting their vast skills at filing, storing, and retrieving voluminous accumulations of data on reels of tape, microdots, gigabytes, and other cybernetic phenomena. But frankly, I was not impressed then or now with "the knowledge business" because I'm not interested in *knowledge* alone or its sheer acquisition. It's not information, data, or facts alone I seek to convey to students, their parents, or their teachers. I hope to open their eyes to *wisdom* and *understanding*: wisdom from the vantage of God's perspective as revealed in His Word and understanding in the application of wisdom to one's life. I'm not as interested in dispensing knowledge on how to make a living as I am in helping people discover how to make a life. If "a little learning is a dangerous thing," a lot of learning without moral character, without principle, without the redeeming grace of God is a disaster. For such learning lacks the wisdom of God, the understanding that the Holy Spirit imparts.

So then, what matters in our vocation as teachers is not just a commitment to learning but to gaining *wisdom, knowledge,* and *understanding;* learning to discern the genuine from the fraudulent, the worthwhile from the merely gaudy, the permanent from the transitory. As we learn, we do well to recall Geoffrey Chaucer's description of the young scholar and teacher from Oxford: "… and gladly would he learn and gladly teach" (Prologue, *The Canterbury Tales*). I believe that the entire syllabus of most courses on "methods of education" could be summed up in those seven words. For here is the only model for pedagogy that works unfailingly: Glad learners make glad teachers. To this may be added the corollary, No one teaches well what has brought no joy in learning.

Why are so many classrooms places of dismal drudgery? Not because the paint is peeling or the desktops are scarred from many years of use, nor even because the students are ill prepared and the board is callous to our needs. If our schools are barren of delight, is it not because the joy of learning isn't being transmitted as an essential part of the joy of teaching? For when we who presume to teach no longer find joy in learning more about our art or science or discipline or sport, we have forfeited the right to teach or to lead those who teach. We're already over the hill, and our students are the first to know.

But if we keep on learning about the Thirty Years' War or the human circulatory system, the etymology of words or the mysteries of the boundless megaparsecs of space, the infinite variations of meter and melody or the influence of Palestinian agrarian culture on the parables of Jesus, the intricate habits of migratory birds or the relationships between emotional distress and disease—if we keep on learning and finding joy in what we learn, then we shall convey that same joy as we teach and inspire others who teach.

What is it that we are learning and teaching day by day? First, we ought to be learning and teaching the importance of *excellence*. We need to recognize and promote excellence in our Christian schools. I recognize how stale and overworked and ill defined the word *excellence* can be, and I want to avoid being platitudinous. The starting point in measuring excellence is equality of opportunity: Everyone deserves a chance to try, but we must also recognize degrees of attainment: those whose efforts reach the highest standards deserve appropriate praise.

The most fitting definition of *excellence* I know is that framed by a man named Harold Best. What a fine name for someone who defines *excellence*! He writes about art and artists, but with his permission I have made the application to schools and those of us who teach and learn there:

> Excellence is both absolute and relative; absolute because it is
> the norm of stewardship and cannot be avoided or compro-
> mised; relative because it is set in the context of striving,
> wrestling, hungering, thirsting, pressing on from point to
> point and achievement to achievement.

Best concludes as follows:

> Furthermore, we are unequally gifted and cannot equally
> achieve. Consequently, some artists [I would add, some
> schools and their boards, some heads of those schools, some
> teachers, some students] are better than others. But all artists

[all schools, boards, heads, teachers, students] can be better
than they once were. This is excelling.

But in all our talk about excellence, we need also to talk about something else we must learn and keep on learning with joy: humility—not
false modesty but genuine humility in the face of how little we know and
how much remains for us to learn. I say again, the paradox of our vocation
is this: we are both learning and teaching, and when we stop learning, we
lose the power and the moral authority to teach. But we must bear in
mind what the great Moravian pastor and educator, John Amos Comenius,
wrote (Simon S. Laurie, *John Amos Comenius, His Life and Educational Works*
[Cambridge: Pitt Press Series, 1895]):

> God does not call us to heaven asking us smart questions.
> It is more profitable to know things humbly than to know
> them proudly.

Finally, I encourage you to make a total commitment to people. We
don't lead a school as an impersonal structure or teach mathematics or
music as impersonal subjects. We teach something important to people
who need to learn mathematics or music. We teach algebra to human
beings, physics to people, literature to individual students, chemistry to
young men and women, history to that child in the third row near the
bulletin board.

How do we go about making and sustaining a commitment to
people? By *teaching who we are*, not merely what we know. And we don't
even have to try: That's precisely what happens, whether we wish it or not.
I know because of a humbling experience I will tell you.

As my second year at The Stony Brook School was beginning, my
administrative superior, Marvin Goldberg, called me to his office and said,
"I need your help in keeping a very homesick and disheartened boy from
leaving school." His name was Roger, and he was a new ninth grader, the
son of much older parents who had overindulged their little genius and
turned him into a perfectly wretched fourteen-year-old. I wasn't at all
surprised to learn that he was unhappy, because he made almost everyone
else unhappy just by being around him.

"What troubles Roger most," my administrator continued, "is your
English class and the afternoon athletic period you supervise." No
surprises there either. Roger classified himself as a scientific whiz kid, and
held language and literature in disdain. He lacked the most elemental
interest in sport and thus suffered painfully through our daily physical
exercise and competitive games.

"What are you prepared to do to help this boy?" my senior colleague asked. That was easy: I was prepared to go to his room in the boarding school residence hall and assist him in packing his gear, then carry his luggage to the train—or even drive him all the way home myself! But that was not what my colleague had in mind.

"What do you know about chess?" I told him that I didn't know a rook from a pawn. "Roger is a nationally ranked junior chessmaster"—why was I not surprised?— "and I want you to invite him to teach you how to play chess." I could not have been more startled—or angry.

But I took that to be an order, and I obeyed. For the next six weeks, until Thanksgiving recess, I met with Roger every afternoon, and after he suffered through my athletic regimen, he got even by making me suffer through his chess lesson. In thirty sessions and countless games over that six-week period, I never came close to beating him even once. My only success was a single draw. Usually he was calling out "Checkmate!" after only a few moves. All the while he kept up a stream of banter and insult, saying things like, "That was a typically stupid blunder!"

At last, Thanksgiving vacation came, and with it my deliverance from the prison of chess lessons with Roger. He and I never played chess again. I wondered if he would return to school after Thanksgiving, but he did. And he kept on returning—for his sophomore year, his junior year, then for his senior year. Once again, he was enrolled in my English class and my after-school physical exercise group. But now he was also a resident of the dormitory where my wife and I lived with our three children. It seemed there was no escaping my least-favorite student Roger.

Furthermore, the years had done nothing to improve his personality. At seventeen, he was a spoiled and selfish brat. But adding to his disagreeable nature, Roger had decided to exceed his father's agnosticism; in fact, he had become a scoffer. I think it's fair to say that, as an act of self-defense, Roger and I did our best to avoid each other. At the end of that academic year, Roger won several academic prizes and graduated *cum laude*. I did not lament his departure.

He went to a selective university and there met two older graduates of The Stony Brook School, both of them devout believers. In spite of that, Roger fell in with them, mostly to provide himself with someone to be the butt of his jokes about God and faith. One evening, the two friends invited Roger to attend the InterVarsity Christian Fellowship meeting on campus. He went, only to tease and provoke them with his ridicule. But God had the last laugh, for that same evening, upon returning to his college residence hall, Roger got down on his knees and trusted in Jesus Christ to be his Savior.

Not long thereafter, as a passenger in a car involved in a collision, he was killed instantly. Imagine my shock when his parents—with no church or pastor of their own—asked me to conduct his funeral and burial services.

I had done nothing to win the respect or affection of that young man; I had only obeyed the directive of my academic superior. I hadn't consciously witnessed to Roger about his spiritual needs; I had only been submissive to the authority of my administrator. I hadn't sought any opportunity to befriend that awkward and antisocial boy; I had only fulfilled what was demanded of me. God did the rest.

As a result of Roger's death, I believe my temperament softened somewhat over the remaining decades of my time at Stony Brook. For better for worse, I didn't teach reading and writing at Stony Brook; I taught Bruce Lockerbie as reader-and-writer. The same is true for you: you also teach *who you are* as a man or woman whose life is shaped—imperfectly, perhaps—by your relationship with God in Christ and enhanced by your love of the Latin language and its culture, or your passion for Asian art and architecture, or your thrill over marine biology or whatever else it is you teach.

Someone has said, "The poor teacher *tells*, a good teacher *explains*, an outstanding teacher *shows*, but the great teacher *inspires*." We need Christian teachers in our schools who breathe hope and encouragement into our students, who can inspire our students to rise above and beyond our own accomplishments and reach their higher goals.

Recently I watched reruns of the PBS series "Creativity with Bill Moyers." In one episode, the camera follows Maya Angelou as she returns to her childhood home of Stamps, Arkansas. That film ends with Miss Angelou speaking to a classroom of children in that tiny and culturally limited village. Her final words to them—this cosmopolitan woman, this artist and poet, a person who must have seemed to those children like a creature from another planet—her benediction upon them went something like this: "When I look at you, I see who I was. When you look at me, I hope you see who you can become."

This is the essence of the "moral education" that is the goal of Christian schooling; this is what I mean by *teaching who you are*: holding up before your students a model worthy of emulation; presenting them with "the habitual vision"—daily, hourly, moment-by-moment—of what it means to be a mature adult committed both to your Christian faith and, because of your vocation and your love of learning, to those you teach. The English statesman Edmund Burke said, "Example is the school of mankind and they will learn at no other" (John Bartlett, *Familiar*

Quotations. From Letter i, On a Regicide Peace. Vol. 5, p. 331). What is your example in the office, in the classroom, or on the soccer field?

And what is "the habitual vision of greatness" you set before your students? Is it merely great books, great ideas, great inventions by great figures in history? Sad to say, Alfred North Whitehead—towering intellect that he was—knew and offered nothing higher than the classic myths of Greek and Roman deities. At your Christian school, may there be a more sublime vision of the abundant life, a life made possible by obedience to the commandments to love the Lord our God and to love our neighbor. May God enable each of us to live what we teach so that when our students look at us, they see what they can become—and more!

8

SOWING THE SEED, REAPING THE HARVEST

This was the keynote address at the New England Sunday School Association's Christian Education Conference, held in Springfield, Massachusetts, on November 2, 1985.

Some years ago, when I was regularly writing Sunday School lesson materials for an evangelical publisher, I had one of those disquieting experiences every educator and writer dreads. I'd been invited to preach at the morning service of a local church and arrived early enough to be ushered into the adult Sunday School class. There, much to my chagrin, I sat through thirty minutes of excruciating boredom as the alleged "teacher" read word-for-word from the teacher's manual that I had written six to eight months earlier. My own words came back to haunt me. I realized how dull a lesson can be unless it's energized by a Spirit-directed and Spirit-illumined discussion of the Scriptures.

You are likely a Christian school administrator or faculty member, and you believe in the power of the Scriptures to shape a child's life through its precepts and the example of those who live by those precepts. But if we care about children and their nurture in a Christian school as much as we claim, it's time that we began thinking-and-acting like Christians ourselves. It's time that those who stand in our classrooms know and live by what the Scriptures teach. It's also time that those who occupy desks in administrative offices and seats at the board table do their work according to the standards of Scripture.

Everywhere I go, I issue this same call for a reaffirmation of formal Bible study in the curriculum of evangelical education. Why is it so hard to persuade reasonably intelligent deans, other administrators, and professors at Christian liberal arts colleges? Many of them seem not to understand that their often expressed goal, "the integration of faith and learning," is impossible without rigorous Bible study.

Let me offer Lockerbie's Laws on this matter, the first of which is this: *You can't integrate biblical truth into daily living and learning without a knowledge of biblical content.* And the second is like unto it: *You don't learn biblical content without studying the Bible.* Or to put it simply, *You can't integrate out of ignorance.*

But there's another maxim I'd like to include in my canon of laws for Christian education, and this one applies to all phases of Christian education, starting with family devotions and going on through Sunday School teaching, pulpit preaching, informal Bible studies, the Christian school, college—including Bible college—and seminary. It's this: *Thou shalt not make the study of the Bible dull and boring.*

I intend to demonstrate how it's possible to avoid dullness and boredom by discussing one of the most familiar passages in the Gospels.

Of all the parables told by Jesus Christ, only the parable of the sower receives such thoroughgoing explanation from the Teacher Himself. This explanation is both general as to the nature of His teaching in parables and specific as to the meaning of this particular agricultural story. I want to concentrate on the second aspect of our Lord's explanation, His own interpretation of the parable.

Wherever the parable appears—in Matthew 13, Mark 4, and Luke 8—and whenever it's preached or taught, the usual reference is to the parable of the sower. Indeed, the parable begins with these words, "A farmer went out to sow his seed." Yet Jesus makes no further reference to the farmer, the sower, or his identity. He's certainly necessary to the story, as he was and is necessary to the actual process of planting, cultivating, and harvesting on which an agrarian economy depends. There's nothing deeply mysterious or symbolic about this farmer; he's simply an instrument, broadcasting the seed from his bag slung across his shoulder and hanging at his hip. He has no special qualifications—no degree in agronomy from Palestine A&T, no certificate showing his membership in the local Farmers' Cooperative. He's simply a farmer going about the business of his work.

When it comes to the seed and its meaning, the Gospel narrators become more specific. Matthew calls the seed "the message about the kingdom," Mark says that the farmer sows "the word," and in Luke's version, "The seed is the word of God." I'll return to this point a little later.

For me, the most interesting element to this parable and our Lord's explanation of it lies in His description of the ground on which the seed falls. Rather than calling this the parable of the sower, I suggest that it be considered, more accurately, the parable of the soils because the four plots of ground and the differences among them give this parable its development and depth. Furthermore, by reading and prayerfully applying to our own situations the meanings of these different soils, we can begin to see our part in sowing the seed and reaping the harvest.

We need to understand, first, that Jesus takes for granted the farmer's good intentions and aspirations for success. We're not given to believe that the farmer is anything less than wholly conscientious about his work. He proceeds with his planting in the customary manner of his time, walking his property in rows, throwing the seed back and forth across his line of progress, shooing away the birds as best he can. Perhaps, some would charge, the farmer might have been less wasteful of the seed, more selective in aiming his throws, instead of casting it broadly from side to side. The text, of course, doesn't say.

What the text does say is that four different types of soil received the same seed with dramatically different results. The soil bordering the path, just at the edge of the farmer's field, had probably been walked on by many. It was hard as a concrete sidewalk, and the seed just lay there, waiting to be scooped up by hungry birds. The next category of soil will be familiar to any who know the terrain of the Holy Land: rocky, difficult for a plant to penetrate or take root. The seed does its best, but eventually the rocks prevail and the plant dies. Thorns spoil the third type of soil. It has sufficient earth to receive the seed and allow plants to take root, but as they grow, the thorns stifle their growth, eventually killing them. Finally, there's the good soil, and from it springs an abundant crop. In fact, both Matthew and Mark describe the size of the crops produced as "a hundred, sixty, or thirty times what was sown." A bumper crop indeed!

These four soils are different precisely because of their natural or cultivated state. They are as the farmer finds them on that day when he takes his bag of seed and goes a-sowing. Note that as Jesus interprets His own parable, nowhere does He accuse any of the first three soils of being unreceptive or antagonistic toward either the farmer or his seed. No plot of ground rises up to curse the farmer and spit the seed back in his face. Why, then, such disparity between the harvest from the good soil and the crop failure of the other three? In other words, *what made the good soil good?*

The interpretation Jesus offers His disciples teaches them and us—as Christian disciples and disciple-makers—that, ultimately, we aren't in charge of the results of our planting. Which soil is hospitable to the seed, which soil permits the seed to flourish and grow to harvest, and which doesn't is not this farmer's concern. He simply goes about his task in the time-honored manner, the way his father and grandfather have always done—and with the same almost predictable results.

But is that good enough? Just as the science of producing food has advanced over these 2,000 years, from broadcasting seed by hand to implanting it through a mechanized and computerized process, so too our methods and skills as Christian evangelists and educators ought to have improved with the centuries.

First, we're responsible for *preparing the soil*. The answer to my question above is this: What made the good soil *good* is the fact that it had been properly prepared to receive the seed. Its rocks had been dug up, its thorns uprooted, its earth ploughed and fertilized and cultivated. Perhaps the farmer had even fenced off a particular patch of ground, just so that it wouldn't become a shortcut and harden like the path.

Preparing the soil means removing obstacles to growth. The great Anglican historian of missions, Bishop Stephen Neill, told of the pioneer missionary to Iran Robert Bruce. Despite his discouragement at not finding a single convert, Bruce wrote (Adam Matthew Publications, www.adam-matthew-publications.co.uk/),

> I am not reaping the harvest; I can scarcely claim to be
> sowing the seed; I am hardly plowing the soil; but I am gath-
> ering out the stones. That, too, is missionary work; let it be
> supported by loving sympathy and fervent prayer.

We can all think of comparable instances in our own experience. As a Christian teaching English or any other subject, I am called on to do more than merely cast the seed of knowledge and truth indiscriminately and untargeted. I am also commissioned to eliminate any impediments to my students' learning—not just grammatical deficiencies or a lack of interest in reading but also some teenager's latent suspicion of adult motives, another's despair over earlier experiences with unreasonable teachers, a son or daughter's contempt for the example of faithless parents. How can the soil of a student's heart and mind become good and productive if it has already been befouled as some adults' favorite dumping ground?

And so, it is part of my job to do everything in my power to over-come the obstacles that will otherwise block my students from learning what I am trying to teach. I need to be transparent and consistent in dealing with a student cursed by cynicism. I need to be patient with a teenager whose hostility is a defense against further disappointment in adults, showing the resisting son or daughter that some adults, at least, can keep their word and fulfill their promises.

That, for me, is hewing out rocks, or "gathering out the stones," as Robert Bruce said.

For you in your school context, the act of preparing the soil may mean giving of your time to chaperone a class party or to help build a stage set or to drive a sick child home. In a broader sense, it may mean giving up your Saturday morning to take a child to the zoo or to listen to a lonely and confined older person's endless reminiscences. Or it may mean serving on some local committee or volunteer agency, or attempting to help a slovenly neighbor find order in his chaotic life, or comforting an abandoned woman and her frightened children—all in quietness and without any overt evangelism. It will *not* mean passing out tracts or quoting the Four Spiritual Laws in an ostentatious display of piety. Rather, it will simply be the steady, persevering work of readying the soil for planting, work I believe we customarily refer to now as "lifestyle evangelism."

Let us always remember that the surest indication that we've begun thinking like a Christian will be evidence that we're also acting like a Christian, demonstrating an aroused sensitivity to the needs of others. Loving God with heart, soul, strength, and mind goes hand in hand with loving our neighbor. Furthermore, loving God by loving others begins at home—often the most reluctant soil from which to garner a harvest. We show that love for God by loving the members of our own family, by showing love and gratitude, respect and honor to our parents; love and graciousness, respect and fidelity to our spouse; love and patience, respect and responsibility for our children.

Christian educators of my generation, by our increasing laxity in thinking like Christians about our own domestic relationships, are failing to give others a model to emulate. Instead of preparing the soil by hauling out its boulders, too many professed evangelicals are doing Satan's work for him, throwing obstacles to belief back into a potentially fertile field. I refer to the shame of our sinful neglect of biblical standards for loving each other.

If the apostles Peter, John, and Paul were to return and visit our evangelical community today, they would be stunned at the havoc we're wreaking on the Christian family, the Christian church. We've permitted a shoulder-shrugging, noncommittal neutrality toward marriage vows to infect our homes, along with an abdication of authority with regard to bringing up our children. We've declined to oppose the decadence of a sinful world; instead, we've taken to our bosoms its cheap and corrupt values. Can our generation be far removed from having inscribed as our motto the word *Ichabod*, "The glory of the Lord has departed" (see 1 Samuel 4:21)? We need to return to the task of removing hindrances to growth—of ourselves as well as of those we would presume to teach.

We must also work at creating an atmosphere in which mutual respect may flourish into love. I think particularly of those of us who work with children and teenagers. When I was dean of faculty at The Stony Brook School, one of my principal duties was to acquire a pool of candidates from which to select and hire new faculty members. Often I interviewed eager young men and women whose motivation in applying for a position at Stony Brook was *ministry*. By this term they generally meant talking with teenagers, witnessing to them, counseling students, leading them to faith in Jesus Christ, discipling them through Bible study—all of which are commendable in a Christian teacher. But frequently these same candidates seemed puzzled when I asked them to indicate which activity would have priority on a given evening, conducting a voluntary Bible study for a few interested students or preparing the next day's lessons in algebra or European history.

You see, it's my conviction that, no matter how earnestly an algebra teacher wishes to serve Jesus Christ by conducting student Bible studies, his primary mission—his "reasonable service"—is to be the best teacher of algebra he can be. If his primary calling suffers because of other activities—and who could doubt that time spent in Bible study with animated teenagers is more engaging than time spent correcting algebra homework?—then the algebra teacher is shortchanging his students. The worst condemnation a Christian teacher can hear is to have a student, believer or otherwise, say of him, "Oh, yeah, Mr. Jones is a really nice guy and, I guess, a committed Christian, but when it comes to algebra, he doesn't know his stuff."

Christian school administrator, teacher, or staff member, be sure you *know your stuff*! Whatever it is you presume to do as a means of preparing the soil—if you're coaching a junior high basketball team, know your stuff; if you're offering photography classes, know your stuff; if you're directing a handbell choir, know your stuff; if you're leading a backpacking expedition in the mountains, know your stuff; if you're preparing a mailing to parents, know your stuff; if you're teaching the principal parts of an irregular verb, know your stuff. It's all part of removing the obstacles to faith and growth. It's essential to creating an atmosphere in which initial reticence develops into respect and on to love.

And all the while, you'll be *spreading the seed*. Yes, even as you give instruction on how to pitch a tent so that a sudden rainstorm during the night doesn't wash its occupants away, you're spreading the seed. Even as you work at correcting homework papers so as to return them to students in a timely fashion, you're spreading the seed. Without quoting Bible verses? Yes. Without explicitly stating the plan of salvation? Yes.

But, someone else says, doesn't Jesus interpret the seed as "the word of God"? Doesn't that mean the Bible and its teachings? Of course, "the word of God" means primarily the Bible and its teachings. But the seed is more than the sixty-six books in our canon of Scripture; the seed is "the message," "the word," the truth. The seed is certainly the redemptive truth about Creation, the Fall, the covenants, grace, atonement, judgment. The seed is also the disciplining truth about the Lordship of Jesus Christ, service to Him, accountability to Him at His second coming.

But there is other truth beyond what theologians call "salvific truth," or truth that pertains to salvation. There's also truth about human responsibility, what Reformed Christians know as "the cultural mandate." So, while driving a group of teenagers within the posted speed limit won't save their souls or minds, I have no doubt that my careful, responsible, lawful driving is part of spreading the seed; and it may preserve their physical lives in order to save their souls!

The truth about Christian education and evangelism is this: if we're to be effective sowers of the seed, we can no longer content ourselves with aimless scattering; we must work at preparation and cultivation. Some of my work as a consultant for Christian schools involves assisting schools to do a better job of enlisting gift support. I know of few instances in which a person makes a worthy gift after being taken by surprise, accosted by a stranger, or embarrassed in public. Obtaining financial support takes time because the act of giving requires a foundation of mutual respect and trust on which to build confidence. Soliciting gift support requires cultivation before seed-planting, and cultivation takes time.

The same is true for sowing the seed and reaping the harvest. Yes, it's true that God is able to use all sorts of odd and even bizarre methods of evangelism. He can use a ranting street-corner preacher, and wonder of wonders, He can use you and me with our idiosyncratic ways of planting. The seed is hardy and can take root anywhere, despite adverse conditions. But how much more fruitful our harvest will be if, unlike the farmer in Jesus' parable, we are able to produce expanded acres of cultivated soil ready for planting, good soil so that we can concentrate on creating a hospitable atmosphere *before* we plant the seed.

In equipping yourself for serving God through your own gifts, always remember who is the Lord of the harvest—Lord over our budget deliberations and plans for a capital campaign, Lord over hiring of new teachers and establishing an equitable salary scale, Lord over our classrooms and cafeterias, Lord over our leaking roof and losing basketball team, Lord over our school's most laudatory achievements and—yes—even our greatest disappointments.

But in our acknowledgment of the Lordship of Jesus Christ, let's recommit ourselves to sound teaching of the Bible in our schools. Let's rid our schools of the blight of boring Bible teaching by boring teachers. Let's find the most animated, imaginative, industrious, exciting communicators on our faculty and, if necessary, train them how to teach the Bible in ways that bring the text to life and energize students to read it with eagerness.

Let's raise our sights above all that so often disturbs and distresses and distracts us from our work as Christian educators. Let's discover a renewed vision of the importance of sowing the seed and reaping the harvest, because that's our calling as tenant farmers in God's wheat fields. When we do, we are promised the eventual joy of reaping a bumper crop—a certainty because God calls us to joyful service, and He will not fail to deliver on His promise.

9

A *REAL PERSPECTIVE* ON CHRISTIAN SCHOOLING

The Mid-Atlantic Christian School Association is a regional organization founded more than a half-century ago that retains its membership and schedule of annual events. One of these is a "White Paper Conference"—a day devoted to the discussion of a single topic. On February 26, 1999, at Eastern University in St. Davids, Pennsylvania, this address initiated the White Paper discussion on the nature of belief and unbelief within a Christian school.

In the spring of 1957, I was introduced to Dr. Frank E. Gaebelein and invited to join the faculty of The Stony Brook School. I was twenty-one years old, teaching English and coaching track at Wheaton College. My wife and I arrived at Stony Brook and were assigned a faculty apartment in the residence hall occupied by some forty seniors, the oldest of whom were only two years younger than we were.

I'll never forget my first experience with those guys. A week before the school term began, football players and cross-country runners arrived for early practice. They were full of their summer's exuberance and excitement at the prospect of their final year in confinement at an all-boys' school. That zest spilled over into the dormitory corridors just outside our rooms—and some of their language also bombarded our sanctuary. Like the police officer in the film *Casablanca*, I was shocked, shocked at what I heard.

I recall going to my immediate superior, the academic administrator—a wise soul named Marvin Goldberg—and confessing to him that I had no idea that students in a Christian school would talk that way. It was he who reminded me that, while their speech was unacceptable and not to be overlooked, these boys were demonstrating one of the reasons why Jesus died on the Cross. I'm forever grateful to my colleague for helping me avoid sentimentalizing Christian schooling in favor of a real perspective.

One of the highest goals we can set for ourselves in Christian schooling is to bring "a real perspective" to our work. And I believe our failure to obtain and uphold such a perspective has led, in some part, to a triumph of postmodern intellectual and spiritual bankruptcy whereby, in a nation that boasts of massive church attendance and a high percentage of professing "born again" believers, so many seem baffled by what to do about public immorality and deceit.

Let me cite six observations from an intriguing book called *Reality Isn't What It Used to Be* by Walter Truett Anderson (Harper San Francisco, 1992):

> These are some of the givens of life in the early postmodern era:
> 1. The society itself is a social construction of reality. All the things that identify and define a "people"—such as its boundaries, its culture, its political institutions—are the (usually reified) products of earlier inventions.
> 2. Individual identity is also a social construction of reality, and the concept of a "self" is different in different societies and at different stages of history.
> 3. We regard the collective beliefs of individuals (rather than the mind of God or the laws of history) as the ultimate repository of social reality (what is true is defined by what we all believe), and we know that beliefs can be modified.
> 4. Consequently, all sectors of society are deeply interested in finding out what people believe (public opinion) and modifying those beliefs (advertising, propaganda, brainwashing, public relations, and so forth).
> 5. In a postmodern society we perceive life as drama, and our major issues involve the definition of personal roles and the fabrication of stories that give purpose and shape to social existence.
> 6. Public happenings have the quality of scenes created or stage-managed for public consumption. They are what Daniel Boorstin called pseudoevents.

Where and how do these observations manifest themselves, and with what effect on our Christian schools? Within the limits of this white paper, I can hardly claim to address fully any of the points raised, so I'll focus on a narrower band of concern. I suggest that we look at only one issue: a teenager's loss of faith and the relationship of that tragedy to a postmodern worldview. I hope thereby to address the implications of such an event for our Christian schools.

Let me frame this part of the piece by affirming that, of all the unsolved mysteries of human experience, none is more perplexing than this: how is it that—of two children reared in the same home, schooled in the same environment, presumably given the same nurture and example— one develops a warm and devout relationship with God in Christ while the other turns away in unbelief, disbelief, and dismissal? I make no claim to have any satisfactory answer to this agonizing reality. Rather, I ask these questions: Why do some never seem to take hold of their beliefs altogether? Why do they choose the vacuum of unbelief? Why do others, more aggressively, seem obsessed by a warring spirit against belief that compels them to challenge God's supremacy? Above all, why do some drift even further, into the vast wasteland of cold contempt for the very notion of faith?

Tracing that decline from a convinced and convincing faith, the first step is often skepticism brought about by an inexplicable circumstance. Doubt may lead back to faith, but it may also point to agnosticism, a word coined by Thomas Huxley, who professed merely not to know whether or not God exists. From skepticism and agnosticism, the next step down is unbelief, the refusal to believe. And beyond unbelief lurks disbelief, characterized by militant opposition to God and those who do believe. (This last is a form of intolerance rarely cited in the catalogs of "hate crimes.")

Why, we may ask, do some individuals—academic persons in particular—feel compelled not only to reject belief in the existence of God for themselves but also to challenge anyone else's belief with total hostility? Why are they seemingly so vexed by someone else's choice to put faith in Christianity or in some other religion, as if such a decision were an act of effrontery against their own personal dignity? But such disbelievers are not at the end of the continuum of faith and its absence. Yet another category exists beyond disbelief: the vast and vacant tundra of cold contempt for the very notion of faith—a sneering rejection of the validity of the religious impulse so adamant as to deny the slightest reason even to argue against religion.

I would contend that we who work in Christian schools or on their behalf see the full spectrum, from faith to cold contempt, in both our present student body and among our alumni. Call me a cynic if you will, but as I often say—somewhat facetiously—having been a teenage saint myself, I'm ever more suspicious of presumed adolescent sainthood! Would that my suspicions were not justified, but they are. And the tragedy I see is that too many Christian school administrators, teachers, and parents seem to be in a state of perpetual denial. This observation pertains especially to those parents who are unprepared to acknowledge that both sin and grace abound in the life and experience of their own children.

Thus, too many parents who send their children to our schools are afflicted by a moral myopia; like the proverbial ostrich, they have their heads buried in the sand. This ostrich syndrome is most apparent in those schools that demand a faith profession from students, and it is almost equally apparent in schools that require that at least one parent be a believer. Armed only with these admissions criteria, gullible parents and naive educators somehow form unrealistic expectations, giving them a false sense of security. We have the signature of the kid, affirming his commitment at age fourteen to whatever creed we've spelled out. We have the parents—or at least one of them—nodding vigorously when we ask if they are faithful witnesses of Jesus Christ and communicants of some evangelical fellowship. So then, how can it be that this child is arrested for shoplifting, or that the sponsoring church's pastor's son makes the front page of the newspaper for some infamous act, or that those same godly parents have just introduced us to their notoriously litigious attorney?

Whenever I meet a head-of-school whose admissions policies restrict entrance to believing students or the offspring of believing parents, I find it hard to resist a little teasing. "Oh, it must be wonderful," I say with tongue in cheek, "to lead a school where the students don't lie or steal or cheat or cuss or use drugs, where the girls don't get pregnant and the boys think only pure thoughts and the parents don't sue!" To which the standard response is, "That's not my school you're describing"—at which point, the jaws of my trap spring shut! "So then, what's the point of your restrictive admissions policy?"

What is the point of excluding someone—a student we'd invite to Sunday school or vacation Bible school or youth group or Christian camp—from our Christian school classroom? If enrolling only presumably believing students makes no difference in the tone and behavior of our school, why are we doing so? And aren't we, in fact, defying the One in whose name we hold school, who said, "Let the little children come to me, and do not hinder them" (Matthew 19:14)?

One of the principal metaphors of the New Testament is growth to maturity, pictured as human development from a toothless and nursing infant, dependent for nourishment on milk and mush, to a strong and virile adult capable of chewing steak. Because the spiritual analogy fits so well with the familiar physical growth of children, from babes in arms to young adults, we have no difficulty accepting the fact that persons of any age may be either more or less mature in spiritual matters. In and of itself, chronological age isn't the issue. St. Paul knew this well enough to specify, in his instructions to Timothy, "Don't let anyone look down on you because you are young" (1 Timothy 4:12). At the same time, the apostle declared that a leader in the church "must not be a recent convert" (1 Timothy 3:6), lest his spiritual immaturity govern his actions.

Once in a while, we come upon a youthful believer who is spiritually developed far in advance of his or her years. We are blessed as a school to have such an influence in our midst, but such persons are rare. Jesus of Nazareth Himself could not produce one out of twelve who possessed such traits. In fact, a friend of mine has pointed out that, when Jesus called the apostles, not one of them was a Christian! We need to be realistic about our spiritual assumptions. We need to reject the tendency toward expectations of sanctification and the unavoidable disappointment that results when we demand more than is reasonable in social, intellectual, or spiritual maturity.

Only God knows whose names have been written in the Book of Life, but I venture to observe that the remarkable words attributed to John Newton may well dampen the typical Christian school's spirit of triumphalism regarding its students and graduates. Newton wrote, "There will be three wonders in heaven: There will be people there I never expected to see; there will be people absent I expected to see; and wonder of wonders, I shall be there" (source unknown). Since none of us knows for sure who is in what state of grace, let us not assume that all our present students and eventual alumni are already enrolled.

Instead, let's retain a measure of reserve. Once I became aware of the dangers of assuming too much about a teenager's spirituality, I developed a habit regarding public prayer. Rather than saying, "Let's all pray," I'd say, "Will those of you who are committed to the Lordship of Jesus Christ please join me in prayer." Like it or not, everyone in that public gathering is instantly summoned to a moment of self-examination: "Is he talking to me? Am I included among those invited to pray? If not, why not?" It's a way of overcoming the error of taking someone else's spiritual state for granted.

At the same time, whatever the admissions policies of our school, we do well to recognize that, while the students are under our care, they are passing through periods of emotional and intellectual change. The most obnoxious teenager can develop into a radiant believer. So too an earnest fourteen-year-old can turn into an honest doubter at sixteen and an angry scoffer at eighteen. What must we do in such circumstances? Without attempting to lay down a "law of the Medes and Persians that altereth not," I would simply say this: our Christian schools need to be places that offer inquiring and searching teenagers what I call *the dignity of dissent*.

Thus we will welcome the skeptic, the doubter, the unconvinced. Sure, we can require courtesy and a respectful tone in expressing dissent, but we need to remove from our adult attitudes any fear that somehow this adolescent may discover the weak point in our Christian faith that will bring the whole superstructure tumbling down. We need to eliminate from our language the sarcasm and hostility that attempts to bully and bulldoze into oblivion the honest—or even the smart-alecky—questions about the Bible's integrity or the Bible's historicity or the church's failings. No teenager is going to overturn the fact of the Resurrection by asking awkward questions. We need to welcome those questions as evidence that the Holy Spirit is keeping that student's heart and mind prepared so that the seed of the Word will eventually take root and flourish. And we need to rid ourselves of the notion that we must be able to answer every question.

Let our school never in any way be a stumbling block to a young person's coming to faith and retaining that faith. The place to begin is with our curriculum, which too often has been one of the failings of our Christian schools. The problem is not that we haven't been pious enough or that our teachers haven't set a good example. But we have failed to demonstrate what T. S. Eliot means when he calls for Christians to be "able to think in Christian categories" (T. S. Eliot, *Christianity and Culture* [New York: Harcourt Brace, 1949]). As a consequence, too often we prove the accuracy of Harry Blamires' arresting opening sentence, "There is no longer a Christian mind" (Harry Blamires, *The Christian Mind* [Ann Arbor, MI: Servant Publications, 1978], 3).

Often the course of study we teach is little more than a sanctified version of what can be found in any state-supervised or Middle States accredited school. We hold daily or weekly chapel, yes, and in many classrooms a prayer is said before the lesson begins. But where is the biblical perspective? Where is the biblical world-and-life view? Where is what Frank Gaebelein called "the pattern of God's truth" woven into the fabric of what we teach (Gaebelein, *The Pattern of God's Truth* [New York: Oxford University Press, 1954])? Where is the reality of the wholeness of truth in our curriculum? Where is the challenge to our students to "think in Christian categories" about physics and physical education? about words and the Word? about politics and policy? about the difference between science and scientism? between ethics and morality? between the relative and the absolute? Where is the challenge to "think in Christian categories" about sports and music and sex and money and death?

I'm prepared to make a bold statement. Unless our schools are teaching their academic content specifically from a dedicated and intentional point of view—by which I mean a biblical world-and-life-view—our schools are worse than inadequate; they are a sham. If all we have to offer is piety, then we are less than a school. If all we have to offer is example—no matter how worthy of emulation—we are less than a school. We need piety, example, and academic content from the vantage of a biblical understanding of truth and reality.

But what about the masses of students who aren't rebellious, aren't scoffers, aren't blasphemous but are just inert, apathetic, and bored—like many of their parents in the pew on Sunday—because our students, like their parents, aren't receiving instruction that transforms and renews the mind? What do we say about our Christian school's typical graduating senior?

Several years ago, I had the honor of giving the Jubilee address at the fiftieth anniversary of the Association for Biblical Higher Education. In preparation, I conducted a survey to determine the relationship between those Bible colleges and Christian schools. I wanted to know what the current pool of prospective students thinks about Bible colleges as a viable continuation of their formal education, as a place of preparation for Christian vocation. My message to the assembled dignitaries from these colleges was not encouraging. What do Christian school twelfth graders think of Bible colleges? In a word, nothing. For the most part, only a tiny portion of twelfth-grade students give any Bible college any consideration in their postsecondary plans.

These perceptions had been derived from a poll that PAIDEIA Inc. conducted of some five hundred graduating seniors in Christian secondary schools. We surveyed specifically college-bound seventeen- and eighteen-year-olds in long-established evangelical schools—the very context in which one might expect to find a population compatible with the purposes of a Bible college. Their responses to our five questions are telling:

1. Why do you plan to attend college? By far the greatest number of reasons offered reflected purely utilitarian and occupational values. Only two or three out of the entire group wrote anything like this: To get training to serve the Lord and go on the mission field.

2. Have you applied to a Christian college? If so, is it a liberal arts college or a Bible college? One percent of these college-bound students had applied to a Bible college. The college-placement counselor at one of the leading Christian schools—himself a graduate of a Bible college—tells me that he has not had one Bible-college applicant in the last fifteen years.

3. What is the difference between a Bible college and an evangelical liberal arts college? In order to discern why these students might not have chosen to apply to a Bible college, we asked what they knew about the difference between a Bible college and an evangelical liberal arts college. Those who gave the most thoughtful answers were convinced that a Bible college offers little besides biblical studies. They knew nothing about the breadth of the curriculum offered, and they assumed that the Bible college exists only to prepare pastors and missionaries. They also assumed that Bible colleges are highly restrictive in their expectations of student behavior. This response is representative of the high end of this student population: "Bible colleges are more geared to people going into ministry of some sort; liberal arts colleges help prepare you for other jobs with a Christian worldview."

4. Which of the following list of colleges and universities can be recognized as explicitly evangelical Christian? Our poll listed ten regional universities and colleges, and asked students to identify which are "explicitly evangelical Christian." Two of the ten in each list were Bible colleges, so they were generally identified— although one respondent noted only that Lancaster Bible College "might be." Of the rest, Messiah and Cedarville were the most readily recognized. Again, a single respondent commented that Messiah "used to be" Christian. Not one respondent recognized Eastern University as "evangelical Christian." Highly disconcerting was the fact that fully 21 percent of the responses carried a handwritten message informing us that the respondents did not understand what we were asking; they did not know what we meant by asking them to identify a college, whether liberal arts or not, that they recognized as "explicitly evangelical Christian."

5. If your family could afford any college and your grades qualified you, which college would you most like to attend? Overwhelmingly, the answers were the Ivy League, the NCAA Final Four

basketball colleges, and so forth. Very few of these seniors in Christian high schools were content with their college choice. Only one whose first choice was a Bible college indicated that she would choose it over all other available options. (That college, by the way, was Philadelphia Biblical University.) Fully 10 percent of the responses included a gratuitous note to the effect that, wherever the anonymous student enrolled, it would be a place where he or she could indulge in the most notorious sins of the flesh.

I pass along this information for what it's worth—and what it's worth, I believe, is a careful scrutiny of adult attitudes and convictions at two levels of education and over the full range of institutional mission and marketing. At first, as someone who spent thirty-four years in a Christian preparatory school, I was appalled—even ashamed—at how grossly under-informed these twelfth graders were, only two months before graduation. How could they be so ignorant of issues pertinent to their own future?

Then I tried to gain some perspective and shifted my ire from them to their teachers, counselors, and administrators—which meant me in my former roles. Clearly, those of us in Christian schooling need to do a better job of conveying to our students the universe of higher education, the distinctives among the several types of institutions, and the particular distinctives within Christian higher education. First, however, we must bring a real perspective to Christian schooling.

Perhaps we can begin to understand why—for those who lack the gift of belief—many professing believers seem to have all the right answers to the wrong questions. Perhaps those of us who believe need to ask why our conventional methods of evangelism seem so corny or staged; why religious broadcasting is so predictable and sometimes even phony; why the altar call smacks of something straight out of *Elmer Gantry* or Robert Duvall's film *The Apostle*. Those of us in Christian schools need to ask why we insist on suffocatingly common expectations when the Lord Jesus Christ Himself was so unconventional. Remember this: The disappointed father looks up through his sorrow and sees the wayward son returning— and what does he do? He throws a party! He kills the fattened calf and hires an orchestra. He doesn't impose regulations, and he accepts his younger son's repentance at face value. It's worth our noting that the only wallflower—the only person invited who doesn't join the dance—is the self-righteous and unforgiving elder brother.

Like our Lord, we too need to look for other ways of communicating the Truth, other ways of taking the unbeliever—and even the disbeliever—

by surprise. And what a marvelous surprise it is to discover that, after all, the Truth is no arcane philosophy subject to current approval, nor is it a systematic theology requiring categorical intellectualizing. The Truth is but a simple fact of history, and the most elementary starting point in personal evangelism—the Good News that this Man Jesus receives sinners and eats with them.

In 1998, on the fortieth anniversary of their graduation from The Stony Brook School, my first group of senior students gathered at our home for their reunion. We welcomed them because, as I told them, Lory and I were eager to see how much they had aged! Bald and portly, these fifty-eight-year-old grandfathers hugged and wept as they saw friends and roommates some hadn't seen in two-score years. All of them hugged my beautiful wife; some even hugged me. And as the evening went on, we shared stories. Some were revealing of how naive and gullible I'd been as a rookie teacher among these veteran students. Everyone laughed at the recollection.

But there were other stories as well—stories of a long rebellion against home and church and God and Christ and the Bible and everything that Stony Brook had stood for. And yes—in more cases than not—stories with a happy ending, not unlike that of Luke 15. In the late hours, after most of the alumni had departed, a few remained to tell my wife and me what our youthful and immature marriage and parenthood had meant to them. It was far too humbling for us to comprehend, but it was also another reminder of what my older colleague Marvin Goldberg had meant when he told me—forty years earlier—"Bruce, that's why Jesus died on the Cross."

After all my years in Christian schooling, I'm thoroughly convinced that what matters most is not the testimonies given by students at the commencement exercises but their witness on Alumni Weekend ten or twenty or forty years later. What matters most is not how well we combat the worst elements of popular culture but how well we equip our students for the years that lie ahead by giving them the resources to "think in Christian categories," to gain a biblical perspective on reality.

The task is ours, the challenge is ours, the hope is ours.

10

JERUSALEM, JUDEA, SAMARIA: CONCENTRIC CIRCLES OF CHRISTIAN SCHOOLING

*The Hoboken Group is a loose federation of urban schools brought together origi-
nally by Mustard Seed School in Hoboken, New Jersey. The Hoboken Group met
on December 2, 2000, at Spruce Hill Christian School in Philadelphia,
Pennsylvania, where this keynote address was delivered.*

Jesus Christ made the following promise to His disciples: "You will
receive power when the Holy Spirit comes on you; and you will be my
witnesses in Jerusalem, and in all Judea and Samaria, and to the ends of the
earth" (Acts 1:8). The text is familiar; it is a corollary to what is often
referred to as "the Great Commission" to the church, "Go and make disciples of all nations" (Matthew 28:19). The reason these two texts stand side
by side is that one provides the *mandate*—"Go"—and the other provides
the *plan*—start here in the city, then go to the suburbs, then to the countryside, and finally "to the ends of the earth."

There can be no avoiding the mandate. The risen Lord doesn't offer
His apostles a recommendation for them to consider and debate and
perhaps revise. He puts it to them straight: "Go and make disciples of all
nations." He doesn't suggest that they offer a seminar on comparative religion or a workshop on self-discovery or a meditation on finding the god
within each one of us. He says straightforwardly, "Make disciples."

What does Jesus mean when He talks about making disciples? To
answer this question, it's important for us, as Christian educators, to know
and understand both the denotation of the word *disciple* and its connotations. At the basic level of the denotation, or dictionary definition, a disciple is a pupil, someone who, according to the ancient custom, sits at the

feet of a teacher and takes in every word—literally, reciting back in rote fashion what the teacher has just said.

What are the connotations to be drawn from that picture? Among those that come to mind is the teacher who is superior to the pupil because the teacher knows far more; the teacher who sits above the pupil and speaks down to him, both literally and figuratively; the teacher who dictates what the pupil is to learn. Similarly, we have the connotations of *pupil* as one who absorbs like a sponge the teacher's every utterance, repeating not only the teacher's words but every inflexion, every intonation, every emphasis, every pause. In other words, the ancient relationship between teacher and pupil, teacher and disciple, is didactic and overpowering. In some classrooms today—including some Christian school classrooms—the authority of the teacher expresses itself as *authoritarianism*—as in the old TV series and movie *Paper Chase* (20th Century Fox, 1973), in which the actor John Housman played an intimidating law professor.

Combining these connotations, what impression do we get of the disciple of an ancient teacher? Simply this: The pupil accepts the *discipline* of absolute obedience to the teacher. But is this what it means to be a *disciple* of Jesus Christ? Is this the mandate of the gospel? "Go and make mindless clones ..."? "Go and create little robots who will follow orders"? "Go and brainwash ..."? Indeed not. If we read the New Testament carefully, we find an entirely new method of teaching and its entirely revolutionary results. For in the mandate to "go and make disciples," we also find the command to go and free the slaves, go and liberate the minds and hearts and souls of those who now believe that Jesus Christ is Lord.

When we go and invite someone to become a disciple of Jesus Christ, we go in the name of freedom and liberty. A favorite inscription on academic buildings is the statement from John 8:32, "The truth will set you free." There's a liberating sound to those words. But there's also a context, and it is in the preceding statement, recorded in the preceding verse. Jesus doesn't imply that somehow or other each of us can come independently to a knowledge of the truth that sets us free. He is very specific about how we are to gain that knowledge: "If you hold to my teaching," He declares, "you are really my disciples. *Then* you will know the truth, and the truth will set you free" (John 8:31–32, emphasis added).

And what was that teaching? Unlike a lot of religious leaders after Him—gurus and mind-control experts and swamis and manipulators—Jesus did not present a series of declarations to be memorized and regurgitated on demand. Rather, he taught primarily by asking questions.

"But," someone will say, "doesn't the Bible tell us that the crowds were astonished at Jesus' teaching because He did so with authority, not like the teachers they were accustomed to?" Yes, the Bible says this—but we need to understand that the authority of "the teachers they were accustomed to" was the authority of standing on the shoulders of those who had gone before them—very much like the expectations of a scholarly dissertation today, that the writer will use a lot of footnotes to document and verify the scholar's thesis. Nobody today expects to be awarded a graduate degree on the basis of his own independent claims to scholarship.

But Jesus was different from those teachers. In fact, Jesus of Nazareth got off to an early start in His method. Remember the story at the end of Luke 2, when Joseph and Mary take Jesus to Jerusalem for His *bar mitzvah*? Somehow He becomes separated from them, and they suppose that He is with the extended family in the city. Not until they are returning home do they realize that He isn't present. Greatly agitated, they retrace their way to Jerusalem, where they finally find Him "in the temple courts, sitting among the teachers, listening to them and asking them questions. Everyone who heard him was amazed at his understanding and his answers" (Luke 2:46–47).

Why? Because it was unheard of for a pupil to pose his own questions to a teacher; unheard of that a mere student would dare to think outside the prescribed series of questions to which there were prescribed answers, quoting the prescribed authorities, the rabbis and prophets of old. Yet at age twelve, Jesus was already overturning the conventions of teaching and learning. He was demonstrating the freedom that comes when the Spirit of God imbues the mind.

So it was throughout His ministry. Yes, in the Sermon on the Mount, He made a series of declarations we call the Beatitudes; yes, He taught by directive, even didactic, statements. But He also asked questions, drawing the answers out of His audience. In fact, like the Greek philosopher Socrates four hundred years earlier, Jesus taught by feigning ignorance, pretending not to know the answer Himself in order to draw an answer from His disciples.

For instance, when He and His company of followers were at the Roman shrine called Caesarea Philippi, He almost gave the impression of someone suffering from an identity crisis. "Who do people say the Son of Man is?" and "Who do you say I am?" (Matthew 16:13, 15). Had Jesus lost track of His mission, His purpose, His identity? Why did He need to ask mere men to confirm who He is? Why didn't He simply declare Himself? You know the obvious answer: He wanted His followers—His *disciples*—to answer His question with their own affirmation: "You are the Christ, the Son of the living God" (Matthew 16:16). For them, this was a freeing moment of intellectual insight as well as spiritual enlightenment.

How about another example? It's a few days after the Passover, and two devout Jews, one named Cleopas, are walking from Jerusalem toward Emmaus. Suddenly they are joined on the road by a fellow traveler who asks them why they are so morose, so downcast. They say to him, "How can you be so uninformed! Don't you know what's been going on? Weren't you watching CNN Headline News this weekend? Did you miss your copy of *USA Today*?" Does Jesus step away from playing dumb and declare who He is? No, He continues to profess not to know what they're talking about and turns the discussion to what the prophets had written about the Messiah. Later, Cleopas and his companion recognize who has been asking them questions.

The method of inquiry—asking questions—is Jesus Christ's preferred method for winning disciples: not hammering a set of rubrics to be memorized and recited but teaching by asking questions whose purpose is to evoke the disciples' own confession of faith.

Let's go back to John 8:31–32: "If you hold to my teaching, you are really my disciples. Then you will know the truth, and the truth will set you free." Those who are mathematicians or philosophers will note the use of *if ... then*. Such reasoning is familiar to us in the cliché, "*If* it looks like a duck and it walks like a duck and it quacks like a duck, *then* it must be a duck." Same thing: *If* you hold to—meaning, if you respect and act upon—the teaching of Jesus, *then* you qualify to call yourself a disciple, someone who has put herself under the regimen of discipline that the teacher or the coach imposes. What makes successful basketball coaches? Their insistence that players *hold to* their teaching.

After the *mandate* comes the *plan*: "Go and make disciples.... Be my witnesses in Jerusalem, and in all Judea and Samaria, and to the ends of the earth." Jesus knows what it takes to make disciples. It takes discipline. Jesus knows what it takes to acquire the liberating blessing of *truth*. It takes discipline, the rigorous and repetitive practice of essentials until they are mastered; the equally rigorous question-and-answer technique of assessment and self-examination that leads to understanding. And where better to learn such discipline, such essentials, than in school? And who better to make disciples than those whose life of witness sets the example of discipleship?

From the earliest days of the Christian faith, the church fathers understood the importance of teaching discipleship. We know from the early chapters of Acts that instruction was fundamental to the growth of the young church. This instruction was not confined to children but extended to all those professing faith in Jesus Christ. The first classroom was the Upper Room—perhaps the same place where Jesus had instituted the memorial we know as the Last Supper, the celebration of which we call Holy Communion, or the Eucharist.

But soon the group of believers had grown too large to meet in such a space. They took to the streets of Jerusalem, to the Temple Mount, to Solomon's Colonnade. There they heard the sermon that Simon Peter gave on the day of Pentecost, or the testimony of the formerly lame beggar who was healed by the power of Jesus' name. When the believers dispersed, it was not to return to a single meeting place but to many homes, where the teaching continued around the table as Christian families shared their meals together. In fact, Acts 4:32 tells us that these first Christians shared far more than a potluck supper; they shared "everything they had." What better lesson could they have taught their children?

In time, the plan to make disciples took the apostles beyond the city limits. In most instances, they were driven out of Jerusalem by persecution, beginning with the martyrdom of Stephen. But even such hardship didn't diminish their sense of mandate and plan, for we read that "those who had been scattered preached the word wherever they went" (Acts 8:4). For instance, Philip preached in Samaria, then met the royal official from the court of Candace, queen of the Ethiopians, and won him to faith in Jesus Christ.

After the conversion of Saul of Tarsus, we discover that Christians had fled all the way from Jerusalem to Damascus in Syria. Later, we find converts in Lydda and Joppa, and even among the Roman garrison at Caesarea. Furthermore, we read, "Now those who had been scattered by the persecution in connection with Stephen traveled as far as Phoenicia, Cyprus, and Antioch" (Acts 11:19). In Antioch, by the time Paul and Barnabas received their call to missionary service, there were already "prophets and teachers" there, men like Simeon the black man (could he be the same person who carried Jesus' cross?) and Lucius from Libya, and Manaen who had been a member of the household of Herod Antipas, who helped to condemn Jesus to death. From Antioch, Paul and Barnabas took the gospel to Cyprus and the rest of the Mediterranean and Roman world.

And so the gospel expanded. But what about formal schooling? Before the end of the apostolic age, Paul was already using the language of the Greek school to instruct Timothy, himself a graduate of the *gymnasium* in Lystra. As the first century came to an end, a believer named Clement had opened a school in Rome. In the middle of the second century, in the city of Nablus—made notorious today by the frequent atrocities committed there by Palestinians and Israelis against each other—a teacher named Justin came to faith in Jesus Christ and continued his work in a school in Rome. In time, he argued the case for Christianity before the Roman

Senate. In the city of Alexandria, another Clement and Origen held school. In Rome, a North African named Augustine—the greatest mind among the church fathers—wrote *On Christian Doctrine*, a handbook for Christian teachers, in which he argued that nothing is foreclosed from a Christian believer's study and learning because, said Augustine, "wherever he may find truth, it is his Lord's."

The roster of Christian teachers and schoolmasters is rich with honor. Another North African named Tertullian argued that too much of worldly culture adulterates the Christian faith. But Basil in Constantinople countered by urging the Christian student to be as selective as a honeybee, taking the good here and rejecting the bad there. All these teachers and schoolmasters set an example for others to follow the *plan*: They taught their students what it means to be a disciple of Jesus Christ; and they did it in the major cities of their time. They grew and nurtured the growth of others precisely where they had been planted.

There is a logical reason why Christian schools began in the ancient cities of Rome and Alexandria and eventually Athens and Jerusalem. Those were the urban centers of government and commerce, the places where the educated lived. As more and more schools were founded, they tended to be in the palaces of kings and bishops, and in the great centers of trade and manufacturing. After the collapse of the Roman Empire and the spread of the Christian faith throughout the known world, the pattern continued: schools were founded in the major cities. Thus, if a prospective student wished to learn, he journeyed to the city to find a teacher and a school. And if someone founded a school, it was in the city, where the children were. Not until the great missionary movement sponsored by Gregory the Great in the fifth century did Christian teachers found schools in the *pagus*—the remote regions, the suburbs, the countryside inhabited by pagans.

Sometimes royalty demanded the presence of a teacher. At the turn of the ninth century, a famous teacher in England named Alcuin was summoned by the Emperor Charlemagne to his royal home in Aachen. Alcuin had been teaching in York, the second most important city in England. Now he was hired to teach the son of the emperor, a youth named Pepin. How did Alcuin proceed? He set his lessons to music and taught his student to sing what he was learning. So the text of the Apostles' Creed was learned first as a sing-along.

Six centuries later in 1423, Gianfrancisco Gonzaga, the Duke of Mantua, learned about a renowned teacher named Vittorino da Feltre. He ordered Vittorino to his palace to teach the children of royalty. But Vittorino declined unless certain conditions were met. He demanded that he and the students be housed together, away from the corrupting influences of the palace, and that he be the sole authority as to what his students were taught. The Duke agreed, and Vittorino set out to find a suitable site. What he found may be of some encouragement to you who have struggled to find adequate space for your school. Vittorino found an abandoned brothel known as "The House of Pleasure." He claimed it and renamed it *La Giacosa*, "The House of Joy." There for twenty-three years, he led his students in what came to be known as the finest school in Italy.

At the beginning of the seventeenth century, when Europeans began arriving in the New World, they too brought formal schooling with them. In the Massachusetts Bay Colony, the legislature stipulated the necessity of schooling to combat "ye olde deluder Satan." The founders of Harvard College chose as its motto the Latin words *Veritas pro Christo et ecclesia*, meaning "Truth for Christ and the Church." They declared that the purpose of its education was "to know God and Jesus Christ, which is eternal life." The founders of Yale College set as their motto the words "Light and Truth." Sadly, today most of the institutions that once enshrined truth or engraved the words of Jesus on their buildings have long since abandoned the discipleship that was their purpose. And that's where we must differ from them, by remaining true to the One who is the very source of truth.

But even as we choose to differ from those who have apostatized, we can also learn from our ancestors about the importance of beginning our mission in the city, where the children live. That's where our American schools began: Boston Latin School in 1635, the Collegiate School in New York soon thereafter. By 1750, in Philadelphia, the Quaker Anthony Benezet, who taught at William Penn Charter School and founded the first girls' school in America, was teaching the children of African and Caribbean slaves. Through his influence, in 1770, the Philadelphia Meeting of the Society of Friends voted to construct a school for slave children, which Benezet headed until his death in 1784. A century later, Russell H. Conwell, the pastor of the Baptist Temple in Philadelphia, began a school in his church as a means of teaching English literacy to immigrants. That school is today's Temple University.

Of course, much has changed since the 1880s. There has been a series of migrations in the last 120 years: first, from the farm to the city, from the plantation to the ghetto, from the islands to the *barrio*; and more recently, an opposite retreat from the urban center to the suburbs and beyond. But our mission is to found and sustain schools *wherever the children are*.

The plan for a broadening gospel witness, set forth by Jesus Christ in Acts 1:8, creates in our imagination a picture of ring upon ring of circles moving outward from the center, like the ripples made by a stone thrown into a quiet pond. We call these rings *concentric circles*, for not only is each new circle outside the old, but each new circle has the same center as the old.

What is that center that every circle holds in common? It's not a matter of geography or a location such as Jerusalem. It's not a place; it's a Person. In giving the mandate and the plan to His apostles, Jesus isn't saying that there is something magical about staying put in the upper room in Jerusalem. He simply promises that, if they are obedient to His mandate and plan, power will come to them. That power—the Greek word is our word for *dynamite*—derives from the person of the Holy Spirit, who testifies to us that Jesus Christ is Lord.

Whatever your school's written mission and philosophy—or lack thereof—it's likely that the common spoken or unspoken element is a biblical awareness of God the Father and of His Son Jesus Christ. The basic element that distinguishes Christian schooling from other forms of schooling, public and nonpublic, is this: commitment to Jesus Christ as Lord!

Jesus Christ is Lord! *Iesus Christos Kurios!* These Greek words in English express the earliest Christian creed, the formulaic password that gained admission to the secret meetings of the followers of the Way, who first became known as Christians in Syrian Antioch. Eventually, the single phrase would be expanded into a baptismal confession of faith: "I believe in God the Father almighty, maker of heaven and earth, and in Jesus Christ his only Son our Lord . . . ," known to the ancients in Latin as the *symbolum apostolorum*, the apostles' passport or symbol of authenticity. In the Roman Empire, when an official message was transmitted by courier from one dignitary to another, the messenger carried half of a broken disc. The recipient had the other half, and because the two halves fit perfectly, he knew the message was authentic.

But before the framing of the Apostles' Creed came the three Greek words *Iesus Christos Kurios*. What did this phrase mean to them, more than nineteen hundred years ago? What does it mean to us? It ought to mean nothing less than that Jesus Christ is the very center of all that constitutes our universe. He is the cosmic center.

In our schools' mission and philosophy, it is important that we put Christ at the center and that we learn to live in His peace. Our students will never be prepared for their adult lives unless we who administer and teach in their schools stand firmly on that watchword, that Jesus Christ is Lord, and unless we ground them in that reality. The real difference between Christian schooling and public schooling, or any other form of elementary and secondary schooling, must be this: In our Christian schools we bring every thought, every theorem, every act, every axiom, every aspect of teaching and learning—with rigor and without apology—into captivity under the sovereign Lordship of Jesus Christ, at whose coming in glory every knee will bow and every tongue confess that He is Lord to the glory of God the Father.

This is the mission of Christian schooling. We have no other. This is our common mandate and plan: to go wherever there are children and make disciples in the name of the Lord Jesus Christ.

11

TRANSFORMING CHARACTER: THINKING-AND-ACTING LIKE A CHRISTIAN

This address was presented to the ACSI South-Central Region's convention in Dallas, Texas, on November 24, 2003.

Teaching that transforms character—one of the core goals of Christian schooling—presupposes the inherent and indelible relationship between *thinking* and *acting* like a Christian; the connection between how we speak and act and who we claim to be; between language and character, between appearance and reality. Nothing else about our lives is more important than this: that we should demonstrate by our thinking-and-acting that we are subject to the Lordship of Jesus Christ.

In the interest of full disclosure, I should point out that I've written a book titled *Thinking-and-Acting like a Christian.* When it came time to issue a second edition, I changed the title ever so slightly: I added hyphens to connect the three words *Thinking-and-Acting.* Why? I wanted to suggest visually that, for the mature believer, *thinking-and-acting* ought to be both sides of one coin; *thinking-and-acting* should more often be simultaneous rather than sequential.

The reason is that how we think and what we say or do stem from the same source. Our Lord Jesus Christ put this idea plainly when He said, "For out of the overflow of the heart the mouth speaks" (Matthew 12:34). The apostle James asks, "Can both fresh water and salt water flow from the same spring?" (James 3:11). The French naturalist Comte de Buffon said, "Style is the man himself" (*Diacours de Reception* [Recueil de l'Academie, 1753]). There is no longer any escape clause to separate what we say and do from who we are. When a professional football coach has to go on national television to apologize to his wife and daughter for his sidelines behavior during a game, including foul speech, it does little good to blame that behavior and speech on the emotions of the moment. He *is* what he *says*. So are we all.

I'm reminded of an old chorus we used to sing in Baptist youth groups:

> I wanna be more than a Sunday-go-to-meetin' Christian:
> I want religion that thrills me every day.
> Sayin' "Amen!" to the preacher is fine
> If every day I let my light shine.
> I wanna be more than a Sunday-go-to-meetin' Christian.

That's what I mean by *thinking-and-acting like a Christian*. Someone else might call it "authentic Christianity."

The main challenge of our vocation in Christian schooling is to be men and women of God before the children and youth who are in our care. This challenge—especially in our essentially God-dismissing culture—is to remind some and inform others of an unbreakable tie that binds into one our thought, speech, and action, because it is our thought, speech, and action that together and in concert define our character and give evidence as to whether or not we are truly Christlike and therefore Christian.

What about Thanksgiving Day, for instance? Do we permit it to be called "Turkey Day," as is becoming increasingly common? Do we instruct our students about the history of the event, dating from 1621, when the few survivors at Plymouth Plantation gave thanks to God for their very lives and celebrated God's grace among them in the provision of food? Do we teach our students—and their parents—a rudimentary lesson in logic, rhetoric, and grammar, profoundly apparent in our God-dismissing media. The point being missed by the secularists is simply this: You can't celebrate Thanksgiving Day in a vacuum. In fact, you can't even speak the word *Thanksgiving* without two accompanying prepositions and pronouns: Thanksgiving *for what?* and Thanksgiving *to whom?*

Again, as we celebrate Jesus' Incarnation at Christmas, do we succumb to the vapid secular holiday custom of gift giving without valid meaning? Do we utter the banalities of "Season's greetings" without questioning why Christmas should be "merry"? Do the cards we send cater to the Hallmark commercialism of the times, or do they express our belief in a Savior born as a child in order to suffer death as a man? Do we heed the words of Reginald Heber's carol, "The Infant King," as he points to the real reason for the Incarnation?

Sing lullaby! Lullaby, Baby, now reclining,
Sing lullaby! Hush, do not wake the Infant King,
Dreaming of Easter, gladsome morning,
Conquering death, its bondage breaking: Sing lullaby!

What we say and how we say it means something. Yes, there are limits to language. We can never adequately express ourselves, and a word is not the thing itself. But the God who reveals Himself to us as the *logos* is the eternal Word Himself; He is the everlasting *Yes*, the affirmation of all meaning. Therefore, if we profess to believe in who He is—and if we claim to be staking our lives on that belief—we will speak somewhat differently from those who do not share that faith. In short, our use of language will be transformed along with our character.

Obviously, we will cease and desist from profaning the name of God and will demand that others under our care and supervision do the same. I believe I can date almost exactly the beginning of the scourge that is so popular among the young, the exclamation "Oh, my God!" with its rising intonation of surprise and dismay. It started with a television sit-com heroine whose family caused her a steady stream of anxious moments, to which she characteristically responded by smacking her forehead and declaiming, "Oh, my God!" Soon an entire generation of teenagers and children were mimicking her.

At The Stony Brook School, where I was at that time, I urged my colleagues to challenge our students each time they said the phrase by asking, "Is that a prayer or a curse?" Typically, the student looked confused and wondered what the adult was talking about. Typically, the student had no awareness of having said anything at all remotely resembling a prayer or a curse; he or she had simply spoken mindlessly or casually the name of the Supreme Being. So what?

So what, indeed! And so what if a coach of a team representing a Christian school wishes his athletes "good luck" before a game? So what if a teacher at a Christian school informs her class that her reason for being late this morning is that she had an "accident" while driving to school? Do we have to be *that* picky about the words we use? After all, isn't it enough for our speech to convey the general idea of what we mean?

No, it is not enough. I remind you that the Scriptures are full of injunctions about words, *words*, *WORDS*. We are urged to utter only "worthy words" and to speak a "timely" word. We are warned against "bitter words" and their sting. We are cautioned about the damnation that awaits those who swear oaths and do not keep their word. And most important, the prologue to St. John's Gospel does not say that "in the beginning was the General Idea" or that "the Vague Notion became flesh and dwelt among us."

So let us covenant together ourselves to *think-and-speak* like the Christians we profess to be; for only then can we begin to urge our students to develop their Christian character in accord with their speech. Let us place a premium on words and the Word. Let us use the power of memorizing and reciting Scripture to fulfill what I used to tell my reluctant students was my duty: to serve as the interior decorator of their souls by hanging beautiful texts on the walls of their minds. And let us—once and for all—rid ourselves of the silly notion that, somehow, spelling and the precise use of language doesn't matter outside the English classroom. Precision in usage and accuracy of expression do matter. In science, in mathematical word problems, in history, in Bible, an incoherent written response is never the right answer. There never was a battle at G-e-t-i-s-b-u-r-g, and the last book of the Bible isn't *Revelations*.

Language is character; so too action is character. What we say affects what we do. But the greater truth is this: What we *do* may cancel out all the grandeur of what we *say*. Our actions convey the essence of our character. That's why, in telling the parable of the Good Samaritan, Jesus uses action to make His point. He shows how the behavior of the priest and the Levite—both of whom ignored the victim's plight and left him on the roadside to die—contrasts with the behavior of the despised Samaritan. No doubt both the professionally religious priest and Levite were reciting the Torah as they journeyed to Jericho; but what was the effect of merely saying those words? To what extent did what they said determine their willingness to act in accordance with the Law? How willing were they to delay their progress by taking time to show mercy to the man who had fallen among thieves? Apparently not at all.

And so it is with us who claim the transforming power of Jesus Christ on our life and character. Someone has rightly said, "What you *do* speaks so loud that the world can't hear what you *say*." And someone else has written,

> We are writing a Gospel a chapter a day
> By the deeds that we do and the words that we say.
> Men read what we write, whether faithful or true:
> Tell me, what is the Gospel according to you?

But even as language and action are inextricably tied, so both language and action stem from thought, and thought stems from a worldview. From earliest childhood we have been warned by our elders to "think before you speak" and "think before you act." But what governs our thought life?

What determines the process and filtering of our inner being, the mind and soul and spirit? My answer is that our *worldview* governs our perception of reality, how we see the external and internal world and act according to that reality. Governed by a biblical worldview, our thought, our speech, and our actions take on a different set of criteria, a different standard. The God-dismissing secular world finds this amusing or confounding or irritating, but the fact remains that—for someone who holds to a biblical worldview—the simple question is, *What would Jesus do?* To the degree that we respond in answer to that question, our thought, speech, and actions will reflect our Christian character.

But is it all really that easy, that straightforward? Living as we do in what some would call "a post-Christian, postmodern age," can we reduce how we think and speak and act to a mere formula? Certainly the secular world doesn't think so. One of the reasons why the challenge of staking out a biblical worldview is so daunting is that modern society knows nothing of—indeed, appears to want nothing to do with—a wholly consistent vision of life, especially when that vision is based on claims of authority revealed from a divine source. Here is a sure way to be accused of "fundamentalism" and classified as a potential terrorist. Here is a sure way to be charged with "hate speech," especially if the topic at hand is what the Bible teaches about human sexuality.

A biblical view of reality—whatever its application—demands blending personal moral values with public acts. It argues against the sort of mixed behavior whereby what is proclaimed in the marketplace is violated in the privacy of one's own home, or *vice versa*. It requires a consistency of character, which our society prefers to honor more in the breach than in the observance.

In fact, to most Americans the personal morality of a public figure seems irrelevant. A vast disconnection exists in the American populace between the public *persona* and personal behavior. I say again, it's clear that, while our society despises and scorns hypocrisy among professing Christians, most are fearful of any authoritative vision calling for moral order, choosing to label "narrow-minded" any suggestion of moral consistency.

Meanwhile, many evangelical Christians are equally divided in their ability to grasp what wholeness of character might represent. The inculcation of a biblical worldview, therefore, seeks to transform character by replacing such *dis-integration* with a perspective of wholeness. The truly intentional Christian school desires to instill and promote in every person coming into its sphere—board members, administrators, faculty, staff, students, alumni, parents, friends—the joy of knowing that the God we worship is the One who is consistently "the same yesterday and today and forever," the One in whom "all things hold together."

If our school is to offer a truly valid Christian education—an education that can help to transform character—we will work to achieve that goal by being consistent with biblical truth in every aspect of our institutional life. First, we will seek to demonstrate by our own institutional character how the truth of Scripture bears upon and pervades every decision, every facet of institutional action. Second, through our curriculum, we will seek to develop in our students a worldview in which the truth of God's Word permeates all other knowledge and understanding. Third, our faculty and staff will exemplify what it means to be transformed by biblical truth, through their example of Christian community lived out with collegiality, companionship, and compassion. And fourth, our mature and maturing students will learn to become whole persons in the privacy of their homes or in the anonymity of downtown, in a chapel service at school or in their parents' church.

To achieve this kind of wholeness of life that transforms character, we need teaching that exemplifies a wholeness of vision, a vision unbroken by cheapening and distracting values. But we also need a real vision of the world obtained by knowing the difference between God's call to obedience and Satan's summons to rebellion. We need to know the two great paradoxes of a life lived according to a biblical worldview: first, that submission leads to freedom; second, that license leads to slavery.

All around us and our students are the lures and traps, the siren calls, urging us to gratify ourselves first, to do what pleases ourselves, no matter the consequences to anyone else. All around us are the promoters of self-interest telling us that you only go around once, so you should deny yourself nothing. Rarely do we hear a call to self-sacrifice or self-denial; instead, *Carpe diem*—"Seize the day!"—is the secularist's cry. We are a society of conspicuous consumers, devotees of licentiousness, bound to earthly delights.

How different is the call to discipleship issued by Jesus of Nazareth: "Follow me"! He leads us into a life of obedient discipline to His Lordship, a life "whose service is perfect freedom." He offers to show us how our submission to His will becomes liberating. He provides a place to stand and see the world in true perspective. He rids us of the fragmented and broken life, the disintegrated life, and replaces it with wholeness.

Sometimes the Christian's worldview is mistaken for a joyride through Lollypop Land. Nothing could be more inane. Yes, there are sincere Christians who practice a quarantine mentality, living their lives in total isolation from the world's contagion. Others go to the opposite extreme, exposing themselves to reckless and foolish endangerment. In your authentic Christian school, I trust, you have found a middle ground we might call vaccination or inoculation against contagion, where your students have limited and controlled exposure to the toxic infections of the world and are thus better able to avoid their lethal effects and make discriminating choices.

I hope that your school isn't afraid of unpopular ideas or even of revolutionary notions but wants every idea, every strategy, every fad, every thought to be subject to the Lordship of Jesus Christ, as St. Paul urges in 2 Corinthians 10. To bring every thought into subjection, we need to be asking penetrating questions: *What does Jesus Christ think about this issue? What is His view of the matter?* After all, education according to a biblical worldview is thoughtful, analytical, critical, and consistent with biblical revelation.

I must be faithful in reminding you that there are some worldviews that are incompatible with Christian discipleship; some lifestyles that Jesus summons us to abandon when we choose to follow Him. Matthew and Zaccheus, white-collar tax men who lived off their graft and corruption, were called away from sin to a new vision of reality, a new way of thinking-and-acting like a Christian. Mary Magdalene left her harlot's practice and gave up the very stuff of her profession—her precious perfume—to fall in tears at the feet of Jesus.

The principle of teaching that transforms character by thinking-and-acting like a Christian means more than merely adopting a philosophical perspective. It also means standing up against whatever would usurp the rightful authority of Jesus Christ to demand our willing submission to His will. It means standing against what St. Paul calls "every pretension that sets itself up against the knowledge of God" in an attempt to overpower the Christian; it means to "take captive every thought to make it obedient to Christ" (2 Corinthians 10:5). It means thinking-and-acting like a Christian: that is, thinking about your life's work, your life's partner, your call to serve God by serving others—and then acting on what you know is right.

Students sometimes ask me how they can come to know the will of God for their future. My counsel always begins by asking this question: Do you know, first, what God's will is for you *now*—this semester, this week, during today's classes? When—as often happens—I get blank looks, I ask permission to inquire further and ask two penetrating questions: *What's your current GPA?* and *What's your relationship with your current classmates?* Then one final question: *Are both of these representative of all they can and should be?* For our students are not yet called to fully developed action or service. Rather, they are called to acquire a solid world-and-life view, a place to stand that will give them a true and balanced vision of reality and will shape their character in the mold and model of Jesus Christ.

God's will for every student is simple to define. It is not to be living on the ragged edge of mental and physical breakdown because of participation on every committee to reform society and the church. Neither is it necessarily a full-time role in campus politics or worldwide evangelism. Nor is it setting the goal of making the first million by age thirty or becoming a presidential candidate by age fifty. God's will for every student in every Christian school is twofold: first, to make the best possible use of one's intellect to achieve the best possible academic preparation—which means attending classes faithfully and doing one's academic assignments whole-heartedly; and, second, to make the best possible effort to live in respect and love for one's neighbor. This is the will of God in Christ Jesus for every student in your school at this time.

In fact, it's the will of God in Christ for every student at every Christian school, college, university, and seminary; for every believing student at any academic institution. It is also God's will for every one of us who administers or teaches or coaches or fulfills other duties: do your work well and live at peace with your neighbor.

Once upon a time, the primary purpose of education in Western civilization was for students to know God and the Scriptures. In 1636—only fifteen years after the first Thanksgiving celebration—a few scholars gathered in the primitive New England village called Cambridge on the Charles River where they founded Harvard College for such a purpose. At the celebration of Harvard College's 350th anniversary (June 6–7, 2001), a college president lamented the fact that today's colleges and universities no longer have the same rallying point they used to, having become godless institutions. Far and wide, today's colleges have forsaken the worldview that places God at the center and us as created beings whose chief end is "to glorify God and enjoy Him forever."

I thank God for the schools whose biblical worldview remains intact. I thank God for the schools that have not become godless. For many years, students have come to learn what it means to learn to love the Lord with heart, soul, strength, and mind. These schools still believe in and teach submission to the will of God, "whose service is perfect freedom."

So, do you really believe what you profess with your mouth? Are you ready to acknowledge your own need to transform your thought and speech and action to conform to a biblical worldview? Are you ready, with renewed devotion, to let the Spirit of God enable you to shape in your students a new vision of reality that transforms their character? Are you ready to affirm the truth, that in Christ are hidden all the treasures of wisdom and of knowledge—hidden in the arts and sciences, in the skills and techniques of professional studies, in the rigors of competitive sport, in the blessings of collegiality, companionship, and community that mark the life and witness of your Christian school—hidden and waiting to be found!

12

TEACHING TO TRANSFORM CULTURE

In the immediate aftermath of the 2004 presidential election, the secular media were astonished that "faith and moral values" had such an impact on the reelection of President George W. Bush. My opportunity to present a keynote address to the ACSI Ohio Valley Region's convention on November 11, 2004, in Dayton, Ohio, came in this context of national and international challenge for biblical Christians to be transformed and renewed in order to be more effective witnesses to the world.

I begin my remarks this morning with several quotations. The first is from a movie review by A. O. Scott, film critic for the *New York Times* (www.nytimes.com, May 28, 2004). In the spring of 2004, a movie called *Saved* depicted Hollywood's version of a Christian high school called Eagle Christian Academy. The head-of-school, Pastor Skip, is having an affair with a senior student's mother. Meanwhile her daughter—the heroine of the movie—is helping her boyfriend overcome any doubts about his own sexual preference by becoming pregnant with him. Other *dramatis personae* include a self-righteous snob who leads a group called Christian Jewels; the pastor's son, a rebellious skateboarder; and a sure candidate for eventual expulsion—who also happens to be the only Jew in the school. Of course, Scott commends the movie's message, which is that "religious morality should be tolerant of human fallibility and differences."

A second quotation comes from a similar source (www.religionnews-blog.com, August 17, 2004). In 1995, a Denver pastor named Keenan Roberts wrote a play called *Hell House* that was presented in his church as a Halloween vehicle for evangelism. The play depicts the consequences of sin as teenagers plunge into hell. The pastor-playwright decided to market the play, and he sold the script and stage directions for $200 to more than 500 churches. But a wily Los Angeles producer named Maggie Rowe also obtained a copy of the script and staged the play with comedian Bill Maher in the starring role as Satan and actor Andy Richter as Jesus. Maggie Rowe said the play would be used to "lampoon (Christian) fundamentalist beliefs about hell. It will be a parody of itself. It will be very funny. We're having a hoot."

The third quotation appeared in an editorial in *The New York Times* on August 14, 2004. As you might suppose, this newspaper has been a noisy advocate of so-called "same-sex marriage." When the California Supreme Court invalidated all such ceremonies by the San Francisco mayor and others, the *Times* lamented the action as if it signaled the final demise of freedom, although liberal editorialists found reason for hope: "The road toward greater fairness is already being mapped in the 50 states.... Just as California was the first state to strike down its own laws against interracial marriage, we expect that it will ultimately find a constitutional basis for the human right to same-sex marriage."

I could go on with this sort of bad news. But let me offer a different set of quotations with which to begin this convention: first, the Great Commission, given by our Lord Jesus Christ to His followers, and our theme verse for this convention: Go into all the world and proclaim the gospel to every creation (Mark 16:15).

Next, hear the words of St. Paul to the Christian believers in Rome: "Therefore, I urge you, brothers, in view of God's mercy, to offer your bodies as living sacrifices, holy and pleasing to God—this is your spiritual act of worship. Do not conform any longer to the pattern of this world, but be transformed by the renewing of your mind. Then you will be able to test and approve what God's will is—his good, pleasing and perfect will" (Romans 12:1–2).

Last in this series of quotations is this profound declaration to us who serve in the vocation of Christian schooling, uttered almost five hundred years ago by Desiderius Erasmus, the greatest mind in Christendom: "All studies, philosophy, rhetoric are followed for this one object, that we may know Christ and honor him. This is the end of all learning and eloquence" (*The Collected Works of Erasmus*, J. K. Sowards, ed., 1985).

My purpose in citing these six quotations is to set a context for this keynote address on "Teaching to Transform Culture," a goal deserving to be commended and encouraged and more importantly, affirmed and acted upon by each one of us, both institutionally and personally. But to do so, we need to understand what is being asked of us. Quite specifically, we are being summoned toward a tremendous task. Notice the three principal words in this summons: *teaching, transform,* and *culture.*

ACSI is committed to *teaching* in schools whose purpose is something more than the mere acquisition of data or information or computer skills or how to answer multiple-choice questions. Like my consulting firm PAIDEIA Inc., ACSI is committed to helping schools grow stronger, a task that ACSI refers to as "enabling" schools.

Because our schools are academic institutions, we have entered into a social compact with parents who enroll their children. Occasionally, I still meet well-intentioned people in Christian schools who are confused about this point: they haven't yet come to accept that the primary and only legitimate reason for their school's existing *as a school* is to be a place of teaching and learning where Jesus Christ is honored as Lord. From time to time I still meet people who say, "We want our school to be academically rigorous, but we don't want to lose our fervor for Christ." How sad! As if the latter were an automatic consequence of the former! It is far better to say, "We want our school to be academically rigorous *because* we don't want to lose our fervor for Christ!"

The Great Commission is to go and tell, go and proclaim, go and *teach* all nations, as the version in Matthew 28 reads, "teaching them to observe everything I have commanded you." This is the reason why God's sovereign plan called for leaving the apostles behind when Jesus Christ was transported bodily out of their sight. They were commissioned by the very Lord of the universe to carry the Good News everywhere. Within the extended lifetime of the early church, one of those means of proclaiming the gospel was through Christian schooling. Paul of Tarsus makes this purpose plain in his admonitions to Timothy ("command and teach these things," 1 Timothy 4:11) and to Titus ("teach what is in accord with sound doctrine," Titus 2:1). In addition, Paul uses Greek educational terms such as *paideia* (curriculum), *nouthesia* (discipline), and *paidagogos* (the adult male slave who escorted the student to school).

So teaching is integral to proclaiming the gospel, the Good News of God in Christ. Those of us who have been called to teach need never to apologize for the fact that we are not medical missionaries or jungle aviators or Bible translators or church planters. We are *teachers,* and thus we too have a role in proclaiming the gospel.

The second word to note is *transform.* ACSI is not asking its membership to do anything less than to become primary agents of change that is so fundamental that it alters our world. We're not talking here about a botox treatment or a face-lift or some other kind of cosmetic adjustment. To transform any object or living creature requires an inherently radical act. Indeed, transformation starts at the very root of any entity, the very heart—the core—of the matter and works outward from there. The result of transformation is this: once a substance has been transformed, it's no longer recognizable to those who knew it in its former state.

What might there be about *teaching* that carries with it the power to transform? Surely it isn't the content of the teaching alone. Ideas have consequences, as we know, but it's highly unlikely that anyone's life is going to be transformed simply by being taught the Pythagorean theorem or the rhyme scheme of a Shakespearean sonnet. Instead, what will transform any student will be the *character* of the teacher and the demands made by that teacher's example for new and fresh and creative thinking.

That's the message of the apostle Paul to the Romans and to us: be transformed, says Paul in Romans 12:2. Then he tells them how this change can be accomplished: "by the renewing of your minds." In other words, change the way you think in order to change the way you act. I call this *thinking-and-acting like a Christian.*

Changing the way we think begins with changing the way we approach the whole range of intellectual behavior. Suppose we accept the biblical teaching that human beings are made in the image of God—then our grasp of the human phenomenon called *thinking-and-acting* will have a very different description from the mechanistic secular explanation of how a human being thinks and acts.

Because we are made in the image of God, like Him we have the threefold power to *will*, to *speak*, and to *reason*. God the Father *wills* the world into being by His divine fiat: "Let there be. ..." God the Son—the divine Logos—*speaks* the world into being and upholds it by His Word. God the Spirit illumines the world with the light of reason and love. If this is how our worldview is shaped, we come to recognize and differentiate among the *wisdom* that belongs to God alone, the *knowledge* that God commissions every human being to acquire, and the *understanding* that is the Holy Spirit's gift to help us discern and discriminate and decide— through the transformation of a renewed mind.

Such a worldview has its own power to transform the way we learn and teach. Indeed, if all this were so, then our sixth and last quotation would make eminent good sense, especially for those of us who are called to the vocation of Christian schooling. Listen again to Erasmus: "All studies, philosophy, rhetoric are followed for this one object, that we may know Christ and honor him. This is the end of all learning and eloquence."

When we examine the scope of what Erasmus is saying, it almost takes our breath away. He is comprehensive, all-encompassing: "All studies," declares Erasmus—not just Bible studies but algebra, biology, chemistry, drama, English, French, geography, history, industrial arts, and every other area of formal study—"are followed for this one object," says Erasmus. And what is that one object, that single-minded goal? "That we may know Christ and honor him. This is the end"—the consuming purpose—"of all learning and eloquence."

This is what must distinguish Christian schooling from godless or unintentional education: "That we may know Christ and honor him." Why must we honor Him? Because He is Lord of the universe. Christ's supremacy over the cosmos, over all created things in heaven and on earth, as St. Paul told the Colossians, is what language and art and mathematics and science and the record of human history reflect. If we believe anything less, we have not learned the first lesson of our calling to serve in Christian schools. So, says Erasmus, "This is the end"—the goal, the objective—"of all learning and eloquence."

I'm reminded of another wise believer, the World War II martyr Simone Weil, who starved herself to death by refusing to eat more than was being fed to the inmates of the Nazi concentration camps. In an essay called "Reflections on the Right Use of School Studies," she specified why we teach our students Latin or physics: not simply to learn Latin or physics but to learn how to concentrate the mind for the purpose of prayerfully waiting on God to speak to us. Speaking of a geometry problem to be solved, she writes that "it is the image of something precious. Being a little fragment of particular truth, it is a pure image of the unique, eternal, and living Truth, the very Truth that once in a human voice declared: 'I am the Truth.'" Then she says, "Every school exercise, thought of in this way, is like a sacrament" (Simone Weil, *Waiting for God* [New York: G.P. Putnam's Sons, 1951). What a challenge to us as we prepare our lessons and assign our homework: to make each act of teaching and learning an act of worship of God!

But ACSI isn't calling on us to change the way we think-and-act in a vacuum; we're given a context for both teaching and transforming. That context is *culture*, a word that gathers into itself every element of human existence, every shared experience—whether universal or societal, ethnic, tribal, or familial. Culture is what we do by custom and by habit and by learned experience that marks our identity as distinctively Americans or Italians or Bangladeshis.

For centuries, culture was contained within the village, within the region, within the territorial nation. Then came the era of exploration and travel. Marco Polo brought home from China evidence that people in that distant land eat far differently than people in Mediterranean Europe. Christopher Columbus returned to Spain with proof of cultural differences in the New World. Sir Walter Raleigh first amused the Elizabethan court with his findings from the Roanoke Island experiment. Then, in 1616, John Rolfe brought back to England his princess bride Pocahontas. Thereafter, the English-speaking world was never again its own isolated culture, as any tourist to London can see.

We in the United States of America have our own culture, our own customs and habits and traditions. As a conglomerate of immigrants, we have borrowed and adapted elements from other cultures, reshaping them, making them our own. Still, we continue to export as "American culture" the products and fads and ephemeral trinkets and toys of our ever-declining imagination.

Unhappily, around the globe "American culture" means *an excess of everything*—too much money, too much sex, too much noise, too much violence, too much food, too much leisure, too much freedom. We are notorious as "the ugly Americans." We have allowed American culture to be overtaken by materialism, lust, greed, and a secular disdain for what, more than eighty years ago, Frank E. Gaebelein called "the eternal verities" (*The Christian, the Arts, and Truth: Regaining the Vision of Greatness*, D. Bruce Lockerbie, ed. [Portland, OR: Multnomah Press, 1985]). The secular mentality sees all of life as limited by space and time, with no allowance for the spiritual or eternal dimensions. The ancient pagan philosophy is back, and its slogan could not be more modern: "Eat, drink, and be merry, for tomorrow we die."

As my first three quotations this morning indicate, American culture has been overrun by the most aggressive secular mentality. Perhaps you watched the PBS presentation called "The Question of God" (Tatge/Lasseur Productions, September 2004). Armand Nicholi, an evangelical scholar from Harvard, contrasts the spiritual journeys of Sigmund Freud and C. S. Lewis, and discusses their opposite paths with a roundtable of educated Americans, one of whom, Michael Shermer—a former professing believer educated in Christian schools—states the secular case quite directly. His worldview now is *naturalism*, by which he means the total exclusion of the transcendent, the spiritual, the eternal, the divine, leaving only two explanations for life: first, what we can observe and attribute to natural causes, and second, what has not yet been explained but will eventually yield to naturalistic reasoning.

In my book *Dismissing God*, I have traced the course of rising hostility against God from conventional piety and skepticism to agnosticism and atheism; then to militant disbelief, meaning the belligerent attack against someone else's desire to believe; and finally, cold contempt for the very *idea* of faith. This last is the level to which American culture has now declined.

Why was President George W. Bush so strenuously opposed by the so-called Hollywood elite and other entertainers? Because his simple profession of Christian faith was a rebuke to their lascivious and licentious living. Whoopi Goldberg's foulmouthed tirade at Radio City Music Hall, Bill Maher's HBO crudeness, and Michael Moore's accusations are more than political opposition. They and others have mounted an unrelenting assault on biblical virtues as currently represented by the one man who bears the brunt of an attack that is intended for biblical Christians throughout this nation.

This, then, is the culture that our teaching must transform—a culture debased by sin and condemned by God in the words of St. Paul to the Romans. In the first chapter of his Roman letter, at the end of his catalogue of wickedness, Paul writes, "Although they know God's righteous decree that those who do such things deserve death, they not only continue to do these very things but also approve of those who practice them" (Romans 1:32).

How are we to begin teaching to transform culture? I believe our starting point is to recognize and understand the lethal culture of secularism we inhabit. Then we must declare ourselves to be in a state of war against that culture, which has surely declared war against anything that stands for Jesus Christ and His kingdom.

Here is one more piece of evidence from that cultural barometer of all things hostile to Jesus Christ, the *New York Times*. Earlier this fall, the *New York Times Book Review* granted most of a full page to praising a new book, *The End of Faith: Religion, Terror, and the Future of Reason*, by an unknown graduate student named Sam Harris, who writes, "We have names for people who have many beliefs for which there is no rational justification. When their beliefs are extremely common, we call them 'religious'; otherwise, they are likely to be called *mad, psychotic,* or *delusional*" (New York: W. W. Norton, 2004).

The *New York Times* has determined that it can deride those of us who are so insane as to believe in a transcendent and holy God who made Himself known to us in the Person of Jesus of Nazareth and summons us to faith in His gospel. Of course, there is nothing new or modern or even postmodern about the accusation of insanity against Christians. When Paul of Tarsus gave his witness before the court of Roman and Jewish rulers, he too was accused of madness for claiming that Jesus of Nazareth had been raised from the dead.

But having declared war against the culture of secularism, we cannot stand aloof from its appearances or hide from its manifestations. As mature adults, we need to know the reality of its infectious grip on children and adolescents before we can inoculate or even quarantine them against its deadly effects. We cannot afford to be naive about the deviant and rebellious behavior going on in and around our schools. For instance, rampant sexual experimentation among middle school children includes a prepubescent girl's wearing bracelets of various colors to indicate which sex acts she is prepared to offer. We cannot ignore the reality of some barely shaving youth's being the principal dealer in hard drugs.

One of the greatest griefs we share is the sorrow of our own children gone astray. Why is it that our schools, like our homes, cannot prepare some of our youth to withstand the lures of secular culture—what the King James Bible calls "the lust of the flesh, the lust of the eyes, and the pride of life" (1 John 2:16)? In the 2004 convention issue of ACSI's *Christian School Education,* Nancy Pearcey ("The Mandate to Transform Culture") and George Barna ("Living and Learning with the Mosaic Generation") document how perniciously the secular worldview has overtaken a large number of professing Christian young people—including those educated in our schools.

I am reminded of the story of one such young man named Brian Warner, who spent quite a few years in a Christian school in a nearby city. In his autobiography he tells of an incident in his elementary years, when a music teacher invited students to bring to school a favorite recording. He brought an album whose music scandalized his teacher and flouted the school's rules against such music. He was taken to an administrative office and given corporal punishment, as was that school's policy. And did that incident cleanse him from sin? He writes, "When I saw what happened when I was bad, I kept on doing it" (*The Long Hard Road Out of Hell,* [New York: HarperCollins, 1998]). We know him as the personification of rebellion, Marilyn Manson—whose influence, thank God, seems to have been eclipsed recently but only by another Christian school dropout named Britney Spears.

No, we cannot transform culture by ignoring the fact that its attractiveness to our students is rooted in rebellion. Adolescents are fascinated by the outrageous—the more so, the better! And while most of us would prefer not to become adulterated by the contents of the dumpster, some few of us in every school need to know firsthand the corruption that lurks in our schools.

So, what must we do to ensure that we are teaching to transform culture? We must teach toward developing a biblical culture of *discipleship,* an environment in which adults as well as children are learning-in-order-to-teach; a culture in which what we are learning is obedience to the Master-Teacher so that we may be worthy disciples, ready to proclaim the

Good News throughout every human society and every culture. I offer several recommendations—to be expanded, perhaps, in another setting:

1. Know your subject matter inside and out. Do not allow inadequate preparation to hamper your effectiveness in communicating truth to your students. Do not give Satan a foothold in the minds of your students, who will discredit your teaching if they perceive factual inaccuracy or a limited imagination or an unwillingness to continue learning even as you teach them.

2. Know your Bible inside and out. Don't merely proof-text your lesson or play some pedagogical trick like "Pin the Tail on the Donkey." Know how the Scriptures relate to the content of your discipline. Know how the very essence of your subject participates in the mystery of God's truth. Like Simone Weil, know how to find the "unique, eternal, and living truth" in a geometry problem or a Latin lesson.

3. Know how to fuse your faith and your subject matter. Integration begins within and moves deeper toward the core. Integration must never be superficial and commonplace. So probe and test your mind, rejecting the easy answer and the cheap connection. Look instead for the beauty of complex relationships and discover their simple grandeur.

4. Know how the culture in which you and your students participate has been, and can still be, shaped by the example of earnest Christian faith and the uncommon sense of biblical truth. We are blessed by direct and forceful examples among persons our students know and perhaps admire. The Boston Red Sox pitcher Curt Schilling says after a courageous victory, "Seven years ago I became a Christian, and tonight God did something amazing for me" (http://bostonredsocks.mlb.com). The two-time Masters golf champion Bernhard Langer says, as the famous green jacket is fitted on him, "I can think of no better way to celebrate this victory than to dedicate it to my risen Lord and Savior Jesus Christ" (*Bernhard Langer: My Autobiography* [London: Hodder & Stoughton, 2002]). And even though I dislike some of the music and musicians our students admire, the fact is that godly people playing and singing their music can have a remarkable influence

on the way today's young people think about spiritual issues and the Person of Jesus Christ.

5. Know that the ultimate transforming act was begun on the Cross and continued in the empty tomb. The ultimate transformation will be ongoing until the consummation of history and "the glorious appearance of the great God our Savior Jesus Christ." We are not in charge of the universe, nor of God's timing.

6. Finally, know that if we are to mold the minds of young people to serve God and transform their culture, we must give them the model of biblical norms for maturity among Christian believers and point them to consistent examples.

Recently, my wife and I joined alumni from The Stony Brook School's class of 1964 at a reunion dinner. These men, now grandfathers, had come from far and near—from England and Korea and across North America—to see each other, some for the first time in four decades. Of course, they had stories about humorous incidents and pranks and pratfalls, some of which included me. But they also had testimonies of how—years after they had left the Stony Brook campus and its Bible classes and chapel services—God broke through and transformed their lives. Now they are ready and able to participate in transforming their culture.

We cannot change the world by ourselves. We can only be faithful to what we know and are convinced is God's truth ... then leave the rest to His sovereign grace.

THREE

HELPING SCHOOLS GROW STRONGER

INTRODUCTION TO PART 3

A clearly enunciated philosophy of Christian school education is absolutely essential to effective Christian schooling. So too is an affirming sense of God's call in the life of each person who serves in a Christian school.

But these two attributes are not enough to found and sustain a thriving Christian school. We must also have leadership that understands the principles of school governance, executive authority and responsibility, managerial accountability, fiscal integrity, marketplace savvy, cultivation and solicitation of donor support, and—under God—a plan to put these assets to good use for the future of the school.

The governing board of a Christian school is its most important component. No individual head-of-school, however gifted and energetic, can lead well unless the board is strong, united in its support of the school's mission, generous in its individual and collective financial support, and committed to the school's plan. In the strongest schools, the board will not consist exclusively of parents of current students, nor—in a church-sponsored school—exclusively of members of the host congregation, nor even just a few strong-minded individuals: rather, the board will consist of *the best people for the job* of serving on a not-for-profit governing board.

In the strongest schools, the board will choose and appoint as its head-of-school a person qualified to act as chief executive officer, the board's sole employee, the one responsible for leading the school in fulfilling its mission according to the board policies. The person will be more than a gifted classroom teacher or coach elevated to an executive office. The head-of-school will also be a public *persona* in the immediate and broader community, the school's chief representative and advocate, and its foremost solicitor of major financial gifts. For the fact is that, while a Christian school must be bathed in prayer and energized by hard work and imagination, its success is fueled by money that is needed to pay its employees and vendors so that it will grow stronger and fulfill its mission.

In today's environment, the head of a nonpublic school is no longer able to be the quiet scholar who emerges from his study or her laboratory to take an occasional phone call in the office or preside at an occasional faculty meeting. The twenty-first-century head of any Christian school will often find herself or himself away from the building and off campus, doing the external work that is critical to the financial stability of a nonpublic school.

These are some principles of a Christian *paideia* that every board member and head-of-school needs to consider. They are also important to every teacher and coach who may aspire to leadership as well as to every college undergraduate or graduate student who is preparing for the vocation of Christian schooling.

13

THE UNPLEASANT TRUTH ABOUT CHRISTIAN SCHOOLING

This address was presented at a regional meeting of Christian Schools International, held on March 16, 1990, at Union Theological Seminary in New York City. A few days after this speech, one of the most prominent headmasters present called me and said, "I sat listening to you last week, thinking that what you were saying was entirely irrelevant to me. Yesterday, I learned otherwise." He too had received his "first performance review, written on a pink slip."

The American writer James Baldwin once said, "I love America; that's why I reserve the right to criticize her" (*James Baldwin: Collected Essays* [New York: Penguin Putnam, 1949]). I would say the same about my affection for Christian schooling. I admire the work of Christian schools and their leaders, but I respectfully reserve the right to be a loving critic and exhorter toward better schools and conditions. I ask you to bear that in mind, even as you read what may be uncomfortable words concerning the unpleasant truth about Christian schooling.

If you heed only the Christian school triumphalists, things seem to be just fine, thank you. Certainly, the enrollment statistics are glowing. More important than sheer numbers, however, is the impressive work that Christian schools are doing, even those that are struggling. In fairness, most Christian school advocates will affirm that our schools could and should be better in many respects: better governed, better managed, better funded, better at developing critical thinkers and godly disciples. But these advocates seldom are willing to go into detail as to *why* and *how* such improvements must be made. To do so, it seems, is nit-picking.

Therefore, I offer as my words of encouragement to you this declaration: *Our schools should be stronger than they are,* and here's *why* and *how.*

There are several significant reasons *why* Christian schools must grow stronger—if Christian schools are to thrive. Other chapters in this book address some of these matters, including a school's lack of a distinctive curriculum, or its refusal to fund fully its own mission with cost-based tuition augmented by gifts for financial aid, or its apparent self-satisfaction with a mediocrity that contradicts its claims of "excellence." But here I wish to concentrate on the single greatest threat to a Christian school—broken relations between the head-of-school and the governing board or pastor of a sponsoring church.

If you have a candid yet affirming relationship with your board, your pastor, or your head-of-school, lay down this book and count yourself and your school among the singularly blessed! In many schools, it isn't exactly that way. In fact, it's no secret to anyone in positions of responsibility at the head office of Christian Schools International or the Association of Christian Schools International or the American Association of Christian Schools or any of the other organized bodies that the turnover among heads-of-schools in their membership is appalling in both the brevity of their tenure and, often, in the brutality of their departure.

Why is this so? One reason is that few people—including board members, pastors, and parents—seem to understand the complex and dynamic organism that is any Christian school. By definition, the Christian school is both a ministry and a business. It is a service to parents and their children and at the same time a marketplace competitor that must succeed in attracting and retaining its clientele. It is an idealistic educational institution, yet it is also a practical enterprise that must be able to pay its employees and its vendors.

A second factor is the failure of many Christians to hold to a Reformed understanding of *vocation.* In too many situations, Christian schooling is weakened by a pervasive fallacy that abounds throughout evangelical North America: if you profess faith in Jesus Christ, you can certainly teach in a Christian school, perhaps even serve as head-of-school. In holding to this bromide, we have given too little place to a theology of vocation and the specific call of God to men and women to become teachers and leaders. The fact is, some ardent believers lack this call: they can't communicate well with anybody's children, including their own. Some ardent believers may be wonderful scholars, but they have no understanding of how to break down a topic and rebuild it before a child in such a way that the child learns for herself. In short, some Christians just can't teach. That's why, in many church-sponsored schools, we find a youth pastor who is ill at ease in the formality of a Bible classroom or the minister of music incapable of managing a junior high class in music appreciation.

Others who have the gift of teaching don't seem to have been granted "gifts of administration" (1 Corinthians 12:28). These are women and men who perform with stellar results in their own classrooms but have no ability to inspire and motivate others to follow their example; or they lack the ability to plan and fulfill their plan; or they have no stomach for asking others to support the school's mission with financial contributions. Yet, for whatever reasons, we often find some of these very persons transferred from the classroom, where their gifts are demonstrable, to the office of head-of-school, where they can never succeed. Some victims of this awkward appointment are self-deluded and fail to recognize their own inability to perform well in an administrative position. Others are simply unwilling substitutes, aware of their liabilities but bravely filling in until the board makes a permanent appointment. Meanwhile, of course, the school languishes for lack of leadership.

My late friend Werner Janssen, who led the New York Philharmonic and other great orchestras, once told me that a conductor is someone who "can look one hundred musicians in the eye at the same time and still keep the beat." His description applies as well to today's head-of-school, who fills a far different role from that of the typical school principal a half-century ago. Like an orchestra conductor, today's head-of-school must be able to do many things at once: relate to each member of the board and/or to the pastor while professionally overseeing each member of the faculty and staff, nurturing every student and calming the parents, and representing the school to the larger community, especially current and potential donors—all without missing a beat!

Admittedly, service as a pastor is one of God's most demanding callings. Service as a volunteer on a school's governing board—whether church affiliated, parent approved, or independent—is often a thankless task. But both of those are easy in comparison with heading a school in contemporary North American society. To put matters succinctly, the job of heading a Christian school in North America deserves combat pay for its frontline dangers, of which the most pernicious is the possibility—no, the *likelihood*—of being dismissed at the whim of a new board chairman or under the pressure of disgruntled parents or a dissatisfied pastor.

Of course, if a head-of-school is derelict in his duties or guilty of moral turpitude—if he or she runs the school poorly or consistently makes rash and silly decisions—there are legitimate reasons for concern. The board may justifiably choose not to renew a contract, or even to make a dramatic change during the course of the school year. But I'm not referring to such cases.

How many horror stories do you know about good and decent professional educators in Christian schools who, with no warning, have been summarily dismissed—the slang word is *fired*—without recourse? Their termination generally happens because, in some amorphous way— and often without any documentary evidence to support its decisions— the board loses faith in or respect for the head-of-school.

PAIDEIA Inc. conducts a dozen or more executive searches each year, most of which are for Christian schools of quality. In this work, we encounter numerous such victims. One person was fired because, his board chairman told him, he just didn't fit; no specifics were offered. Another was told that he was too high-powered and sophisticated for the board's tastes. A third, after thirteen years, was told that he had never *not* been on probation! Another lost his job because he was reported to have danced at his own daughter's wedding.

The headmaster of a large school found it necessary to dismiss a business administrator, whereupon her husband did a search into the headmaster's past and discovered a court case in a different state involving the headmaster—a case so frivolous that it had been dismissed by the presiding judge with a warning to the other litigant never again to appear in his courtroom. But the husband of the fired business officer ignored that detail; he simply informed the board of its headmaster's brief notoriety. Foolishly, the board acted without due diligence and fired the headmaster on the husband's say-so. That headmaster promptly sued and won a justified settlement against all parties. The school has yet to recover from its folly.

Why don't other heads-of-schools sue for "wrongful termination"? While some few have, most of those we know are repelled at the very thought of bringing suit against a school for which they still have deep affection; or they have biblical scruples against lawsuits between believers; or they have accepted their mistreatment as part of the inexplicable mystery of God's will for their lives. Others have been intimidated by the very board chairman who fired them, who happens also to be a leading local attorney with a reputation for overpowering his opponents.

These conditions would be bad enough, but what makes them intolerable is the cruel manner in which some school boards treat their former employee. I know one headmaster who sat with his board chairman at the school's Christmas concert but the very next morning was ordered out of his office and off the campus with thirty days' pay and no health coverage.

Why? To save money by having three board members assume the head-master's duties.

A Christian school's boardroom is no place for slaughterhouse tactics. No one with proper Christian compassion enjoys firing someone from the security and stability of his position. But the act of terminating someone's job can be done with grace, compassion, and a spirit of brotherly love and even with provision for maintaining the emotional and economic well-being of the person and his family.

What, then, is the solution to this problem? How can we reverse these negative patterns in regard to those who lead and those who govern Christian schools? How can Christian schools improve relations between the head-of-school and the governing board and, in some cases, the sponsoring church's pastor? I offer these ten steps to reform and redeem the unpleasant into as-painless-as-possible:

1. Change the board chairman's term from annual replacement and the board membership from three-year rotation (or other brief tenure) to more extended terms.
2. Offer a contract to the head-of-school that stipulates expectations and conditions.
3. Identify the head-of-school as chief executive officer.
4. Eliminate the need for the head of a church-sponsored school to report to the pastor as well as to the board.
5. Provide mandatory ongoing instruction to all board members and candidates for the board.
6. Schedule a regular performance review for the head-of-school based on mutually agreed criteria.
7. Appoint or elect the best persons to serve on the school board, not some arbitrarily restricted group.
8. Among these best persons, look for those who have had prior experience on the board of a not-for-profit institution or agency.
9. Remind every board member and candidate for the board of the universal expectation that board members of a not-for-profit institution or agency take the lead in generous giving to the cause.
10. Prepare in advance against the necessity of dismissing a head-of-school with policies and a contingency fund to deal justly with the former employee.

To begin, PAIDEIA Inc. urges our client schools to reexamine their bylaws in reference to a board member's term of office and automatic rotation off the board. In too many instances, a new head-of-school is hired by the outgoing board chairman, then introduced to the succeeding board chairman, who is replaced twelve months later by yet another board chairman. This revolving door creates havoc in board governance and policy decisions. It leaves the new head feeling abandoned and vulnerable to the preferences of the third chairman in little more than a year, a person who may or may not have any emotional investment in the head's initial appointment.

Similarly, a board of nine members has only three years before all nine have rotated off, and that board is history. Stability in a Christian school ought to begin with a stable board whose members encourage stability in the office of head-of-school. We prefer to have an executive committee that is semipermanent (subject to internal board discipline) with the rest of the members having renewable four-year terms.

Second, the head-of-school should be offered a written contract that clearly states the terms and conditions for continuing employment. Some schools use a rollover method of retaining the head-of-school: If both the board and the head-of-school are satisfied to continue, by such-and-such a date the present contract automatically rolls over into a new term of agreement at a prearranged increase in salary, unless otherwise negotiated.

Third, PAIDEIA Inc. insists that our clients recognize today's head-of-school as *chief executive officer* of a not-for-profit corporation called *school*. When this appointment or renamed appointment is secure, many good results follow. Board members who are themselves in business—especially those who are CEOs or work with a CEO—will hold the office of head-of-school in higher regard.

Furthermore, the head as CEO is—or ought to be—the only employee reporting directly to the governing board and as such is the chief decision maker, whose decisions reflect the policies of the governing board and advance the mission of the school. The board no longer hires and fires any other employee. Rather, the board holds the head-of-school as CEO responsible for the succession of wise decisions or their opposite.

In exchange for this recognition as CEO, the head-of-school may have to sacrifice some of the very blessings that brought him into Christian schooling. He may well have to give up teaching calculus; she may have to turn over the volleyball team to another coach. To be sure, some heads still insist on teaching or coaching to keep themselves current with faculty and students, but they do so at the expense of their multiple other duties.

Executive responsibility for these duties needs an executive title. "Principal" is no longer an executive title; it signifies the *manager* of a certain grade level, such as "middle school principal" or "secondary principal." "Director" suggests the appointment of someone without academic credentials to *direct* the affairs of the school. "Administrator" is too bland, too indistinguishable from the many others who *administer* in the school, from admissions and business to development and custodial maintenance.

Increasingly, we find Christian schools using the old terms "headmaster" or "headmistress." "Head-of-school" with or without hyphens, or simply "head," is a preferred title to denote the office and connote its executive authority. "Superintendent" may be used if, as in a public school district, the CEO oversees several schools on several sites.

Fourth, we need the boards and pastors of churches that sponsor schools to understand the mandate of the head-of-school and CEO to report to the board, not to both the board and pastor. No head-of-school can serve two masters. The pastor of a church with a related school must delegate his pastoral authority to the board and not hold private and separate standards for the head-of-school to meet.

Fifth, each Christian school needs direct and ongoing instruction on the role and responsibilities of board members, and pastors if applicable, distinct from the role and responsibilities of the head-of-school. None of us is born knowing how to act like a school board member, and some candidates misconstrue their volunteer's role for that of a professional involved in the intricacies of day-to-day operations. Before their appointment, potential board members should have served on a committee of the board and received ample orientation to the principles of governance by policy—which PAIDEIA Inc. summarizes as answering the question, *Who's* in charge of *what*?

Sixth, we must end the sorry practice of dismissing a head-of-school who has never been evaluated against mutually agreed criteria. Why is it that so many heads-of-schools receive their first and only performance review *written on a pink slip*? Instead, we need boards that are willing—even eager—to grant the head-of-school the professional courtesy of a regularly scheduled performance review, measured against stated goals. The focus of a performance review will be to answer the question, To what extent has the head-of-school met these goals and advanced the mission of the school?

Seventh, we need boards whose membership consists of a broad spectrum of the best persons to sit on the governing body of a not-for-profit institution. Board membership should not consist exclusively of parents of current students, or members of the host congregation—especially when, as some pastors have confessed, a hierarchy for church appointments exists that places the most "godly" on the deacon or elder board, the most "business-oriented" on the church's trustee board, and the leftovers on the church's school board!

Eighth, among these best persons should be those who have had experience on the board of another not-for-profit agency or institution—the local symphony orchestra, museum, library, hospital, or helping agency. These people will already understand that no board member plays in the band or chooses the concert program; no board member arranges exhibits or performs surgery. These are the tasks of the professional whom the board hires to lead the enterprise.

Ninth, these experienced board members will also know that every not-for-profit cause expects its board members to take the lead in generous financial support of the cause. We still meet Christian school board members who have no notion of their obligation to be among the first to support the school on whose board they sit—generously and "according to [their] means" (2 Corinthians 8:11).

Tenth, perhaps the most unpleasant truth about Christian schooling is that few school boards have considered in advance how best to deal with a difficult personnel problem. For Christian schools to grow stronger, the board must set aside time to prepare policies in advance of an emergency, including the unhappy prospect of a sudden termination. Similarly, Christian school boards must consider in advance of such a catastrophe how to fund their act of fair dealing with a brother or sister in Christ whom they cannot retain in their employ.

For those of us in Christian schooling who claim to honor the Word of God as our standard for Christian behavior, a rereading of the Golden Rule might be appropriate: "In everything, do to others what you would have them do to you, for this sums up the Law and the Prophets" (Matthew 7:12). In dealing with their head-of-school, members of Christian school boards can do nothing less.

14

PERTINENT AND IMPERTINENT
QUESTIONS ABOUT CHRISTIAN SCHOOLING

This was the keynote address at the ACSI Southeast Conference for board members and administrators, held in Atlanta, Georgia, on July 25, 1991. Following this presentation, a man said to me, "I've been a headmaster for nineteen years. By what right have I been kept from knowing these things?"

In June 1991, I completed my thirty-four-year career at The Stony Brook School, freeing myself to devote my full energies to writing, lecturing, and serving schools, colleges, universities, and seminaries, and other institutions around the world, through my role as a consultant. In my travels, I've seen much for which to give thanks, much for which to be encouraged. But recently, a funny thing happened on my way to becoming a senior citizen: I seem to have lost my sense of humor, my capacity to laugh—except in despair—at the well-intended incompetence, inefficiency, and pious indirection that seem endemic throughout so much of Christian schooling.

So I resolved, "No more Mr. Nice Guy!" No more speeches solely about the high calling of God to the role of Christian teacher. No more high-sounding homilies on the glorious heritage of Christian education in Western civilization. No more platitudinous talks about integrating the truths of Scripture with all aspects of human knowledge. I have become, instead, a crotchety and irascible scold, a gadfly to associations and individual schools, their boards and administrators.

Not that I no longer believe Erasmus when he says that a Christian educator's calling is "the noblest of occupations." Not that I no longer honor the historic legacy of Justin Martyr and Augustine of Hippo, Alcuin of York and Vittorino da Feltre, John Amos Comenius and William Augustus Muhlenberg, Cornelius Van Til and Mark Fakkema, Jonathan Blanchard and Frank Gaebelein. Not at all. I simply believe it's time for a prophetic and radical reassessment of Christian schooling's operating premises in the twenty-first century.

To that prophetic and radical task, I've committed the rest of my own life and the resources of those who work with me. I've promised the Lord whom I serve to use every such opportunity to address clearly and candidly the issues in Christian schooling that are stifling its growth and robbing its integrity. I refer specifically to the iterating and reiterating of pious and self-congratulatory claims of excellence without substance in fact to support such claims.

I am fully aware that my words may be regarded by those whom they unintentionally offend as arrogant and even self-serving, and for that I must accept the blame for not having expressed myself with greater evidence of humility and sincerity. I have never professed—nor do I now profess—to have all the right answers, but I certainly do not shrink from requiring us all to look boldly and self-critically at our practice of Christian schooling in order to determine how we all might serve Christ more fully.

To do so, I call on all of us to ask what may seem to be both pertinent and impertinent questions about Christian schooling.

Curiously, when I raise such questions, I often discover that my strongest critics are those who are entrenched in power within Christian schooling; those for whom *change* represents a threat; those with the most to lose by the intrusion of new ideas; those whose mouths can formulate the phrases that always seem to mark the rhetoric of Christian schooling— terms such as "Christ-centered education" or "education from a biblical worldview" or my favorite, "excellence in education"—but whose check- books have yet to be dedicated to the same high purposes; those who have grown so accustomed to mediocrity that they can't even recognize their schools' desperate and inevitable slide toward inferiority.

Curiously also, I discover that many persons new to Christian school- ing tend to agree with me. Among them are new administrators who have come to Christian education from a background in secular independent schools, new board members whose educational standards are not so read- ily satisfied by a patina of piety, parents who have chosen to enroll their children in the Christian school because they accepted at face value what the school's literature promised and are now wondering why their expec- tations are not being met—even classroom teachers, some of whom inform me that they've often asked the same pertinent and impertinent questions themselves—usually with the lonely impression of one hollering into the Grand Canyon and hearing in reply only the echo of one's own voice.

Among my prophetic and radical concerns, which lead to simple and straightforward pertinent questions that some find impertinent, are the issues I've come to classify as "the five *M*-words of a stronger school." Here are the *M*-words and some of their accompanying questions:

1. *Mission* What's this school's reason-for-being? Why does this school exist? For what extenuating reasons are we willing to cease to exist? What's our primary and only legitimate reason for existing as a school? How does our mission differ from our philosophy?

2. *Management* Who's in charge of what? What's the structure of governance and accountability in this school? How does one become a member of the governing board? What responsibilities accompany such membership? Who sets policy? Who implements policy? Who has the final word on any matter at any given level of authority?

3. *Marketing* What are the "publics" or constituencies that this school seeks to serve? What are their needs? How do we know? How well are we meeting those needs? How well are we communicating with our various constituencies? How well are we reaching out to other public spheres to discover their needs and whether or not we can meet them as well?

4. *Master-planning* Where, in God's providence, is our school headed in the next five to eight years? What plan is in place to give us direction and assure us, as far as possible, that we will reach our goal? What are the implications of having no such plan?

5. *Money* How much money does our school need to fulfill its present and future promises to parents and students? Where will that money come from?

My hope is that the text of these pertinent and impertinent questions concerning mission, management, marketing, master-planning, and money may stimulate further consideration of the prophetic and radical vision of the high and holy calling to Christian schooling. But here, I wish to focus specifically on the need for *marketing* the Christian school, then providing the *money* to fund its mission.

It comes as no secret to any board member or administrator of a Christian school that among our highest priorities must be the task of getting out the good news about our school. In advocating the school to prospective faculty whom we wish to invite to join us, or to potential trustees whose time and energy and resources we hope to enlist, or to possible financial supporters, we need to be able to speak honestly of the school's progress toward fulfilling its mission.

In admissions, we speak of the retention of current students and the recruitment of new students as the two most critical elements of our school's well-being. Never mind attractive classrooms and textbooks and brightly lit gymnasiums and sparkling faculty and delicious lunches and a successful annual giving campaign: first, you must have the students, keeping them challenged and invigorated and happy, and you must draw others to take their place when they leave. In fact, wouldn't it be wonderful to have a waiting list, to have young parents, upon the birth of a child, paying a deposit for that child's enrollment five years later?

But, unhappily, too few Christian schools enjoy that luxury. I'd like to offer without comment a catalog of reasons why many Christian schools aren't overcrowded. Perhaps you'll agree, perhaps you won't.

1. Many Christian schools were founded for the wrong reasons, in a frenzy of fear or reaction against problems in the public schools or in society at large, such as busing to achieve racial integration.
2. Many Christian schools were founded by an enthusiastic inner circle who either never communicated their enthusiasm to others or else kept all decision making to themselves. When their own children left school, their interest died and with it the school's quality.
3. Many Christian schools have never been able to articulate a mission statement that sets them apart as offering a distinctive education.
4. Many Christian schools are inveterately committed to under-funding their own mission by charging too little in tuition.
5. Many Christian schools have never been able to achieve more than a church-basement quality to go with their bargain-basement tuition and salaries.
6. Many Christian schools were deceived by prepackaged formulas and curriculum into thinking that they could offer a genuine education in an exclusively programmed training environment.
7. Many Christian schools deprecate a Christian *paideia* in all its fullness in favor of a protected curriculum with "safe" text-books—which in some instances are biased, even bigoted.

8. Many Christian schools presume that corporal punishment by persons other than the child's parents is an acceptable form of discipline.
9. Many Christian schools suppose that only children of tested and proved academic achievement should be enrolled.
10. Many Christian schools operated by churches insist that the sponsoring church retain all powers, even though fifty, sixty, or even seventy-five other churches may be represented in the enrollment.
11. Many pastors of sponsoring churches are threatened by a strong head-of-school, especially when funding the school becomes an issue.
12. Many Christian schools have difficulty in teaching the text of the Bible without promoting one doctrinal view over others in such matters as baptism, the nature of the Lord's Supper, and eschatology.
13. Many Christian schools seem almost uninterested in expanding their market by changing any of the foregoing negative observations into positive ones that will lead to institutional advancement.

And to this baker's dozen I would add the following:

14. Many Christian schools suffer from evangelical apathy that devalues Christian schooling.
15. Many Christian schools display an attitude toward teaching-and-learning that sentimentalizes it into something only a little more challenging than vacation Bible school and so drains its rigor.
16. Many Christian schools offer limited and limiting programs. How many Christian schools offer Advanced Placement courses or a third year in two or three foreign languages or a full athletic program for girls as well as boys?
17. Many Christian schools lack a program to fund need-based financial aid—not tuition discounts.
18. Many Christian schools represent an appalling duplication of effort among schools unnecessarily competing for the same constituents.
19. Many Christian schools restrict admission in ways that no other Christian outreach does. How many Sunday schools turn away children whose parents aren't professing believers? How many Christian Service Brigade or Pioneer Clubs or Awana groups

reject children whose parents are not churchgoers? How many pastors permit only believers to assemble for worship? Why don't administrators and boards of Christian schools heed what Jesus Christ Himself said: "Let the little children come to me, and do not hinder them" (Mark 10:14)?

20. Many Christian schools ignore the hundreds of thousands of children nationwide who are currently homeschooled. How many of these might eventually become candidates for Christian schooling? What are we doing to ensure that, when the time is right, these children will be enrolled in our school?

These are just some of the issues one faces in marketing the Christian school. But I realize there's a problem in the very use of that phrase "marketing the Christian school." For many educators—Christian and otherwise—the very mention of the word "marketing" is offensive; it smacks of sleaze and squalid salesmanship. Of course, that's an impression left by a misunderstanding of what marketing is and how the term is applied. The marketplace in a Greek city, the *agora*, was the place where products, services, and ideas were exchanged among those whose needs were being met by something someone else had to offer. The Greek verb form of the word for marketplace appears in the New Testament in St. Paul's writings; in the New International Version, it is translated as "making the most of every opportunity" (Ephesians 5:16; Colossians 4:5)—in other words, marketing what we have to offer to those who need what we can supply.

What, then, is marketing? It's not primarily advertising, not selling, not hawking or huckstering a product. Marketing begins with the recognition of someone else's need: finding a need and filling it! Marketing looks around the community and asks the right questions: What does this community need to make it a better place to live? What do the families of this community need to assist them in becoming stronger, more resistant to the pressures that corrupt and destroy many families? What do Christian families and churches in this community need to enhance and encourage the good work they are trying to do for their children?

In time, this answer may come: what this community needs is a Christian school, a place of teaching and learning committed to academic integrity based on the example of Jesus Christ and the mandates of Scripture modeled in the lives of godly men and women. That's a marketing answer to a marketing question.

The next step, and the first priority in marketing, is to meet that need. But in order to serve the needs of others, we must know what those needs are. We must also be sure that the needs we perceive are genuinely other people's needs, not just our own needs. For instance, in how many towns are there small and struggling Christian schools competing with each other to satisfy the ego or denominational biases of pastors? Exactly whose needs are being met? How much better if a consolidated Christian school could draw on the strengths of cooperating churches and pastors and provide for its students an authentic quality education! Thus marketing depends on research that provides a needs analysis and interpretation, followed by planning and the conscientious implementation of those plans.

But marketing is more than doing research and then announcing a solution to somebody else's problem. Marketing gurus speak of marketing as a "voluntary exchange of values." Often you must convince the needy of their need. Many people with weight problems never try Ultra Slim-Fast, never sign up with Weight Watchers. Why? Because they don't feel the same need others feel for them. Thus, marketing is also a matter of alerting the needy to their needs.

This fact appears to be true for many evangelical Christian families. Kenneth O. Gangel points out that, even after all these years, a huge majority of Christian families have not yet accepted the idea of sending their children to a Christian school (*Called to Lead* [Colorado Springs, CO: Purposeful Design Publications, 2002]). So marketing means attracting, magnetizing, wooing, winning, and holding on to those whose needs we seek to meet. Marketing also means pricing its services fairly, prudently, and competitively.

Marketing knows its limits and targets its energies. Does your school know its mission? Are you striving to fulfill that mission, or are you so preoccupied with sending letters to missionaries overseas that your math program is on hold? Have you found the point of balance between concern for the world at large and concern for the education of the specific child in the second row next to the window? Too many Christian schools, it seems to me, are trying to do more than they can do and are therefore failing to do as well as they ought the one thing that is their responsibility—provide the very best blend of academic and spiritual nurture a school can offer.

Finally, marketing depends on many elements blended into a *marketing mix*. Marketing begins with the school's mission statement. Indeed, where there is no mission, there can be no marketing. But there must also be strategic planning to take your school to the future you hope for rather than the future you fear.

On a visit to client schools in Florida, I was listening to a radio preacher and heard him say, "I know a lot of Christians who waste time sitting around a table making plans. Wise men don't have to plan; they know what to do!" I thought to myself, "What a foolish and unbiblical remark!" But how familiar that folly is!

Among our clients was a hundred-year-old school. Its enrollment had dropped to less than half what it had been in recent years. It faced a deficit of a quarter million dollars. Faculty had been furloughed for four days without pay. Music students and athletes were charged a fee of thirty dollars for the privilege of playing in the band or on the basketball team. And in the middle of this chaos, the board had launched a 1.3-million-dollar capital campaign—until someone asked the board chairman, "Where's your strategic plan?" He had none to show. What counsel did we offer?

Is it surprising to learn that this century-old school had no mission statement? Is it any more surprising to learn that its philosophy of funding had been to keep the tuition as low as possible and make ends meet by selling candy bars and other products week in and week out?

Which brings me to some other pertinent and perhaps impertinent questions about *money*. Why are most Christian schools struggling under a self-imposed burden brought on by what PAIDEIA Inc. calls their "artificially depressed tuition" and their hesitancy to ask for outright gift support? Why are other schools thriving with rates of tuition aggressively priced to reflect both market reality and the true cost-to-educate? And why are these same schools—without resorting to product sales and fundraising events—receiving gift support in the hundreds of thousands of dollars?

The answer is that these stronger schools have taken a model different from the mass of Christian schools. These stronger schools have chosen to reject the embarrassed, awkward attitude toward money prevalent among so many Christian school leaders. These stronger schools have overcome any reluctance to deal straightforwardly with funding the cost-to-educate and increasing both financial support and financial aid.

Schools that are thriving have confronted the fact that they are in business to fulfill a mission that requires money—lots of it. So they have discarded techniques traditionally employed by poor-mouthing Christian schools, the typical product sales and other torturous methods of raising money to subsidize artificially depressed rates of tuition. Instead, these more advancing schools have made their tuition rates competitive with the best schools in their region, supplementing this income with annual giving campaigns, from which they also derive funds to allocate for financial aid to needy students.

Why doesn't every Christian school do the same? Because many Christian schools have swallowed the impractical notion that every child from every believing family has a spiritual right to attend a Christian school, regardless of cost or ability to pay. Thus we hear pleas for "keeping the tuition as low as possible," instead of calls for providing revenue sufficient to meet the demands of a high-quality education. This attitude translates into a lowest-common-denominator philosophy of tuition setting.

Without endowment or other income to subsidize, low tuition results in limited programs, nonexistent financial aid, and lamentable salaries. Furthermore, most heads of Christian schools have never learned how to ask someone directly for a major gift in support of their school. For this, the blame must fall on college and seminary professors of Christian education—most of whom have never done so either! College and seminary curricula in Christian school administration are strong in history, philosophy, and classroom methods, but they are weak in preparing graduates to determine strategies for enlisting gift support by establishing and promoting an annual giving campaign, like that in place at the college or seminary itself. Instead, budding Christian school administrators learn how to sign up their schools for an unending array of fund-raising projects, from selling magazine subscriptions and candy bars to collecting supermarket receipts and holding car washes.

How can these disastrous trends be reversed? By acknowledging that a high-quality education is expensive but never as costly as mediocrity posing as excellence. Tuition must be increased to meet the real cost-to-educate, which must also include a living wage for teachers and administrators. To survive, Christian schools must settle for nothing but the best and charge what the best costs. For many schools and their constituents, accustomed to artificially depressed tuition, this transition will be as painful as it is for Eastern Europeans to move from their propped-up economies to a market economy, in which quality rises to the top and the shoddy is allowed to go out of business. Sad to say, those schools that refuse to adapt to these realities will simply cease to exist. But if they do, it will be only because they have miscalculated the ability of the evangelical community to support Christian schooling.

An incipient parent revolt may help motivate Christian school leaders to act more wisely. Increasingly, parents perceive their children's need for sound teaching rather than class time spent in each week's new and distracting program for greater sales of citrus fruit or frozen pizzas or Christmas gift-wrapping paper. Given their choice, many parents would rather contribute cash than take time to participate in fund-raising gimmicks. Some parents have even forbidden their children from troubling their grandparents or the neighbors with their block-by-block soliciting in support of their own education. Parents are also beginning to see through the sham argument, put forward by fund-raising vendors at Christian school conventions, that "children learn poise by door-to-door selling."

But the strongest case for funding a Christian school with adequate tuition augmented by generous and sacrificial giving touches a matter of ethics and integrity: A school advertises its program and enrolls children, then informs families that to assure the program's viability, those same children must go out and solicit funds to make that program possible. This practice is as deceitful as false advertising. If the existence of a school program depends on the students' ability to raise sufficient money, how can the school promote that program as part of its curriculum? A school certainly can't satisfy any objective accrediting agency's criteria without adequate budgeted funding.

Frankly, this practice is cowardly. Instead of assuming all costs into the school's budget—then bravely charging tuition that will meet those costs and asking for gift support to make financial aid possible—adults look for some other way out. They shift their responsibilities onto the shoulders of children and make children bear the burden of funding the school. And if these same children don't raise enough money, they are punished by the loss of programs promised to them.

As more and more parents begin to understand that their children are being made to carry financial responsibility for whether or not their school can keep its word, some parents are starting to ask the right questions: How much does it really cost to provide the kind of Christian education we desire for our children? To what extent are we willing to sacrifice in order to pay what it costs?

For while a Christian school must be bathed in prayer and energized by hard work and imagination, it's fueled by money. Here's where thriving schools have made their mark: by promoting the school's mission and declaring, without apology, the correlation between mission and money; by telling their constituents why that school exists—not to save parents money, not to offer as much as necessary for as little as possible—but to offer their students an education based on biblical precepts and modeling the Lordship of Jesus Christ in the lives of those who teach and learn: the best education that responsible stewardship can provide.

With their higher tuition also come stronger financial aid programs for legitimately needy and deserving families, made available through aggressive and productive campaigns for gift support, led by the head-of-school, supported by each board member, managed by a professional development officer. And, may I suggest, this will be the true test of a school that is seeking to become as Christian as possible. The test will not be your orthodox statement of faith, nor your admirable mission statement or motto, nor the cornerstone inscription on your new building, but your record of financial aid, the degree to which you have taken seriously the admonition to "cast your bread upon the waters" (Ecclesiastes 11:1)—the way in which you practice Christian economics, which means *stewardship*.

This is what parents really want in a Christian school. Not the pious poverty of an outdated evangelical inferiority complex—often expressed as, "Oh my, your tuition is high, for a Christian school!"—but an enlightened biblical understanding of mission, management, marketing, master-planning, and the money needed, under God, to make your school's promised excellence a reality.

Let me simply state the obvious: the work of God is above cheap bargain-hunting standards. I believe that Scripture makes clear a natural relationship between *excellence* and *value*, between *quality* and *price*. God demands the best for His tabernacle and temple; not cheap lead but costly gold. When the wayward son returns to his father's house, the father doesn't cobble up a meal of leftovers; he orders a banquet to celebrate his son's return and offers expensive tokens of love, including a ring. When the apostle Paul is looking for a means of contrasting worthy service to God with unworthy, he uses a triad of gold, silver, and precious stones *versus* wood, hay, and stubble.

Perhaps the final question is this: what kind of school are we content to offer to God as our act of stewardship?

15

GUARDING THE VISION,
FULFILLING THE MISSION, IMPLEMENTING THE PLAN

On October 26, 1996, I had the honor of addressing the Mennonite Secondary Education Council, meeting at the Laurelville Conference Center in Mount Pleasant, Pennsylvania. The council represents Mennonite high schools across North America.

Vision, mission, plan—this threefold cord for effective Christian schooling is not easily broken. Certainly, their interdependence is self-evident. No one can prepare a plan without a mission, although I some-times encounter a well-intentioned school board that sets out to do just that. No one can promote a mission-in-a-vacuum. There must be some history, some record of vision fulfilled, to justify the current mission and its claims on potential supporters. There must be some sense of mission for the present and short-term future. So let's consider the implications of guarding the vision, fulfilling the mission, and implementing the plan.

Why does your school exist? What is the vision of your Christian school? *Vision* is the originating purpose that brought your school into being—the historic reason your school was founded. *Vision* also refers to the proposed and ongoing expectations as we go forward, under God. What is the mission of your school? *Mission* is the sustaining purpose, the reason for being that gives impetus to each new day. What is your school's plan for tomorrow and the day after? *Plan* is the strategic purpose to be accomplished in the same manner as a set of war plans in advance of combat or a coach's game plan to overcome the opposing team.

Together vision, mission, and plan represent the key to honoring the legacy of the past, the reason for the present, and the promise of a strong future for your school. Their primary importance cannot be underestimated and must not be undermined.

Consider for a moment the heritage of Christian schooling from which your school derives. When we trace the history of education in Western civilization, we soon realize the correlation between the liberating gospel and a liberal education. In the primitive villages of the French *voyageurs*, across the Southwest and up the coast of Spanish California, as well as throughout the earliest settlements of New England, wherever the Cross was planted, the Academy soon followed. The Jesuits and Franciscans who founded their pioneering mission schools had the same goal as the Pilgrims and Puritans who founded Boston Latin School in 1635. The following year, as a young pastor lay dying, he bequeathed his entire library and half his estate to the founding of a college so that the colony might avoid "an illiterate Ministry to the Churches, when our present Ministers shall lie in Dust" (Samuel Eliot Morison, *The Founding of Harvard College* [Cambridge, MA: Harvard University Press, 1935]).

This fledgling college, set in a village named for the university town across the ocean, on the banks of a river named for their king, was Harvard College. Its purpose was clearly spelled out in the handbook published six years later: "Let every student be plainly instructed and earnestly pressed to consider well [that] the main end of his life and studies is to know God and Jesus Christ which is eternal life, John 17:3, and therefore to lay Christ in the bottom, as the only foundation of all sound knowledge and learning." Its motto became *Veritas pro Christo et Ecclesia*, "Truth for Christ and the Church."

But only two generations had elapsed before Harvard College had lost the support of believing Christians in New England. So, in 1701, a group prevailed upon a New Haven shipbuilder named Eli Yale to help underwrite a new college that would remain true to the gospel. From Yale went forth such graduates as Jonathan Edwards, who was eventually called to be president of what is now Princeton University; and Eleazar Wheelock, who established a missionary training institute to evangelize and to equip evangelists among the native peoples of the western mountains. That school we know today as Dartmouth College. Its original seal is on display in the library: Rimming the seal are the words, "A voice crying in the wilderness, Prepare the way of the Lord."

What was the originating vision of John Harvard? Eli Yale? Jonathan Edwards? Eleazar Wheelock? Why were their institutions brought into being? More to the point, why did those same institutions apostatize? For this is the sorry record throughout American history: apostasy in the academy. Consider the story of Wellesley College, founded by Henry Fowle

Durant, a strong believer in education for women. One of its cornerstones reads, "When this college ceases to proclaim the unsearchable riches of Jesus Christ, let it be torn down stone by stone."

In 1994, the Public Television System carried a documentary about the Wellesley Class of 1969, whose spokesperson at commencement was a young woman from Chicago named Hillary Rodham. Her classmates had gathered to celebrate their twenty-fifth anniversary as graduates, and the television program featured several of them. During the course of the program, they discussed their college's motto, which is the Latin phrase *Non ministrari sed ministrare.* The phrase happens to come from Matthew 20:28, KJV, "The Son of man came not to be ministered unto, but to minister, and to give his life a ransom for many." But to the secularized and politicized alumnae a quarter-century later, the motto of their alma mater had been transformed to mean, in the words of one of them, "Not to be passive but to be active."

After seeing this broadcast, I called the admissions office at Wellesley College and played dumb: I inquired about the motto, which the representative knew immediately in its Latin form. When I asked for a translation, she became uneasy, still more uneasy when I asked for its source, and most uneasy when I asked about the cornerstone inscription and its meaning for the college today. "We regard that mostly as an embarrassment," she admitted.

In the 1890s, John D. Rockefeller determined to found a Christian university in America. Eventually, he invested more than fifty million dollars in the project. A Baptist himself, he sought the leading Baptist educators to work with him and settled on William Rainey Harper and Harry Pratt Judson, descended from Adoniram Judson, the pioneering missionary to Burma. As president and dean of faculty respectively, Harper and Judson set about to recruit teachers. Among their earliest appointments were John Dewey and Thorstein Veblen. Thus did the University of Chicago fail its founder's vision before the first student was enrolled.

I've related these horror stories for a purpose; but all my examples so far are of colleges and universities. What about Christian elementary and secondary schools? In the early 1880s, Dwight L. Moody founded the Northfield School for Girls and the Mount Hermon School for Boys. Many of the students were offspring of foreign missionaries and other Christian leaders. During the summers, the campuses of these neighboring schools in the Connecticut River valley were crowded with people from the great cities of America, hungry for Bible teaching. The Northfield Conferences were renowned throughout the world.

In November 1899, just six weeks before he died, Moody was preaching at Fifth Avenue Presbyterian Church in New York City. During his sermon, he spoke of having founded the two schools in his hometown of Northfield. He spoke of the vision he had for these schools—that they should be for "the training of boys and maidens in Christian living and consecration as teachers and missionaries of Jesus Christ." Could anything be clearer than this? He left them as his legacy "to the churches of America," hoping that they would continue to be "two great, glorious lighthouses of the Lord, beaming out over the land, over the continent, over the world" (Richard K. Curtis, *They Called Him Mister Moody* [Garden City, NY: Doubleday, 1992], 297–98).

Yet within the next decade, these schools had discarded the faith of their founder. If you ask today about Dwight Lyman Moody, someone at the merged Northfield Mount Hermon School will identify him as "a nineteenth-century social reformer."

My own life's work has a direct connection to the Moody/Northfield story. After Moody's death and the faithlessness of his successors, the summer conferences at Northfield so adulterated his intent, that pastors from New York, Philadelphia, and Pittsburgh, who had been sending their people to Northfield, began looking for an alternative. They settled on a parcel of ground on the North Shore of Long Island, in the quaint village of Stony Brook. In 1909, they began summer conferences that led, in turn, to a school for boys, founded in 1922. Thus, my work at The Stony Brook School is a direct result of someone else's infidelity to the vision of a founder.

I repeat my earlier question: what is the *vision*, the originating purpose of your Christian school? And what are you—as board members and administrators—doing to protect and preserve with integrity the founding purpose that brought your school into being? For you can be very certain of this: if the founding vision is not nurtured, protected, and preserved, it will be undermined by what Edgar Allan Poe calls "a barely perceptible fissure" that widens from a crack into a fault in the foundation, until eventually the house caves in (*The Fall of the House of Usher* [Signet Classics, 1998]).

Can it happen at your school? What's to prevent it? What are your responses to these important questions?

1. Who among current board members and administrators and major backers knows the history of your school and its founders' vision or originating purpose? Has that history been recorded in written or oral form?

2. Who is responsible for reminding the current leadership of that vision and the precedents it sets for action in the present and future?

Whenever I meet with the board of a school, I try to encourage them to take most seriously their role as trustees—those to whom has been entrusted the legacy of which Dwight L. Moody spoke. I would urge you to set aside a special time to review your school's charter and other founding documents; to listen to the reminiscences of old-timers who recall why the school was founded and can remind you and your contemporaries of the sacrifices that brought it into being. We owe at least this much to our predecessors; we owe much more to God.

So, as I speak of *vision*, I do so specifically and particularly in a retrospective manner. But we cannot look only to the past; we must also have an ongoing vision to inspire us.

We regard *mission* as the sustaining purpose that builds on the record of the past but accommodates to current needs. Let me share with you some thoughts about mission and mission statements. As before, I offer these questions for your benefit:

1. What is the present mission or sustaining purpose of your school? Who is responsible for articulating that sustaining purpose?
2. How does the current mission statement reflect the original vision and its traditions? Does the current mission statement indicate flexibility beyond that original vision?
3. Who is responsible for revising that mission and mission statement when necessary? What is the process for doing so?
4. Is the mission of your school stated clearly and briefly? Is it published and communicated by the leadership of the school to its several publics, including the community at large?
5. How well is your school succeeding in communicating its mission? How well do its several publics support that mission?

Someone once showed me a cartoon depicting Moses descending from Mount Sinai with the two tablets of stone. Of two who were waiting for him, one says to the other, "Oh no, not another mission statement!" Perhaps you're feeling just so. Perhaps you believe that the primary concern facing your school is the need to raise money in order to support it. May I offer this reminder: "Where there is no mission, there is no compelling reason to give money." So mission will always hold precedence over money; your school's reason-for-being will always be primary to the secondary issue of funding that mission. That's one horse that can never allow its cart to lead the way.

At the same time, your school's mission must be adequately funded, or it becomes little more than empty idealism. Thus, the questions pertaining to mission are utterly straightforward and direct:

1. What does it take to fulfill our mission adequately?
2. Where can resources be found to fund our mission adequately?

In my years of providing consulting services to Christian schools, the *plan* to achieve adequate funding has proven to be the common point of weakness. Most schools recall why they were founded and seek to remain true to that vision. Increasingly, schools have worked themselves up to and beyond the point of drafting a mission statement to express their current purpose. But more often than not, a school has no plan to carry forward its founding vision and its sustaining mission.

There are many different sorts of plan—a plan to increase marketing and admissions, a plan to grow from an elementary school to a middle and secondary school, a plan to separate from the founding church and attain independence, a plan to open satellite campuses, and so on. But nowhere is the absence of planning more apparent than when it comes to anticipating and meeting the school's need for increased revenue from all its logical sources. As is shown in our study—published in the book *From Candy Sales to Committed Donors*—the greatest need for planning is in the related spheres of income production through policy and pricing of cost-based tuition, including need-based financial aid, and voluntary gift support, whether for annual expenditure or for endowment.

Clearly, there are four main sources of revenue for a school:

1. Tuition
2. Voluntary gift support
3. Earnings from endowed investments
4. Extraordinary income from rental, summer programs, and so on

All these sources are important; but the principal dollars that fund a Christian school come from tuition, gift support, and endowment earnings. We need to have a plan to maximize each of these resources.

First and foremost, we need tuition. No one has yet discovered a way to offer automobiles or a Big Mac or a first-rate education at less than it costs to provide such goods and services—and remain in business. But we in Christian schooling have been trying to do so for many years. The only way we can come close to meeting this absurd goal is by paying our teachers less than the cost of living in our own communities, thus forcing many of them to hold after-school and weekend jobs so that their own families will survive. This shameful practice must end! Tuition needs to be set at a rate that covers the fair cost of the curriculum and those who teach it.

Now, why is the problem of raising tuition so troubling for so many school boards? It seems to me that there are three essential problems:

1. An evangelical Depression-era mentality about money
2. The board's mania to keep tuition as low as possible
3. A failure to recognize what tuition ought to cover

My generation, born during the Great Depression of the 1930s, has grown old under the pressure of our "Depression-era mentality," which distorts our attitudes toward money and our understanding of God's intentions for what money can accomplish. Because we were raised to be frugal in a time of economic stress, we lunge for the cheapest, the least costly, the bargain-basement purchase. We assume that God will bless us more if we accept the inferior, and we rationalize that there is really no correlation between quality and price. Lastly, we assume that evangelical Christians like us are equally incapable of affording higher quality—so we don't need to worry about not offering it.

Because my generation has imbued the church with our timid, inferiority-complex attitudes toward money, we have also fostered the fallacy that a board's primary obligation is "to keep tuition as low as possible." Not so. The board's obligation is to provide sufficient funds to fulfill the school's mission. In an emergency, and as an act of integrity, a board may determine to trim back its mission to accommodate some temporary lack of funding. But to set out from the beginning, as most boards do, and deliberately underfund the mission by underpricing the cost-to-educate each student and by so doing, to throw the school into a deficit position six months before the new term begins—this is economic folly.

Instead, the board of any school wishing to grow stronger will set its tuition rate so as to

1. Cover the full cost-to-educate each child
2. Pay adequate salaries and benefits to all employees
3. Express the school's sense of its own worth in the marketplace

Here's a maxim we need to remember: "Lacking other evidence, quality is perceived to be a function of price." It's a fancy way of saying, "You get what you pay for." Few parents I know admit to looking for the cheapest cut-rate education they can provide for their children. Instead, they are looking for the school whose vision, mission, and plan conform to what they believe their children need; then they will find a way to afford what it costs to enroll their children there.

Finally, on the topic of tuition, here's what PAIDEIA Inc. identifies as "the tuition conundrum": *Why is it possible to have a more diverse student body at a higher tuition than at a lower tuition?* The answer is this: setting tuition below the cost-to-educate means "artificially-depressed tuition," picking a number just because it doesn't frighten away too many parents. But it does deter parents who understand that a school can't claim high quality without funding that high quality. They simply won't enroll their children because the lower tuition rate will convince them that the quality will also be lower.

So, in order to attract parents of financial means, we must demonstrate that our school's tuition is realistic for the quality we advertise and is competitive in our local marketplace. Furthermore, only by enlisting such families will we be able to encourage their financial support to provide financial aid for less affluent families. Without the gifts of those who can afford our higher tuition, there won't be any funding to subsidize the needy families.

You notice that earlier I tied tuition policy and pricing to need-based financial aid. I believe that the true mark of an intentional Christian school is the generosity of its financial aid. But the aid should be "need-based," not discounted automatically for every second or third child. So too with all other forms of discounted tuition: no discount for paying in full by July 1, and none for volunteering to clean the schoolhouse or sell tickets to the auction. In fact, we strongly advocate that anyone who does not pay the tuition when it is due—say, by July 1 or so—should be charged a premium percentage for each installment payment.

Voluntary gift support takes one of two forms: funding for current expenditures or preservation of capital to produce earnings in the short- and long-term future. Product sales and fund-raising events are essentially stop-gap measures to meet some current and pressing crisis, or ways to avoid placing the responsibility where it belongs—not with the children but with the adults, starting with the governing board of the school. Just remember this: nobody constructs a building and no bank issues a loan on the strength of candy bar sales, and nobody builds an endowment fund on revenue from a car wash or bake sale. It's time we all acknowledged these truths and ended the cycle of fund-raising sales and events.

The fact is that it's well beyond time for Christian schools to assume the dignity and stature of our colleges and seminaries. I know of no college that sells T-shirts to pay its faculty or provide financial aid. To do so would demean the mission of the college. So it is with our Christian schools. We have a higher calling than to peddle World's Finest Chocolate. Let our friends and potential friends learn more about the mission of our school, and let us plan how best to integrate that mission into our program for funding our school through voluntary gifts and endowment.

Vision, mission, plan. We need a plan to go forward with the full funding of our school's vision and mission. We need a plan to revise the old ways and adapt to new strategies. We need a plan that will provide new models for succeeding boards and administrators to follow, then adjust and adapt to suit the new paradigms for their time. We need a plan to express our school's strategic purpose not only for the current fiscal year but over the next few years and, if the Lord delays His return, for the decades ahead.

It may well be that the leadership of your school already knows its plan, its hierarchy of values, the guiding principles and priorities that govern all key result areas of its plan. If not, then right here at this conference is the time for representatives of your school to ask, Does our board have a strategic plan for satisfying our priorities and implementing our goals and objectives? Does the board have a strategic plan to preserve the viability of our school and ensure its promise for the future?

In short, each school must ask the overriding question: Where (in what economic and educational condition) does our school desire to be five to ten years from now, and how will we get there?

Under God, let's go forward together toward that goal.

16

LEADING BY THE BOOK

On July 28, 1997, at the annual convention of Christian Schools International in Chattanooga, Tennessee, I offered the following keynote address. Because my audience included many Christian school leaders of Dutch heritage, these remarks include specific appeal to their interests.

The theme of this convention is "Leading by The Book." Explicitly, that phrase points to the always-compelling topic of *leadership* and the equally compelling thought of *The Book* as resource and criterion. Leadership is compelling because it seems to be in both high demand and short supply. As I travel throughout North America visiting schools and colleges, seminaries and churches, as well as other Christian institutions, the most apparent weakness—the greatest need—is not for funding alone, although each of these works could benefit from additional financial support. It is not for facilities or more state-of-the-art computers, nor for additional volunteers, nor even for more fervent prayer partners. The greatest need is for imaginative and inspiring leadership.

But true leadership does not derive from merely attending Chester Karrass seminars, nor reading books by Peter Drucker, Tom Peters, Max DuPree, and the other gurus of management science. True leadership is a gift from God, enhanced by our learning from the models and examples of history. These models and their moral character are included in Holy Scripture—recorded in The Book—for our benefit. As St. Paul tells the Romans, "For everything that was written in the past was written to teach us, so that through endurance and the encouragement of the Scriptures we might have hope" (Romans 15:4).

Leadership is, first, a divine gift. Yet the gift of leadership alone is not sufficient; it must be acknowledged and put into action. Think of the example of Moses, the fugitive prince of Egypt, the back-forty son-in-law of Jethro, spending his days and years with sheep while his own people languished in slavery. No, mere leadership is nothing in a vacuum. Money is wasted, facilities are useless, computers are worthless, volunteers are disabled, even prayer is futile—unless people of God who are gifted with the attributes and characteristics of leadership are willing to exercise their gifts according to biblical criteria stipulated in narrative and exhortation.

What are the criteria? We could leaf through The Book, pausing at page after page to note examples and maxims. For instance, soon after Moses takes on the role of leadership, his father-in-law Jethro becomes the first consultant in Scripture and recommends a management plan that delegates authority and spreads the burden of leadership so that Moses will be able to stand the strain. Or we could concentrate on the collection of wise sayings called Proverbs and find ourselves affirming their appropriateness to issues of leadership. But I prefer to offer The Book in context.

Several years ago, sensing that Christian schooling had no common articulated statement of standards for determining excellence in leadership, our firm drafted such a document. We call it *A Covenant for Excellence*. Within its text is this paragraph, spelling out the objective spiritual qualities of Christian living that St. Paul presents as exemplary of the life transformed and the mind renewed:

> humility, sobriety, proportion, love, honor for one another,
> zeal, joy, hope, patience, faithfulness in prayer, generosity,
> hospitality, forgiveness, sympathy, harmony, peaceable behav-
> ior, absence of vengefulness, submission to authority, justice,
> good citizenship, fiscal responsibility, nonjudgmental spirit,
> absence of legalism and license, mutual acceptance

All these are evidences of the powerful work of the Holy Spirit.

This catalog derives, of course, from Paul's letter to the Romans, chapters 12 through 15, which may well be the primary handbook on Christian leadership. Recall the scope of the apostle's address in this portion of his treatise. He begins by describing what it means for professing Christians to think and act in ways different from the rest of the world: transformed and renewed, submissive and obedient. He goes on to evoke once more his favorite analogy of the church as a body with its many healthy and functioning members, and from this comparison he infers the contributions of the believers' differing gifts to the whole church, or body of believers.

Next, the apostle treats two aspects of love—*agape,* or love without strings attached, and *philadelphia,* or brotherly affection. He calls for such simple evidences as deference, courtesy, and exemplary citizenship. He admonishes against the temptation to get even. He sets a high and classically Reformed standard for living under the ultimate sovereignty of God, even if the ruler's name is Nero.

For the apostle Paul, godly leadership extends also to personal relations with other believers. Above all else, we are to avoid a judgmental spirit, especially toward those whom Paul identifies as weak. As a former Baptist preacher's kid, I'm thoroughly familiar with the case made in fundamentalist and many evangelical circles concerning amusements and "the weaker brother." In my growing up, the weaker brother was responsible for depriving me of most of the pleasures in which I wanted to indulge. For instance, no member of my family ever attended a movie theater for fear of causing some weaker brother to stumble. So too with school dances: I was excluded from such events because, surely, my presence and my clumsy-footed participation might injure some weaker brother.

Of course, no one ever bothered to explain to me what made the weaker brother weak; nor was there ever any challenge for the weaker brother to become strong. It was all very confusing to me. Now I understand that authentic biblical leadership recognizes that *agape* and *philadelphia* go far beyond any checklist of legalistic taboos. In fact, *agape* and *philadelphia* are at the very core of leadership gifts and skills. Genuine leadership by The Book follows the apostle's maxim: "Let us therefore make every effort to do what leads to peace and to mutual edification" (Romans 14:19).

Let me apply these biblical principles directly to leadership in Christian schooling. Leadership in our schools comes from a variety of sources. First, there must be *governing* leadership. Much of what I perceive to be the underlying weakness in many schools results from a misconception concerning the nature of a school and its governance. Whoever governs, it is essential to the strength and well-being of the school that both the governors and the governed remember that the school is a corporate entity called *community,* not *family.*

With all due respect to the sweet spirit expressed in the emotional rhetoric we often hear, no institution is an actual extension of the Christian family; it can't be. Only homeschooling, which by design is deliberately noninstitutional, is an accurate model of school-as-family. Once children depart from the sanctuary of their own homes and the presence of their own parents, they enter into a new sphere of learning, one that is controlled by factors other than what their parents might have determined. In fact, the first of these influences may well be a godless school bus driver.

When a school indulges in talk about "the school as family," it means well. It means to suggest warmth and concern and mutual support. But it employs the wrong analogy, for a family is a social unit bound together by identity, consanguinity, heritage, custom, and pride of name. But no school can ever be as socially distinct and unique as a family might be. By its very nature, a school must acknowledge that it is made up of many social units brought together by a single unifying thought: *Together we can be stronger than we would ever be apart.* Thus, a community is formed for mutual benefit and support.

When I enroll my children in your school, I waive some of my family's idiosyncrasies, some of my personal preferences, some of my know-it-all opinions, in order to obtain from the larger social unit called *school* that which the privacy and isolation of my family cannot provide. This is what I mean by *school-as-community*, a social compact of persons held together by common purpose and governed by a school board, not individual parents.

Another element of Christian school leadership by The Book is *executive* leadership. However a governing board is formed, it is not the day-to-day, hands-on, decision-making authority that operates the school. Some boards usurp that role, some boards are innocently unaware that such is not their role, some boards are thrust into the minutiae of a school because of circumstances. But ideally, a governing board appoints a chief executive officer to lead the school. The title given to the position may be one of several: headmaster or headmistress, head-of-school, superintendent, principal, director, administrator—but whatever the title, the office is that of on-site leader of the professional staff.

The head-of-school adheres to board policies and acts in such a way as to implement those policies effectively. Professionally, the school's head is an educator, but primarily he or she is a decision-maker, deciding such major issues as what curricula and textbooks are best suited to carry out the school's mission and educational philosophy as mandated by the board; or such minor matters as school calendar and daily schedule. In the strongest schools, the CEO distinguishes his or her leadership by the quality of such decision making. Of course, a wise head-of-school exercises executive leadership by consensus. Blessed with uncommon common sense, the chief executive officer knows that wisdom derives from the counsel of others.

In some schools, however, the board declines to confer executive leadership on the head-of-school and instead seeks to operate the school itself.

Such a board extends its scope in hiring beyond the one who should be its sole employee—the head-of-school—and makes all faculty appointments, selects prospects for admission, even decides matters of major disciplinary action, leaving the head-of-school without such powers. These schools—I would suggest—have not yet reached full maturity and strength.

A third level of responsibility is *managerial* leadership. In a school, managers may be identified as grade-level principals, deans, business and development officers, classroom teachers and coaches, administrative assistants, clerical workers, custodians, and food service providers. They are loyal to the school's mission, focused on their specific roles, and limited in their spheres of authority. Managers do the work executives assign, and by the quality of their work, managers make executives look good. It goes without saying that no school functions without them.

But in all these differentiations among levels of leadership and responsibility, *agape* and *philadelphia* must rule. Board members must care about the personal well-being of their head-of-school and his or her family. The head-of-school must care about those who work alongside. Other administrators, officers, teachers, coaches, and staff must care about the students and their parents, whose lives and fortunes have been committed to their school. Such leadership, ultimately, will be characterized by a servant's attitude.

One of the more problematic words in the jargon of contemporary Christianity is one that deserves greater dignity than it commonly receives. I speak of the word *ministry*. This word has many applications. Among fundamentalists and evangelicals, a favorite usage appears in the phrase "Christian school ministry." I wish I had a nickel for every time I hear that phrase used. It pours out as a catch-all term for the dedication, commitment, industry, pioneering endeavor, hard work, financial struggle, as well as the joy of seeing young people educated in an environment conducive to their becoming disciples of Jesus Christ.

All this is admirable, but these same speakers seldom pause long enough to edit their own speech. If they were to do so, they might revise the phrase from "Christian school ministry" to "Christian school *mission*." They might also consider this proposition: ministry isn't what we do but the *spirit in which we do it.*

Ministry comes from the Latin root for service. An *ad-ministrator*, therefore, is a professional servant, whose highest duty is to prepare the circumstances and situations in which other people may do their work. No classroom teacher is expected to recruit her class, construct her classroom, schedule when it will be occupied, and raise the funds to heat and illumine the room. All that is asked of her is that she show up prepared to teach. Someone else—a full-time servant—is appointed to make her teaching possible. This servant may have more years of experience and more formal education, and he may be paid a higher salary. If so, it is only because his demanding duties as a servant of others extend so broadly. But each one of us must labor with the attitude of a servant, working in the spirit of service, the posture of ministry. This is leadership by The Book.

Finally, all leadership that finds its source in biblical principles must possess and convey to others a vision of hope. The following memory from my childhood in Canada illustrates such vision. In the early years of World War II, the royal House of Orange Nassau—Queen Wilhelmina and her daughter Princess Julianna—removed themselves from the Netherlands to the small city of Guelph, Ontario, where my family lived. One day in 1942, my second-grade teacher at Central School called me to her desk, pinned a note to my sweater, and told me to hurry home and give the note to my mother. As soon as she read it, my mother went to the bathroom and began running the bathwater for me. "Why am I taking a bath?" I wanted to know. When I emerged from the bath, my Sunday clothes were laid out for me to wear. "What's happening?" I cried. "You're going to sing for someone very special," my mother responded.

We walked back to my school and its auditorium, where on the platform I recognized my father's pulpit chairs—the nearest thing Guelph had to a throne. In one chair sat an old woman wearing a purple dress and hat, and in the other, a younger person. At the appointed moment, I was called on to sing—what else?—"There'll Be Bluebirds Over the White Cliffs of Dover." When the song was done, the Queen beckoned me to her, placed her hand on my head, and said, "I hope so, very soon."

Long ago, I sang a song of hope to a brave woman whose earthly realm had been ravaged by tyranny. She had dared to issue a "flaming protest" against the invasion of her country, but she also encouraged children like me to believe that, under the sovereign providence of God, right would prevail. I have lived my whole life in glad recognition that those of us who call ourselves children of God are never to be characterized as victims, never overwhelmed by pessimism or negative thinking; neither are we to be merely "positive" or "optimistic." If we are men and women of The Book, we are summoned to be the people of hope. It is hope that anchors us in life's storms, hope that carries us beyond Pollyanna clichés, hope that secures a calming vision for the future because our hope is in God the Father Almighty and in Jesus Christ His only Son our Lord.

In this same spirit, speaking nearly fifty years ago, Henry Zylstra, the eminent Christian educator at Calvin College, reminded those of us in

Christian schooling that "our schools must be schools." Such a remark is a challenge to leadership, for in this telling phrase may be found the difference between those who uphold the *mission* of Christian schooling and those who focus on its *ministry*. If Christian schools are to be a force for redemption in the twenty-first century, it will be because they are led by those who understand the purpose of Christian schooling.

To this end, may Christian schooling continue to thrive, and may leaders come forth from the ranks to fulfill the hope that inspires children and their parents.

17

CHRISTIAN SCHOOL OPERATIONS:
MORE THAN A MINISTRY

This address was delivered on October 2, 1998, as the keynote address at the ACSI Northwest Region convention in Anchorage, Alaska.

As I enter school buildings all over North America and observe the work of those called to Christian schooling, I think of the words of Desiderius Erasmus, the greatest mind in Christendom and the leading voice of Christian humanism in the early days of the Renaissance. Over my desk at home hangs this inscription:

> To be a schoolmaster is next to being a king. Do you count
> it lowly employment to imbue the minds of the young with
> the things of Christ and the best of literature and return them
> to their homes honest and virtuous persons? In the opinion
> of fools, it is a humble task. But in fact it is the noblest of
> occupations.

"The noblest of occupations." But what makes it so? And how does that fact affect the way we operate our school? I want to spell out several factors as simply and as directly as I can.

First, ours is "the noblest of occupations" because Christian schooling is a *ministry* ... but more than just a ministry. For a long time, I've reacted negatively against the repeated references to "Christian school ministry" because too often I've found that phrase to be a sop for excusing mediocrity, a euphemism for shoddy institutional management and the absence of adequate financial stability, a sanctimonious circumlocution that avoids acknowledging academic ineffectiveness and business ineptitude. You know what I mean: No, we don't charge what it costs to educate our students; we're just a ministry. No, we don't pay our teachers a living wage; we're just a ministry. No, we don't have the latest technology or even the latest editions of our textbooks; after all, we're just a ministry.

Furthermore, it is often sadly apparent that those who talk most about the ministry of Christian schooling say nothing whatever about the *mission* of Christian schooling. Too often the proponents of Christian school ministry ignore a school's failure to fulfill its mission because of academic inadequacies or poor business practices by speaking in pious terms about its ministry. Thus—all too often—*ministry* becomes not only the catch-word but the catch basin for all the less-admirable elements of our work.

I should also confess that—while I may be right in my assessment of some representations of Christian schooling that use ministry as an alibi and diminish the significance of their mission—I may also have been too harsh, too one-sided in my criticism. So let me try as hard as my God-given powers of reasoning and language will permit to make myself clear. *Ministry* is a noble word, a scriptural word. Its Greek form, *diakonia*, is related to our word *deacon*. In its Latin origin, it means "service." One of the great statements in the Gospels about Jesus of Nazareth is this: "The Son of Man did not come to be served, but to serve" (Mark 10:45). Thus, I honor the concept of ministry as service.

Since to minister is to serve, to be an administrator of a school is to be the chief professional servant. I see this demonstrated whenever I visit a school and am led on a tour of the campus by the head-of-school. We scarcely take ten steps before the headmaster bends over and picks up a scrap of paper or some other litter that has been lying there for three hours. Dozens of others—teachers as well as students—have passed by and somehow failed to notice what spoils the appearance of the campus, but the head-of-school sees it and stoops to remove it—not because it's in his contract to do so, but because he or she is the *administrator*, the chief professional servant.

In the same manner, each teacher in his or her classroom setting is a servant. You are serving God by fulfilling your calling in obedience, but you serve God by serving your students and their parents, providing the children with the services for which their parents are paying tuition. Because those parents have entered into a contractual agreement with your school, they are entitled to the fulfilling of that agreement—which means that their children will be taught. But they have also entered into a covenantal relationship with the school, which means that their children will be nurtured in ways that complement the nurture being given at home and in church. Your task is to serve the children and their parents;

in so doing, you serve God. And to the extent that you fulfill your service as expected, you please God. In that sense, therefore, your work of teaching in a Christian school is a ministry ... but it is more, much more.

So it is, too, for you who volunteer to serve on our governing boards. Because you care about the nurture of children in "the *paideia* of the Lord" and support the mission of the school, you give of your time and wisdom and experience to make the policies that govern the school and its operations. This is your *ministry*, your service to God.

Second, ours is "the noblest of occupations" because a Christian school is an organism ... but more than just an organism. A school is a dynamic, living entity. It isn't just a building or a corporation or a flowchart of names and titles. A school is people, each of whom has a responsible role to play in the organism's life. St. Paul uses this same analogy when he speaks of the body of Christ, by which he means the church. We are all members, he writes, of one body, but all members have different functions. In making his analogy, he specifies various parts of the human body and argues that, just because the hand is not the eye, the hand is no less part of the body (1 Corinthians 12:1–26).

Sometimes, when visiting a school, I ask someone, "What's your work here?" It always pains me to hear in reply, "Oh, I'm just a teacher" or "I'm just an office manager" or "I'm just a volunteer." Most discouragingly, I sometimes hear someone say, "I'm just the business manager" or "I just handle accounts receivable" or "I just manage the maintenance crew." Let me be perfectly blunt: there are no "just-anyones" in the body of Christ, in the Kingdom of God, in the Christian school. You are a child of the heavenly Father, a brother or sister in Christ, and your work is worthy, provided you do your job wholeheartedly and as a service. You are integral to the well-being of the organism that is your Christian school.

A school is made up of many persons, not all of whom teach phonics or Bible verses or geometry; some teach by example what it means to serve Jesus Christ in a business role or as mechanics or as data processors. Such is their ministry; such also is their living contribution to the organism that is your school.

Like every other organism, a school is only as thriving and whole as its individual members—it is also as sickly and fragmented as its individual members. When a school is a place of joy, that joy originates in the attitudes of those who walk its halls and occupy its classrooms. That joy emanates from within. It is the joy of which Geoffrey Chaucer writes when he describes the young Oxford scholar, "And gladly would he learn and gladly teach" (Prologue, *Canterbury Tales*). It is the joy on the face of a young child solving a difficult academic problem. It is the joy on the face of an athlete overcoming the pain of disciplined training. It is the joy on the face of a student artist upon completing a new work. Such joy permeates a school and imbues the organism with joy.

But the opposite condition also applies. When a school is riddled with gossip and backbiting, it isn't the bricks and mortar that are to blame. It's the men and women who inhabit the teachers' lounge and spend their lunch hour in a dyspeptic harangue on the administration and the school board. A school isn't "Christian" because it says so on the cornerstone or signboard. There is no such thing as a biblical brick or a charismatic chem lab or a sanctified schoolroom. Only people can be Christian. A school is Christian—or not!—because of the living members of that school's population. This means that we sanctify the organism that is our school by every single decision we make—whether that decision is financial, strategic, curricular, or personal. So, your Christian school is an organism,... but it is more, much more.

Third, ours is "the noblest of occupations" because Christian schooling is a business ... but more than just a business. For some, this may be the hardest part of this piece to accept. Let me presume to say why: many are in Christian schooling precisely because they chose not to be in business or commerce or industry. And here I am, saying that your school is a business! Because it is. Your school is an economic enterprise that depends on appealing to and satisfying a market niche of customers or clients or constituents who, in return for services rendered, pay a stipulated sum out of which the cost of providing those services is distributed among vendors and employees.

A school must meet its fiduciary obligations; it must pay its bills on time to retain its good standing. A school must meet its legal responsibilities and earn the respect of both civil and accrediting authorities. A school must recruit and compensate competitively the best people it can find to lead and teach and coach. For all these reasons—in spite of intellectual idealism and rhapsodic love of learning—a school must deal in dollars and income and revenue and investments and endowment in the hope of achieving financial stability.

There's nothing dishonorable or unprofessional or uneducational about the business side of operating a school. Yes, your Christian school is a business, and as such it must be conducted responsibly. But it is more, much more.

Yours is "the noblest of occupations" because your Christian school is a school, and we who govern, lead, serve, teach, coach, conduct, or direct its program and personnel must regard its institutional obligations. As a school, it is a place of academic teaching and learning. It is not primarily a soul-saving station, a rescue mission, a drug-rehab clinic, a political store-front, or even a youth ministry. It is a school.

Because your school professes to be a "Christian school," those insti-tutional obligations must reflect the Lordship of Jesus Christ. Indeed, the primary and only legitimate reason for your school's existing as a school is to be a place of teaching and learning where Jesus Christ is honored as Lord. Rather frequently, I encounter someone who thinks otherwise, who supposes that the primary mission of a Christian school is to win souls for Jesus Christ or to plant churches in Haiti. This puts me at a disadvantage, of course, because it appears that I oppose winning converts to faith in Jesus Christ. I don't. But I also don't want to lose track of my ethical and moral obligation as a teacher.

Our role as Christian scholars and leaders of Christian schools—educators all—is not primarily to prepare evangelists or flood the mission field with new recruits. Our role is to teach girls and boys how to read, how to count, how to write, how to listen, how to discern, how to inter-pret, how to think, how to analyze, how to synthesize, how to critique, how to know. And in that act of knowing, how to acknowledge who God is and what His claims on one's life may be. This is what it means to be a Christian teacher, a Christian scholar—a disciple of Jesus Christ.

If I profess to teach geometry, then it isn't honorable of me to make the parables of Jesus the subject of my teaching; I need to teach the Pythagorean theorem. If I profess to teach geography, it isn't ethical of me to teach the parallelisms of the Hebrew psalms. I need to be teaching how rivers and lakes and mountains affect commerce and the economics of a nation. To the extent that I do so, I am fulfilling my role as a teacher. If I concentrate on prayer requests and altar calls, I am defrauding the parents and students who, when they enrolled in my school, entered into a social compact with expectations of receiving an academic education.

In the students to whom we offer the possibility of eternal life with God, we must be able to find evidence that they are acquiring temporal knowledge. We must be able to say to them, "Explain the concept that the square of the hypotenuse of a right triangle is equal to the sum of the squares of the other two sides." "Explain Frederick Jackson Turner's fron-tier hypothesis." "Explain T. S. Eliot's theory of the missing objective correlative in Hamlet." "Explain the powers of magnetic attraction." Only if they have learned these academic principles will we be able to say that we have fulfilled the ethical component of our institutional obligation to be a school.

This was one of the hardest elements of hiring young faculty to teach in a Christian school. Many of them came to us in their eagerness to serve as youth ministers. They wanted to interact with the students, they wanted to "rap" with the kids, they wanted to hang out and be a buddy. The last thing they wanted to do was test and evaluate and grade a paper or write an assessment of the student's academic progress. They had endless hours to spend in late-night discussions but little time for lesson preparation or grading papers. About the middle of the fall, I'd call the rookie in and ask how it was going. Then I'd pose the question, If you have the choice of leading an after-midnight session with a group of students or preparing tomorrow's lesson, which do you think is more "spiritual"? Without fail, I'd get the wrong answer!

The right answer is much less glamorous, much less emotional, much less personal. The right answer is drudgery and hard slugging through a mass of content and details and data and information and strategies for teaching and learning. The wrong answer is easy and laid back and comfortable and unaccountable—and may result in a student's expression of faith in Jesus Christ. But if he fails the quiz the next day or his teacher is unprepared to fulfill the professional and ethical obligation to present academic content in a compelling and discernible manner, then that Christian school is only questionably Christian and is certainly not a school.

Here are some favorite questions from Charles Malik (*The Two Tasks*, Cornerstone Books, 1980): What does Jesus Christ think of the education we offer in His name? Can He be satisfied with our devotion if it means that we don't teach what we're paid to teach? Can He be glorified by our earnestness to save souls if, at the same time, we're wrong about our dates or formulae or theorems or how to spell *potato*? And if you disagree with me and my emphasis on the specific nature of Christian schooling, then I suggest that you reconsider your work, your calling. It may well be that you belong in Young Life or Awana or Christian Service Brigade or Pioneer Clubs or some local church's youth ministry. But you don't belong in the academic setting of a Christian school.

Finally, Christian schooling is "the noblest of occupations" because—like every other form of service to Jesus Christ—it is a calling. What a calling we have! Ours is no less a calling, a vocation, than that of the pastor, the evangelist, or the foreign missionary. We are called by the same God who summoned Moses from the burning bush, Gideon from his father's winepress, David from tending sheep, Ruth from gleaning in the fields, Peter and Andrew from catching fish, Matthew from collecting taxes, Saul of Tarsus from his vigilante pursuits. We are called to govern, administer, teach, coach, or provide support in a Christian school.

Our calling is to joyful service. We cannot hope to inspire young people with "the things of Christ and the best of literature" or any other subject. We cannot hope to "return them to their homes virtuous [persons]" unless we ourselves are imbued with the joy of our work. Again, as Chaucer suggests, glad learners make glad teachers.

What is it that we are learning and teaching day by day? First, we ought to be learning and teaching the importance of excellence. Every athlete knows that excellence is, as Harold Best puts it, "both absolute and relative," that we are "unequally gifted and cannot equally achieve" (Donald Hustad, *Jubilate! Church Music in the Evangelical Tradition* [Carol Stream, IL: Hope, 1981]). Every athlete knows whether or not he or she has fulfilled the personal, inner absolute that is the norm for every match or meet: "have I done my best?" But every wise coach also knows and encourages the athlete to recognize reasonable levels of excellence and reasonable levels of attainment. A city or county championship at 100 meters is a fine and lustrous accomplishment, but it is not quite the state championship.

Excellence is also progressive. Today's excellence becomes tomorrow's minimum standard. And one thing more about excellence: There can be no excellence without integration or wholeness. Integration means the opposite of fragmentation and brokenness, the bits-and-pieces we most often experience. So, for example, a musical piece and its performance succeed as a whole, or else one cannot speak of excellence. As we work toward integration, so we are working toward excellence. And that, with humility.

What is our calling? It is a royal calling, for your school is a ministry but much more; an organism but much more; a business but much more; a school but much more. Your school is an institutionalized opportunity for you to fulfill your calling to help your students become disciples of Jesus Christ and learn obedience to Him. We do this by both precept and example—and mostly by example. The operation of your school is for no other purpose. That's what makes Christian schooling "the noblest of occupations."

18

TRANSFORMING LEADERSHIP IN CHRISTIAN SCHOOLING

This speech served as the keynote address to ACSI board members and administrators assembled at Willow Valley Conference Center in Lancaster, Pennsylvania, on January 23, 2003.

As you know, our consulting firm is named PAIDEIA Inc., which we pronounce *pie-day-ah*. Someone said to me recently, "What a great name for consultants: *Paid-Idea*." Actually, we take our name from the Greek word for "education." In the fifth century before Christ, Greek families sent their sons to the academy to acquire the *paideia*, meaning that they would receive nurture in content and character—unhappily, their daughters remained at home to learn only the domestic arts. Their sons were given instruction in civic responsibility and character development, curriculum and culture and physical fitness. The purpose was to produce men who would be leaders. Plato quotes Socrates as saying, "If you ask what is the good in general of *paideia* [education], the answer is easy. *Paideia* produces good citizens and good citizens act nobly."

Likewise Paul of Tarsus spoke of *paideia* when instructing new believers who would read his letters. To the Ephesian and Colossian parents in particular, he says, "Don't treat your children too roughly—don't expect more of them than is reasonable; instead, bring them up in the *paideia* and *nouthesia* of the Lord."

That is what *paideia* means, but what about that other word, *nouthesia*? Let me explain with a bit of personal memory: When I was a Baptist preacher's kid in Ontario, each June we students learned the name of next year's teacher. As soon as we learned the teacher's name, the major question in our minds was not "How skilled is she at conveying the principles of the multiplication table?" or "How adept is he at teaching phonics?" No, we had only one question: "Does she use the strap?" In the top righthand drawer of every teacher's desk was a three-foot razor strap with specific instructions on its use as an instrument of punishment.

So when that Greek schoolboy went off to the academy each morning, he was accompanied by an adult male slave from his father's household. This slave was called "the child-leader" or *paidagogos*. He spent the whole day sitting in the same classes as his master's son, observing how attentive the boy was to his lesson. The slave held in his hand a leather whip called the *nouthesia*, and if the child failed to respond to his teacher, the slave had his master's permission to apply the *nouthesia* for its intended purpose.

Now, I believe our clients are glad I named the firm *PAIDEIA Inc.,* though I must say that every once in a while, we have to apply some *nouthesia*—especially to obstinate board members who can't quite grasp their proper role as trustees of a not-for-profit enterprise, and to pastors who misconstrue their calling and imagine themselves to be school administrators. So in this piece I intend to provide both *paideia* and *nouthesia* as needed, beginning with "nurture in content and character" before I get to the razor strap!

Let's start with the difference between Christian *education* and Christian *schooling*. Christian schooling is a very special branch of Christian *education*. I regard this distinction seriously. Christian education is the overarching umbrella under which are personal and family devotions; Sunday school and vacation Bible school; youth groups such as Pioneer Clubs, Awana, and Christian Service Brigade; neighborhood Bible studies and other adult groups; Christian radio and television; magazines, books, and a growing presence on the World Wide Web. But Christian schooling is quite different from all of these. Only Christian camping has any parallel with Christian schooling because only Christian camping charges a fee to attend. It costs nothing to conduct family devotions, to attend Sunday school, or to listen to a children's broadcast on Saturday morning.

But Christian schooling calls for parents to *sacrifice*—one of the hardest words in the English language! In fact, the summons to sacrifice is two-edged. First, parents must agree to say to the government, "As citizens, as residents of this community, and as taxpayers, we're entitled to have our children educated in the tax-supported public system. However, because we wish to be obedient to God in seeing that our children are instructed in a framework of biblical integrity, we waive our right to our children's state-provided education in favor of Christian schooling. We'll continue to pay our taxes while at the same time paying tuition to the school of our choice."

That's the first and most obvious sacrifice, but what's the second? Generous giving in support of other people's children, providing need-based financial aid. To me, the weakest and most shameful aspect of evangelical Christian schooling in North America is the absence of substantial, meaningful financial aid. Why is it that godless, secular independent schools can offer millions of dollars in financial aid, while most Christian schools can barely account for such support of needy families wishing to enroll their children? I'll address that question below.

Thus, Christian schooling—unlike mere Christian education—calls for a double dose of financial sacrifice on the part of parents. It's no surprise, therefore, that when parents are called to such sacrifices, they increasingly ask the basic question, "Are we getting our money's worth?"

Let me respond to that question directly. If our calling—as professional educators or voluntary board members or pastors—is to Christian schooling, that becomes our special vocation. As such, we have a social compact with the parents and children who come to us for their elementary and secondary education, as well as a binding obligation to fulfill their proper expectations. One of my strongest assertions is this: The primary and only legitimate reason for your school's existence *as a school* is ...—you fill in the blank.

Usually someone will complete the sentence by adding "to save souls." Now, that's a worthy aspiration. In fact, salvation is essential to the eternal destiny of every boy and girl, every man and woman. I take some risk, therefore, in appearing to differ on the importance of saving souls. But is that the primary reason your school exists *as a school*? If the first and only justifiable reason for your school's existence as a school is to save souls, then I urge you to cease and desist from any further teaching of spelling or American history or the Pythagorean theorem.

I have it on the highest authority that no one ever gained entry into the Kingdom of God by winning a spelling bee or knowing American history or applying the fact that the square of the hypotenuse of a right triangle is equal to the sum of the squares of the other two sides. If saving souls is a school's primary reason-for-being, then instead of teaching how to spell *receive* or how to measure a right triangle or how Henry Hudson sailed into Delaware Bay in 1609—or how Johan Printz founded New Gothenborg in 1643, almost four decades before William Penn's settlement at Chester—we ought to abandon teaching the three R's and dedicate our enterprise instead to sawdust-trail evangelism and soul-winning.

But evangelism is not the primary or only legitimate reason for a school's existence. It's not the foremost reason why parents pay tuition. The founders and current board of your school could have chosen any form of ministry: a drug rehabilitation center, a home for pregnant teens, or a rescue haven for runaways. But your founders and current board have chosen to be a school! So a better completion to the assertion might be this: the primary and only legitimate reason for your school's existence *as a school* is *to be a place of academic teaching and learning where Jesus Christ is acknowledged as Lord.*

In other words, your school is intended to be a place where "the *paideia* of the Lord" is taught to children who need to learn everything they can, arithmetic to zoology, from men and women who recognize their calling to be nothing less than excellent teachers, capable of conveying what Frank E. Gaebelein called "the unity of all truth under God." Here is the mystery that secular learning has not yet probed successfully. Here is the wisdom of God that human knowledge can only apprehend when graced by the spiritual insight called *understanding,* or *discernment.* We are summoned to educate and to do so according to a biblical epistemology that accounts not only for what we know but for *how we know that what we know is true.*

How often I hear well-intentioned but misguided board members say, "We want to be an academically challenging school, *but…*!" They generally go on to say, "*but* we don't want to lose our fervor for Jesus Christ," as if to be academically challenging automatically leads to spiritual apostasy! Where are the brave board members who will say instead, "We want to be an academically challenging school *because* we want to honor Jesus Christ"?

No matter how many Bible verses students memorize, no matter how often they attend chapel, no matter how many professed conversions or missionary projects we see, a school that is less than academically challenging is guilty of defrauding parents who pay tuition to have their children educated. Nothing pious or spiritual compensates for any deficiency in being fully and totally and wholly a *school* to the glory of God, a school marked by teaching that transforms children's lives by pointing toward a more excellent way.

To achieve this goal, we need to reexamine some of the customs and conventions of Christian schooling in North America. Once more, *paideia* gets mixed with another dose of *nouthesia*! It's long past time for Christian schools to stop conforming to the standards of godless schools. It's also long past time for leaders in Christian schooling to content themselves with merely reforming their practices—especially in terms of how

Christian schools are governed. Instead, it's time for transforming the Christian school into an institution that will become the model for education throughout North America and around the world.

Christian schools are increasingly pressured into conforming to state standards with their inherent allegiance to political correctness and the blurring of religious faith and identity. Some Christian schools observe "the law of the Medes and Persians that cannot be changed" (Daniel 6:15)—and consider themselves good citizens for doing so. Many earnest Christian educators and board members and sponsoring pastors point with pride to the fact that their schools meet or exceed standards set by the godless state. They pride themselves on conforming.

And what is it to which they are conforming? Generally, two snares present themselves, especially to newer schools still seeking to establish a reputation for high quality or to schools not quite sure of what it means to be a nonpublic school. The first is state certification of teachers; the second is accreditation by some regional boards.

I realize that not every state is as generous toward nonpublic schooling as is New York State in its recognition of credentials for nonpublic school teachers. In New York State, the chief educational officer of any institution recognized by the Regents of the University of the State of New York stipulates that each member of the faculty—by virtue of his or her eligibility to hold an appointment on that school's faculty—is qualified to teach toward the diploma awarded by that school and honored by the Regents. Therefore, I can declare—for what it's worth—that no member of the faculty of the school where I served for thirty-four years was ever informed that he or she was delinquent in education courses for certification. This fact didn't guarantee that every teacher was superb, but at least it meant that we could appoint as teachers people who had actually concentrated their minds in the area they were to teach rather than devoting time to proving what "studies show."

But even if your state is not so generous—even if your jurisdiction requires some formal documentation—is there not some blessed alternative to the lowest-common-denominator credentials granted by bureaucrats in your state education department? If, as every objective survey confirms, the tested ability of most public educators is laughably below reasonable expectations; if, as the Department of Education reports, twenty-eight states certify teachers who read below the national student average and fifteen states pass those in the bottom 25 percent; if, as the Educational Testing Service reports, the lowest scores on the Graduate Record Examination are recorded by persons intending to enroll in education courses for purposes of state certification; if, as the National

Assessment reports, students of state-certified teachers score ever lower in national tests; if, as the lotteries to gain admission to charter schools show, parents are fleeing the public schools by whatever means possible—then why would any nonpublic school feel proud about the fact that its teachers are certified according to the same disastrous standards?

Furthermore, what parent wants to pay thousands of dollars of tuition to have a child taught by someone advertised as being only as well equipped as the local public school teacher? Why is any Christian school *conforming* to such standards? Christian schools must not join the drift toward eroding standards, or they will lose their distinctive as schools that are deliberately different from government-approved and government-funded institutions.

The same argument applies to school accreditation. Beyond question, our regional accrediting bodies are in cahoots with state university departments of education to guarantee an ongoing stream of graduate students. Some regional agencies dictate that a new headmaster with a degree in classics must return to the classroom and acquire an additional degree in educational administration—or else the school is threatened with the loss of its accredited standing. I say, take the loss and call it a victory! Look for another agency that will recognize the integrity and independence of an educational philosophy that leads your school to appoint a scholar rather than an educational theorist. The last thing to do is worry about *conforming* to such criteria.

Nor is it enough for us to concern ourselves primarily with *reforming* our schools. Not that our schools have no need of improved standards and higher expectations. But merely reforming our schools is no solution to the wave of charter schools in competition with traditional public schools or the rise of homeschooling as a threat to the status quo.

For one thing, merely reforming our schools presumes that the foundation is secure, the footprint is adequate, the rooms are sufficiently spacious, and only the walls need a little redecorating—if you follow my analogy. In too many places where I am invited to visit and conduct an institutional assessment, that very premise is suspect. A few pointed questions with guaranteed confidentiality and anonymity repeatedly confirm that far more than mere *reforming* is needed.

Recently, for instance, we've received several more requests than usual to help schools to separate from their host churches. On the surface, we find a seemingly amicable mood, but probing questions disclose tensions, rivalries, and even ill will. One church-sponsored school placed me on the golf course with its senior pastor, who told me that he didn't find the Christian school in the Acts of the Apostles. I replied, "Pastor, I don't find indoor plumbing anywhere in the New Testament." A few holes later, this same pastor told me, "If you have to have a Christian school—and I'm not convinced you do—you sure don't need to clutter up the curriculum with Bible courses." I asked why, and he responded, "Because they have my preaching every Sunday." At that point, I proceeded to intensify my game.

We find parent-governed schools and independent schools governed by a self-perpetuating board similarly in need of something more than mere reforming. I say this with all due respect to parent-governed boards: we know of no more limiting and suffocating policy than one that restricts membership to parents of current students. At least in the church-sponsored school—where board membership may be open only to church members—it may be possible to find trustees who aren't also current parents. When a board consists exclusively of parents, reforming will never be enough. Rather, what's needed is the legal dissolution of the school's bylaws and their rewriting to specify that the best possible persons—of whom some but not all may be parents—will serve as board members.

In the case of self-perpetuating boards, reforming must go beyond simply extending current members' terms and offices so that newcomers aren't left in charge every three years. The challenge to a self-perpetuating board must also lead to its making new choices as to who best qualifies to sit on the board. This means asking, Among those who hold fast to the principles on which our school is founded, who brings the spiritual maturity and breadth of experience, the wisdom and tact, the financial resources and connections to wealth? Who brings the entrepreneurial imagination and the experience with controlled risk? Who brings the highest level of community respect to our school? And who best understands the difference between a board member as volunteer and the professional head-of-school as chief executive?

Such an understanding leads, naturally, to a board's commitment not to choose, appoint, evaluate, promote, or fire those who teach. Let the board members tend to their responsibilities—including taking the lead in gaining financial support—and let the head-of-school tend to hers or his. Otherwise, how much good can reforming such a school accomplish? Indeed, the school board and pastor who fail to recognize the role of the head-of-school as CEO don't need reform; they need repentance!

Instead of *conforming* to someone else's standards, instead of *reforming* in order to have an "easy fix," our schools need the *transforming* power of innovative minds and changed hearts. The order is important: *Transformation* means *change*, and changed results begin with changed plans, generated by changed goals, preceded by changed thoughts; but it all originates in changed *hearts*. Become transformed, says the apostle Paul, by changing the way you think—by altering your character, your priorities, your vision, by becoming a new creation in Christ Jesus. I'm calling for transforming Christian schools. I'm calling for those of us who administer, govern, and support them to strive toward transforming them by the renewing of our minds—in other words, thinking-and-acting as a Christian school should.

To *transform* literally means to change an object in composition and structure so that it is no longer recognizable for what it was, only for what it has become. Just for a moment, think about your school as it used to be; now think about your school as it is today; next, think about your school *as you wish it to be in the future*. To what extent—in what specific dimensions—has your school changed from what it *was* to what it *is*? To what degree must your school continue to change to be no longer recognizable as the same inferior or mediocre institution?

Let me focus on the single necessity for transforming Christian schooling: financial stability. I'll make three points. First, our firm believes in cost-based tuition to fund the Christian school's mission. We believe that it is irresponsible of board members to approve a budget based on a rate of tuition that is deliberately and artificially depressed below the cost-to-educate each student in each element of the school's educational program. Thus the school must reckon the cost of every aspect of instruction—salaries, benefits, facility use, utilities, books and other learning materials, transportation, field trips, professional development of faculty, and so on—and charge what it costs to provide education to an individual student.

For too long, the Christian school has underrated its tuition—and thereby slighted the worth of its own mission—as if a vast and universal inferiority complex infected Christian schooling. No such inferiority complex compels the member schools of the National Association of Independent Schools to set their tuition at more modest levels. They know that quality costs money. In fact, one of the axioms our firm iterates and reiterates is this: "Lacking other evidence, quality is perceived to be a function of price."

Therefore, what disservice does the board of a Christian school do to its school by setting tuition at a rate below the cost-to-educate? *Answer*: limits the likelihood that the school will fulfill its stated mission and guarantees that faculty salaries will never support a reasonable standard of living. And what moral obligation faces every board member who votes in favor of a deficit budget? *Answer*: to take out his personal checkbook and write a check to help make up the difference.

Second, speaking of board members as donors, we insist that voluntary gift support—in other words, generous giving according to one's means—must take the place of fund-raising through product sales and events. Selling the school's mission for a T-shirt or a frozen pizza or a box of candy or a roll of gift wrap is shameful. If the school is worthy of educating a child, it is worthy of support—direct and generous.

Such support begins with every member of the board. As is true throughout the nonprofit sector, every board member is morally obligated to give in support of the school. That board member who does not support the school loses all credibility in decision making or policy setting. Some board members also serve on local or national boards. Try telling the local hospital or symphony orchestra that you're happy to serve on its board but you have no intention of giving financial support. You won't be invited to the next meeting of that board—nor should you be! Similarly, how many elders or deacons do not give regularly in support of your church? Not to give would be unthinkable, right? Why then is it not equally unthinkable for a school's governing board to permit any member to take a pass on giving?

Third, what is the primary purpose of a school's receiving financial gift support? To fund *need-based* financial aid. Remember my comment above about the paucity of financial aid for most Christian schools, especially in contrast to that of the godless, secular independent schools? Those schools ask their alumni and parents to give in support of economic diversity so as to guarantee that the student body includes qualified young people from impoverished families.

What have Christian schools been doing? For too long, Christian schools have been giving the equivalent of financial aid to every student—regardless of economic status—by underrating the tuition charged. Then come the discounts for the second, third, and fourth children—not to mention the discount for paying tuition in full, and the discount for recommending another family, and the discount for being a church member, and the discount for being an employee, and so on.

We believe that financial aid is the hallmark of Christian compassion, and the support of financial aid is the highest motive for giving to a school. The Christian school that does not offer an abundance of financial aid is less "Christian" than it claims to be. But financial aid should be granted only to those who can substantiate their need. The single mother with her three children, and the nuclear physicist and her pediatrician husband, also with three children, do not equally deserve financial aid in the form of discounts for a second and third child. Even faculty members should apply for financial aid rather than automatically receiving a perquisite they may not need.

I close with one last sphere of responsibility for heads-of-schools, board members, and pastors of school-sponsoring churches: the responsibility to sustain the vision, mission, and plan of your school's founders. Those who founded your school envisioned an institution that would honor God and His Son Jesus Christ. Have you remained true to their godly intentions? Far too often—especially in those institutions founded a century or more ago—apostasy has overtaken godly intent. Across North America we can point to schools and colleges and seminaries whose original documents and even the cornerstone inscriptions on historic buildings make clear the commitment of the founders to faith in Jesus Christ. But in time a succeeding board of trustees has voted to dilute, amend, and corrupt that mission by electing unbelievers to serve on the board and by appointing unbelievers to head those schools. From there, the precipice grows steeper as the unbelieving head-of-school begins to hire faculty. Like him or her, they too are lukewarm at best—hostile at worst—in their Christian commitment. And so it goes.

The lesson to heads-of-school, governing board members, and pastors in both "the *paideia* and *nouthesia* of the Lord" is plain: Don't mess with the founders' intentions. Don't tamper with the spiritual identity, the biblical warrants, the theological mandates that gave the school its original vision and reason-for-being. We need school heads, board members, and pastors willing to accept the guardianship of the school's mission and its plan for the future, under God.

This is our challenge. In our mission statements and in our educational philosophy, we must assert the Lordship of Jesus Christ. We must put Jesus Christ at the center and learn to live under "the *paideia* and *nouthesia* of the Lord." This means that our students will learn to bring every thought, every theorem, every act, every axiom, every aspect of teaching and learning—with rigor and without apology—into captivity under the sovereign Lordship of Jesus Christ, at whose coming in glory, "every knee should bow, in heaven and on earth and under the earth, and every tongue confess that Jesus Christ is Lord, to the glory of God the Father" (Philippians 2:10–11).

We are commissioned by Scripture to avoid exasperating our students; but we are also to make them thinking Christians—young men and young women who know what it means to think-and-act like a Christian. This is the primary purpose of Christian schooling: We have no other. This is our common mandate and plan: to make disciples in the name of the Lord Jesus Christ, disciples who will be able to think-and-act like Christians;

think-and-act with the mind of Christ about algebra, biology, chemistry, drama, engineering, farming, geology, history, industry, justice, kinesiology, literature—and every other letter of the alphabet—because they know and understand that Jesus Christ is Lord over all of these.

Our task—as heads-of-school, board members, and pastors of sponsoring churches—is to lead by example in transforming our schools by the renewing of our minds. That's the *paideia* of the Lord; that's the *nouthesia* I offer here.

19

LEADERSHIP FOR AUTHENTIC CHRISTIAN SCHOOLING: THE EXAMPLE OF LIEUTENANT GENERAL WILLIAM K. HARRISON JR.

The closing address at the 2003 ACSI Leadership Academy was scheduled for July 27, exactly fifty years after the signing of the Korean Armistice at Panmunjom by the United Nations' negotiator, Lieutenant General William K. Harrison Jr. An evangelical Christian, Harrison provided an ideal example of godly leadership and was therefore the focus of this address to Christian school leaders.

I am honored to participate in this celebratory weekend marking the twenty-fifth anniversary of the founding of the Association of Christian Schools International. I'm especially pleased to have this opportunity to address the Leadership Academy of ACSI because I know of no greater urgency in Christian schooling—indeed, throughout the Kingdom of God—than the need for qualified leadership.

This need for leadership is widely recognized and formally noted throughout our society. The New York City school system has announced a pledge of $30 million toward the goal of $59 million to fund its newly established Leadership Academy (same name as ACSI's) for would-be principals. Don't be jealous when I tell you that ninety candidates in New York City are going to spend a year in that Leadership Academy, learning on the job while receiving a stipend of $70,000 and higher.

Fifty years ago today—on July 27, 1953—evangelical Christians, as well as the godless world at large, were given a consummate model of what it means to lead. We were shown what God can do through one man who demonstrates by example what a leader must be.

Today marks the signing of the Korean Armistice at Panmunjom by the United Nations' delegate to negotiations with the People's Republic of China and the Democratic Republic of North Korea, ending combat, if not the war itself. His name was William K. Harrison Jr., and for me he stands as a heroic example of world-class Christian leadership in every sense of those words.

Some years ago, I wrote his biography, titled *A Man Under Orders* (New York: HarperCollins, 1979) You might be interested to know that he was a member of the governing boards of both The Stony Brook School and Dallas Theological Seminary. He was one of the founders of Officers' Christian Fellowship. His younger son Terry headed three Christian schools, and his grandchildren attended Stony Brook or Delaware County Christian School, among others.

Here's a sketch of his remarkable life. Billy Harrison was born into a God-fearing family with a long and noble lineage, including military commanders and one president of the United States. His acquaintances at West Point were Dwight Eisenhower, Omar Bradley, Matthew Ridgway, Joe Collins, and other icons of World War II, including his roommate Mark Clark. For many years Harrison languished at desk jobs in the military bureaucracy. In fact, his most significant accomplishment was almost relegated to a footnote in history: One day in the fall of 1941, when members of the U.S. high command were quarreling over the respective roles of the rival services, Harrison scribbled on a single sheet of paper a plan to reorganize the armed forces. Eventually his plan came to the attention of General George C. Marshall and was adopted as an executive order by President Franklin D. Roosevelt, streamlining the American military just in time to respond to the Pearl Harbor attack.

Following D-Day, Harrison's 30th Infantry Division led the breakout from the Normandy peninsula. When World War II ended, Harrison was sent to Japan to work with General Douglas MacArthur as chief of reparations, where he was able to assist American missionaries arriving in Japan. It was in this role that he first became known as "the Bible-quoting general," at a time when there were few recognized professing Christians in public life and on the front pages of newspapers. As the Korean conflict developed, Harrison was appointed by his friend Mark Clark to head the United Nations' negotiating team at Panmunjom.

Billy Harrison was an enigma to the media, whose attentions he ignored, and a nightmare to his Chinese and North Korean counterparts. The Communists had been relying on daily news accounts around the world to spread their lies and deflect even the most humane proposals for prisoner-of-war exchange. When Harrison discerned their tactics, he shut off the very pipeline on which they depended, refusing to grant a public platform for propaganda. Instead, he boldly walked out of the negotiations.

His first walkout lasted four days. When he returned and the enemy persisted in rant rather than reason, Harrison left again for several days. He kept the pressure on, and when the lesson was not heeded, he called a recess to the negotiations, lasting six months. Left-wing sympathizers in America and around the world demanded his firing, even his court-martial. But General Harrison held fast. When he finally agreed to return to the talks, the enemy faced up to reality and soon signed the armistice agreement—fifty years ago today.

What can we learn from Lieutenant General William K. Harrison Jr. about leadership? How does his soldier's example pertain to this ACSI Leadership Academy, which aims at leadership of a particular kind?

I've been asked to address the topic "Leadership for Authentic Christian Schooling," a title that demands four definitions. I offer them in reverse order: *schooling, Christian schooling, authentic Christian schooling,* and finally, *leadership.*

Schooling is our calling, our vocation, just as plumbing or truck driving or gourmet cooking is somebody else's vocation. We have chosen to respond to God's call by recognizing our natural gifts for learning and teaching the three R's or for organizing and managing others who do so. In his editor's preface to *Called to Lead* (Purposeful Design Publications, 2002) Kenn Gangel writes, "Central to the proper functioning of all Christian schools is competent and spiritual leadership, a cadre of administrators, headmasters, and principals who are *called to lead.*"

One's sense of *vocation* transcends location: the specific setting, or where, is less important than whether or how well we fulfill our calling. But it's also important to note that we represent schooling in the traditional sense of teachers meeting in classrooms with children whose parents have enrolled them for such instruction. Therefore, it is incumbent upon us to honor the social compact we have entered into with those parents, to provide a safe environment in which to teach their children how to read and write, listen and speak, calculate and reason, and interpret, analyze, and synthesize to reach conclusions—not only as a cultural obligation but also as an ethical issue, giving parents their money's worth, or appropriate value for their money.

Because we are intentionally committed to the sovereignty of God, the Lordship of Jesus Christ, the guiding presence of the Holy Spirit, and the authority of the Bible, our focus as educators is specifically on *Christian* schooling. But our calling to Christian schooling does not mean that we teach the three R's with any less rigor or as if we were conducting a Sunday school or vacation Bible school class. It means only that we see and understand what we teach through the lens of biblical revelation. We possess a Christian world-and-life view whose vantage point we find at the foot of the Cross and at the door of the empty tomb.

Parents who enroll their children in our schools do so—for the most part—because they expect our pedagogy to be offered from a Christian point of view. But that doesn't at all diminish their expectations that a *school* is a *school* is a *school*. What parents do not expect, what parents will not accept—what they are unwilling to pay tuition for—is anything less than *authentic Christian schooling*. Never mind how many Bible verses children memorize or how many missions trips they take. Parents will not be deceived by a watered-down curriculum or institutional standards that set "ministry" above the school's mission to educate. While parents will rejoice in their children's spiritual maturation, they also expect and rightly deserve to see evidence of their children's academic progress measured in part by standardized test scores and eventual college admission.

Authentic Christian schooling must be our commitment. We cannot justify a lack of academic rigor. We cannot excuse the absence of Advanced Placement courses or higher levels of foreign language, science, and mathematics by pointing to compensating spiritual factors. Just as none of us would accept as teachers nominally religious persons in place of earnest believers in Jesus Christ; so none of us should appoint to our classrooms persons barely capable of academic rigor and Christian scholarship.

May I cite one example among many? I served a year as acting headmaster at Westminster Schools of Augusta, Georgia. Founded in 1972, Westminster Schools of Augusta set out from its beginning to be an example of *authentic Christian schooling*. Along with a common pre-K–12 curriculum found in most strong Christian schools, Westminster offers both Latin and Greek through secondary school. In that year's worldwide Latin examinations, for instance, Westminster had forty-seven entries, fifteen of whom produced perfect papers, five of them for the fifth year in a row. In fact, Westminster had three of the top ten scores in the world. The results in Greek were comparable. I assure you, no school I know well is more thoroughly steeped in prayer and dedicated to what St. Paul calls "the *paideia* and *nouthesia* of the Lord" (Ephesians 6:2), nor is any school more committed to authentic Christian schooling.

This exemplary model brings us to *leadership for authentic Christian schooling*. Our consulting firm PAIDEIA Inc. conducts executive searches for head-of-school and other administrative positions. We used to offer counsel on qualifications for the ideal candidate—academic preparation, professional experience, personal attributes, and spiritual maturity—all of which you would anticipate as criteria for selecting a new chief executive officer of a Christian school.

Then we came to realize that a PhD with a résumé twenty years long, a perfect marriage, and a scratch handicap in golf, as well as exemplary Christian character, is useless unless he or she can *lead*. So now we counsel our clients to set proven, demonstrable leadership gifts at the very top of their priorities for a new head-of-school. The other credentials are important—indeed, essential—but *leadership* is primary.

What, then, are the characteristics of leadership necessary for authentic Christian schooling? And where does General William K. Harrison Jr. fit in?

We must grant at the outset that leaders are idiosyncratic. Each is different from the other. God graces each of us according to our own gifts and affinities, using the uniqueness of individual personalities and temperaments to the benefit of Kingdom work. But as different as one person may be from another, all leaders hold in common these attributes that I find in General Harrison: a leader must be *humble, prayerful, decisive, committed to discipleship, inspiring,* and *courageous.* Let's spend a few moments on each of these qualities.

A leader must be *humble.* Having risen to the top echelon in his field, General Harrison was unaffected and utterly unimpressed with himself. So too must be the leader of an authentic Christian school: not falsely modest, not diffident about the authority and responsibility entrusted by the board, but genuinely aware that it is the office that deserves unquestioned respect and loyalty, not necessarily the person holding that office.

Someone has said, "Behind every great man stands a surprised mother-in-law!" What should make each of us humble is the realization that no one person can lead an institution without competent and reliable assistance. I'm conscious of the debt I owe to my own wife, Lory, and other family members and friends, as well as supportive board members and headmasters, for whatever work I am blessed to do.

If you would be a leader, be certain that your loved ones and colleagues know how amazed you are to be placed by God in a position of responsibility—and how much you rely on their support for your own professional and personal well-being.

A leader must be *prayerful.* General Harrison told me that he rose at 4:00 A.M. on ordinary days—long before that on days when he was leading troops into battle—to spend time in prayer. Such prayer marks the life and witness of every believing leader; for if our Lord Jesus needed time in prayerful communication with his Father, how can any of us expect to succeed without prayer?

If you would be a leader, be certain that your leadership is prayerful.

A leader must be *decisive*. William K. Harrison Jr. saw the impasse at Panmunjom and decided how best to break it apart. In spite of criticism, he stuck to his decision. Some of his decisions, he knew, cost lives, but he would say, "You don't make an omelet without breaking an egg."

In his book called *Leadership* (New York: Hyperion, 2002) former New York City Mayor Rudolph Guiliani describes the panic and turmoil of September 11, 2001, and how necessary it was for him to be decisive and to be right in his decisions. Nothing alienates, nothing discourages, nothing contributes more to cynicism than a presumed leader's inability to arrive at a decision. Sometimes even the *wrong* decision may be better than no decision.

Not that I'm calling for a rash, impetuous, thoughtless decision-for-its-own-sake. Real leaders take whatever time is possible and necessary to make sure of the facts, to check precedent, to consider implications, to ponder the likelihood of unintended consequences. But then they act! They arrive at the decision that best honors God because it best serves the institution and the persons involved in the decision's aftermath.

Here is how a board informally evaluates the leadership of its head-of-school as CEO. A series of wise, prudent decisions may be interrupted now and then by a questionable or even awkward decision. But for the most part, the board observes the results of effective decision-making and determines whether or not its leader knows how to lead.

Early in my stint in Augusta, I visited a fourth-grade class. Before I left, the teacher asked several students to pray aloud for me. One child—I'll never forget!—asked God to help me "arrive at wise decisions." I kept that prayer before me in all the months that followed, and I repeat it again today for all my choices.

If you would be a leader, prepare to make decisions—hard decisions, decisions between two or three equally unpleasant consequences, decisions that will affect the future of another human being, decisions that will make a difference for eternity. Don't just agonize; *decide!*

A leader must be *committed to discipleship*. Several of General Harrison's aides and other subordinates told me how he had mentored them and thus advanced their military careers. Some years ago, at Estes Park, Colorado, I participated in a weekend dialogue about leadership. We came away from that extended discussion with one clear principle: *Leaders learn how to lead by "hanging out" with other leaders.*

That's why our Lord called a dozen men and lived with them for more than three years, setting an example for those to whom he would entrust the human leadership of His church. That's why the United States Air Force Academy and the other military institutions hire their own officers to teach English and ethics and engineering. They expect these men and women to make disciples of the young people who aspire to leadership. That's why medical graduates, with their freshly granted MDs, spend the next several years as interns and residents before being permitted to open their own practice. That's why any thriving corporation promotes its training program.

Yet we in Christian schooling have been slow to follow this pattern. Perhaps because of the press of duties or the pressure by the board not to fail or an absence of imagination or a shallow pool of qualified persons—or even a jealous desire to keep a strong prospect from leaving—few heads-of-school appear to take an active interest in developing leadership gifts and skills among their key administrators.

We need ACSI's Leadership Academy. But more than this, we need boards and heads of individual schools to be willing to take a chance, to risk a setback, to offer an opportunity for junior administrators to test their fitness to lead by giving them a project for which they are accountable in order to learn the meaning, the burden—yes, even the terror!—of leadership.

If you would be a leader, you must seek out and mentor potential leaders for the future. Otherwise, our venture in Christian schooling will be left adrift in the hands of inexperienced persons who, sad to say, will repeat our own blunders.

A leader must be *inspiring.* When I was writing General Harrison's biography, I met with veterans of World War II and the Korean War—most of them grizzled and godless men who remembered "General Billy" and how he had inspired them. General Mark Clark told me, "Even as a cadet, Billy Harrison was the most positive member of our class. He didn't know the meaning of failure." A veteran of the Normandy invasion said, "I'll never forget the sight of General Harrison riding on the hood of his jeep and calling out encouragement as we made our way across France and into Belgium." Another man said, "I became a believer not because of what General Harrison said about God but because of the way he *lived* what he believed." The president of The Citadel in Charleston, South Carolina, General John Grinalds—a Rhodes Scholar and later a White House aide to President Ronald Reagan—testifies to the inspiration of General Harrison's witness as an officer and a Christian gentleman.

Similarly, by your example to your administrative team, to your faculty and staff, to your students and their parents—even to your board members—you can be inspiring as you strengthen their faith in *Jehovah-jireh,* the Lord who provides.

If you would be a leader, you must offer inspiration that carries forward to action and to victory.

Finally, a leader must exhibit *courage*. To put it crudely, it takes a special kind of "guts" to be a leader, to expose oneself to the judgment and criticism of others by saying, "Follow me." General Harrison had that kind of courage in the face of enemy artillery and a demonic Marxist agenda. Harrison adamantly refused to be intimidated by either the Communist military or their media sympathizers.

If you would be a leader, you must petition Almighty God to give you the courage to lead. As you do, you too will hear the voice of God speaking as He did to His chosen leader Joshua, "Be strong and courageous. Do not be terrified; do not be discouraged, for the Lord your God will be with you wherever you go" (Joshua 1:9).

In 1987 Lieutenant General William K. Harrison Jr. died at age 91 and was buried in Arlington National Cemetery. I had never served as a man under orders in the regular military, only in the Canadian cadet corps. But when the twenty-one-gun salute was fired in his honor, it was all I could do to restrain myself from joining with family members—current or veteran military personnel—in a formal tribute for which I was not qualified.

Respecting the work you do, the risks you take, the challenges you face, the dedication you show to Christian schooling, I salute you as comrades in authentic Christian school leadership. May God bless and prosper the work of your hands!

20

SPEAK TRUTH TO POWER:
CHRISTIAN SCHOOL LEADERS IN A DECADENT SOCIETY

This address was delivered as the keynote to the ACSI Eastern Canada conference of board members and administrators, meeting on February 7, 2004, in Toronto, Ontario. As a native of Ontario—and a former Toronto schoolboy—the topic of this address had and has particular meaning to me, as I hope it will for Christian citizens of every nation.

I'm blessed to be invited to revisit "my home and native land" and especially to be in Toronto, one of my boyhood hometowns. I was born in Capreol, the northern Ontario railroad junction town. My father was a pastor and missionary representative in Hamilton, Beamsville, Guelph, Toronto, and London—where my sister Jeannie and her husband Wally Stephenson now reside. As a middle-distance runner, I held Canadian records—although I missed making the Olympic team in 1956.

But I'm not here to reminisce about those years or to sentimentalize my return to Toronto. Instead, as a naturalized American citizen and a short-term guest in Canada, I wish to talk with you about a subject which, according to the foreign press (by which I mean *The New York Times*), may be too incendiary for you to name without risking arrest in a nation that appears to be careening toward amoral tyranny. That subject is our task as board members and heads-of-schools, pastors and parents, to "Speak Truth to Power" as Christian school leaders in an ever-more-decadent society.

The phrase "speak truth to power" appears in various settings, almost all of them on the political left-of-center, if not anarchist. The exception is a Zionist professor named Troy, a history teacher at McGill University, whose views are quite opposite to those of the pacifists. But the concept of speaking truth to power is biblical to its core. Every prophet in Scripture, every apostolic martyr—even the Lord Jesus Christ Himself—spoke truth to those who, by human standards, appeared to be in power.

The text of Jeremiah 36 is a striking example. Prompted by God, the prophet dictates the Word of the Lord warning of coming disaster. His servant Baruch copies the message on a scroll, reads it aloud at the temple in Jerusalem, and then gives it to the religious authorities, who in turn present it to King Jehoiakim. Because it is winter, the king is sitting in his cold quarters with a firepot to warm him. As he reads the scroll, he takes a knife and cuts out anything that displeases him and throws it into the firepot. Soon he has burned the entire scroll.

So God instructs Jeremiah to send a second scroll with added warnings. Chapter 37 informs us that no one, neither the king nor his courtiers "nor the people of the land paid any attention to the words the Lord had spoken through Jeremiah the prophet" (Jeremiah 37:2). So Jeremiah ends up in a dungeon, his punishment for obedience to God in speaking truth to power. And what of the disobedient rulers of Judah who ignored his prophetic warnings? Read the horror story in chapter 39, and ponder its relevance to current events in today's Israel and throughout the Middle East.

Pontius Pilate asserted his authority when he warned Jesus, "Don't you realize I have power either to free you or to crucify you?" To this Jesus replied, "You would have no power over me if it were not given to you from above" (John 19:10–11). We may well ask, How far above? We know that Pilate received his governing authority first from the Roman general Sejanus, who had been granted control over the eastern Mediterranean by the emperor Tiberius. Pilate had been named procurator of Judea in A.D. 26, but in 31, his patron Sejanus fell out of favor and died, leaving Pilate isolated in the distant land of the Jews. Scholars now believe that Pilate's unsteady political situation made necessary his finding some way to appease the Jewish leaders when they brought Jesus before him. So, for Pilate at least, *power from above* was the power of both politics and patronage, as well as the power of Roman law, the will of the emperor, the Roman senate, and by inference the Roman people.

But we must also read into the words of Jesus to Pilate something even higher, something more profound, for "the power ... given to you from above" is granted ultimately by God alone. As that Roman citizen from Tarsus named Paul wrote in his letter to the Romans, "the powers that be are ordained of God"; or as the New International Version reads, "Everyone must submit himself to the governing authorities, for there is no authority except that which God has established. The authorities that exist have been established by God" (Romans 13:1). So it follows that human authority to govern, to legislate, to rule, to judge, to incarcerate—even to condemn to death—derives from God Himself.

But do the passages in Romans 13 and elsewhere calling for us to respect human authority preclude our speaking truth to power? I don't think so. In fact, as I read Romans 13, I'm very much aware of the context in which Paul writes. Paul is no fool. He is well aware of the current "powers that be"; he knows them by name and title. They are the Roman senate. They are also Agrippina, the widow of the late emperor Claudius I, and her adopted son—a certifiable madman—Lucius Domitius Ahenobarbus, known as Nero Claudius Caesar.

Nero's crimes were legendary, from cheating at the Olympic Games to win a laurel wreath to the murder of the woman who had raised him to emperor. Eventually—after Paul's death at his orders—Nero would blame the great fire that destroyed Rome on the Christians. Yet, says the apostle, "he who rebels against the authority [in this case, Nero] is rebelling against what God has instituted, and those who do so will bring judgment on themselves" (Romans 13:2). Does Paul really expect us to honor Nero as "God's servant, an agent of wrath to bring punishment on the wrongdoer" (Romans 13:4)?

There are several possible interpretations of this text: First, precisely as the words state, seeming to require blind obedience to the state and its authority because it is "what God has instituted" (Romans 13:2). A second reading offers the ideal, which is "do what is right and [the ruler] will commend you," since the ruler is "God's servant to do you good" (Romans13:3–4). Both these views seem to have marked much of fundamentalist and evangelical Christianity during my lifetime, with a commensurate absence of cutting-edge witness in speaking truth to power.

But another interpretation of Romans 13 has made its appearance, accompanied by a rise in civil disobedience with all its consequences. This third reading supposes a layer of irony as subtext—St. Paul speaking with a knowing wink, as it were, to those who perceive his real message. The words say that "God's servant" is "an agent of wrath to bring punishment on the wrongdoer" (Romans13:4). But who really is "God's servant" and who is that "wrongdoer"? An ironic reading reverses the roles so that "God's servant" is none other than the genuinely faithful and patriotic citizen who, by exposing the wickedness of "the wrongdoer"—Nero or any other godless official—and refusing to obey his evil commands, is authentically submissive to the Highest Power.

If such reading between the lines has any merit, then think of the irony of the final sentence: "Therefore, it is necessary to submit to the authorities, not only because of possible punishment but also because of conscience" (Romans13:5).When the apostle introduces the concept of conscience, he is reaching well beyond civic responsibility to the realm of ultimate responsibility to "the powers that be."

If we call ourselves biblical Christians, we too must acknowledge the source of Power with a capital P. Note that when Jesus Christ makes His final post-Resurrection claim, as recorded by Matthew, He states clearly that "all authority [power] in heaven and on earth has been given to me" (Matthew 28:18). "Given to me," not inherent or innate in Him because He is the Son of God, but *granted*, *vested*, *entrusted* by the Father, who alone has power to dispense power upon the Son.

Similarly, if we are biblical Christians, we will recognize that the transfer of post-Resurrection power is God's act through the Holy Spirit. At His Ascension, Jesus tells His remaining apostles, "You will receive power when the Holy Spirit comes on you" (Acts 1:8). In other words, the gift of the Holy Spirit is the gift of power. That gift—Paul assures his protégé Timothy—stands against any human tendency to quiver and quail in the face of fear. Paul writes that "God did not give us a spirit of timidity [fear that resembles cowardice], but a spirit of power, of love and of self-discipline" (2 Timothy 1:7).

Finally, the word Paul uses for *power* in addressing his spiritual son Timothy is the very same word he had used to describe the gospel—the Good News—to his Roman readers: it is the *dynamite* of God! Either we believe this, or we don't! Since we claim to believe in an omnipotent God, how do we act on that belief? And if God is ultimately in control, how then do we account for bad rulers and bad laws that flout God's holiness, God's justice, even God's mercy? And what—someone may ask—has any of this to do with my role in a Christian school?

We live in a time of such astonishing social and legal change as to weary the mind with recounting it. When Mark Kennedy first invited me to an ACSI event in the mid-1990s, neither he nor you nor I could have supposed that we would be facing the social upheaval and legislative shackles that mark North American life today. If I'm not mistaken, the most serious issue facing you in Ontario was whether or not the provincial government would recognize your schools for tuition assistance, as is done in Manitoba and Alberta. The elimination of such assistance by the Province of Quebec spelled financial distress for Protestant schools there— and we thought *that* was a disaster! We in the United States were worrying about what the rise of charter schools might portend.

But hardly anyone I know predicted that, in 2004, we would be facing the imposition of social engineering intended to elevate from their illegal and immoral status behaviors offensive to every world religion—behaviors still deemed too perverse for public viewing, even in an R-rated movie. I speak of the accelerating movement by homosexual guerilla warriors throughout North America to overtake long-standing social norms. By legislation or judicial opinion, they intend to affect common speech patterns, workplace rules and benefits, pulpits and seminary classrooms, movies and television programming, the textbook industry, local school systems, and eventually the family by influencing its youngest members to accept what their parents would not countenance.

You do not need this Yankee to incite you to anger and concern with facts already familiar. Each Sunday's society pages in *The New York Times* now carry accounts and photos of American homosexual and lesbian couples who have journeyed to Ontario to formalize their union, since Vancouver and the Anglican Diocese of New Westminster are too distant. Soon enough—God forbid!—their travels can be shortened to the People's Republics of Vermont and Massachusetts, whose court has now ruled in favor of full marriage for same-sex couples. What is it about the New England states? In my evangelical, Bible-teaching Episcopal, or Anglican, church on Long Island, our parish has been dismayed by the action of the Episcopal Church USA in raising to bishop of New Hampshire a faithless husband and father who divorced his wife, leaving her and their daughters to live in domesticity with another man—and that man participated in the sacred ceremony intended to solemnize the new bishop's election!

Such matters are still beyond my comprehension. Time was when sodomy meant something unspeakable. I knew an Ontario pastor who was driven out of his church for using, by a slip of the tongue, a slang term for homosexual prostitution. Time was when no politician hoping for reelection would advocate making lawful any human behavior so degenerate and essentially opposed to the propagation of the race as are same-sex relations. Time was when no boarding school would tolerate homosexual behavior for insurance if not for moral reasons. Time was when an ordained clergyman of almost any denomination who left his wife and children—never mind in whose favor—would have had his ordination revoked, not be nominated as a prince of the church. Someone has said, "If God does not judge our sinful society, he owes an apology to Sodom and Gomorrah!"

I have spent all this time setting a stage for the real point of my remarks. My real point is not to inveigh against homosexuality or infidelity in marriage or corruption in the church or the abandonment of traditional values. One reason is that, frankly, I'm not interested in "traditional *values*" as much as I am in "biblical *virtues*."

Please note that the distinction I make between *values* and *virtues* is the same as the distinction between *ethics* and *mores*. Social *ethics* reflect the *values* of any *ethos*. I recently attended a hockey game here in Toronto with Mark and Ginny Kennedy. Civilized, respectable, and law-abiding as we are, we chose to enter an ethos in which it is wholly acceptable to applaud villainy, encourage brutality, and hope for signs of bloodshed. As one wag said, "I went to a fight, and a hockey game broke out!"

Within the confines of an arena—or at least on the rink—a player in full pads and helmet can pummel another with legal impunity. His only restriction is that he may not use his stick; to do so would be unethical. But there are exceptions to the self-contained ethics of hockey: as you are aware, there are cases in which a hockey player has been sued for civil or even criminal liability because of his unreasonably aggressive actions within the ethos of the sport.

Why so? Because *moral virtues* rise above *ethical values*. Whatever the National Hockey League may allow, values derive not from what society approves but from those virtues reflecting the higher moral absolutes of a just, holy, and righteous God. So while a hockey player committed to faith in Jesus Christ will play aggressively and hit hard—as the values of his sport demand—he will not deliberately engage in unsportsmanlike acts intended to injure another player. He will honor the biblical virtues of his faith. For instance, he will not need to accept the role of "goon" because his clean, hard skating and stick-handling will be a sufficient threat to his opponents.

No, the issues facing us transcend the so-called "culture wars." It is not enough to identify, recognize, or become aware of the problems in our culture. It is not enough to conduct surveys or take polls and shake our heads in dismay at youthful ignorance or pew-sitters' biblical illiteracy. We must act on our knowledge, and we must attempt—under God—to effect change. This is the call, therefore, to speak truth to power.

Our starting point must be to recognize who our enemy really is. As St. Paul told both the Corinthians and the Ephesians, "The weapons we fight with are not the weapons of the world" (2 Corinthians 10:4) because "our struggle is not against flesh and blood, but against the rulers, against the authorities, against the powers of this dark world and against the spiritual forces of evil in the heavenly realms" (Ephesians 6:12).

The enemy is not the homosexual lobby, for all the energy it devotes to demanding legitimacy of its practices. The enemy is not the politician or judge who passes or overturns laws with which we agree or disagree. The enemy is not the pagan TV news reader or the secular editorial-page columnist. The enemy is not the amoral or irreligious public school teacher or university professor. The enemy is the one who deludes them all! The enemy is the same voice that, long ago in Eden, asked the insulting question, "Did God really say, 'You must not …'?" (Genesis 3:1).

The enemy is Satan, and the clearest evidence of his presence and power is the denial of that presence and power. Satan is never quite as visible as when scoffers discount his reality. But Satan is an enemy whose power is limited and whose destiny is sealed; he has already lost the battle. As Paul tells the Colossians in a passage vivid with ancient imagery, by His victory at the Cross and the empty tomb, Jesus Christ conquered Satan, taking away his power. Paul writes, "And having disarmed the powers and authorities, he made a public spectacle of them, triumphing over them by the cross" (Colossians 2:15).

My wife, Lory, and I have stood in the forum of ancient Rome. Looking down its broad boulevard, past temples and gates built to honor its military heroes and rulers, one could imagine the ticker-tape parade called a *triumph* because the victorious general being honored arrived in a chariot pulled by three horses. Preceding him was his own army with its display of spoils. Then came the captured slaves. But behind the triumphal chariot—either stumbling in chains or dragged as a corpse—came the defeated opponent. That's the picture St. Paul paints: *Christus Victor* making "a public spectacle" of Satan and his defeated, disarmed "powers and authorities."

With this reality in mind, how then do we proceed to speak truth to power? Certainly not as cowering plaintiffs, nor as arrogant and self-righteous moralizers. We need to know who we are and in what voice it is appropriate for us to speak. We are sinners saved by grace. We are alien residents of this nation, subject to its laws, but we are also pilgrims *en route* to the Celestial City. No, not the yellow brick road to Oz but the Way that leads to eternal life.

We are also leaders by vocation in the work of Christian schooling, which means that—whether as board members or professional educators, pastors of sponsoring churches or parents of students—we are summoned to the advocacy and promotion of our work, and when need be, to its defense as well. We are committed to the work of Christian schooling both in theory and in practice, both philosophically and financially.

To be a leader—especially to be a leader of a Christian school, whether as its board chairman or board member or head-of-school—means being willing to risk everything for the sake of preserving the integrity of the mission of your school. It means, literally, being willing—in the worst case—to close the school rather than submit to the ungodly, unbiblical mandates of the state in this increasingly hostile era. It means being willing to "speak truth to power" and accept the consequences.

May God give us that kind of courage!

In the spring and summer of 1993, believing that Christian schooling lacked a common statement calling for excellence in our schools, PAIDEIA Inc. produced A Covenant for Excellence, first signed by delegates to our annual conference at Eastern University, St. Davids, Pennsylvania, on June 30, 1993.

A COVENANT FOR EXCELLENCE

As colleagues in Christian schooling, we hereby solemnly declare and affirm *A Covenant for Excellence* in our calling as Christian educators:

Whereas we acknowledge that we are sinners redeemed by the grace of God through faith in Jesus Christ; and

Whereas we have submitted ourselves to the Lordship of Jesus Christ and to the authority of Holy Scripture as God's Word; and

Whereas God's Word declares that the fear of the Lord is the beginning of godly wisdom, knowledge, and understanding; and

Whereas God's Word commands us to make disciples of all persons everywhere, especially our own children, by the training and instruction of the Lord;

Therefore, we affirm that
- godly wisdom comes only by special revelation through the Person of Christ, Holy Scripture, and the whole counsel of God given by the Holy Spirit through the Church;
- godly knowledge comes by general revelation through formal and informal study and contemplation of nature and human nature, in pursuit of an academic curriculum, and in work and play;
- godly understanding comes only when the whole of life's experience passes through the lens of a biblical worldview, meaning that all truth is framed by biblical reality and everything that is ultimately of God is true.

We further affirm that
- God, who is perfect and holy, commands of us service that aspires to be both perfect and holy, and therefore excellent;
- lacking in ourselves the capacity to fulfill this command, we are nonetheless summoned to know and strive after the highest attainment of our gifts, while humbly ascribing only to God all glory for our lowly efforts;
- to keep back anything that would honor God is sin; to endeavor to achieve less than our best is sin; to commend ourselves for doing what

is only our duty is sin; to judge others whose achievement is either more or less than our own is sin;

- for these our sins of omission and commission, we most earnestly repent.

We further affirm that

- the goal of achieving excellence in any sphere of human service to God is essential to the good stewardship of our gifts and calling;

- both the example of Holy Scripture and the work of God in history commend the founding and sustaining of schools honoring to the Lord Jesus Christ by the excellence of their stewardship;

- both objective and subjective standards of excellence exist for measuring the quality of our schools and our work in them;

- these standards of excellence reflect both biblical virtues and cultural values compatible with Scripture;

- among the biblical virtues are the objective spiritual qualities of Christian living enumerated by St. Paul as exemplary of the life transformed and the mind renewed (Romans12:1–15:13): humility, sobriety, proportion, love, honor for one another, zeal, joy, hope, patience, faithfulness in prayer, generosity, hospitality, forgiveness, sympathy, harmony, peaceable behavior, absence of vengefulness, submission to authority, justice, good citizenship, fiscal responsibility, nonjudgmental spirit, absence of legalism and license, mutual acceptance—all evidences of the powerful work of the Holy Spirit;

- among those cultural values acknowledged by our society and compatible with Scripture are these subjective temporal qualities, exemplary of academic, artistic, athletic, and social attainment, such as personal or communal recognition for scholastic honors, artistic originality, athletic skill and sportsmanship, social maturity and responsibility, and altruistic deeds;

- among other cultural values acknowledged by our society and compatible with Scripture are excellence of professional skills in teaching and administering, business practice and financial management, maintenance of resources, and valid recognition by one's peers of work worthy of commendation.

Therefore, be it resolved by all those undersigned that the schools we found or sustain will be institutions where

- governing boards, administrators, teachers, staff, and supporters recognize the holistic and interdependent nature of our work together, as set forth in St. Paul's analogy of the Body of Christ;

- governing boards, administrators, teachers, staff, and supporters all recognize and act upon their distinct and separate roles and responsibilities in our schools;

- as those called to hone the intellect and shape the will of our students to imitate "the mind of Christ," our calling may be recognized and respected for its own unique contribution to the Body of Christ.

Be it further resolved by all those undersigned that our students will

- be stimulated, challenged, and encouraged to make the best possible use of the intellectual, aesthetic, physical, social, and spiritual gifts given to them;

- be offered every opportunity to excel in academic studies, athletic competition, artistic performance, and social growth, while keeping before them their need for spiritual maturity in proportion to their age and experience in faith;

- be provided with examples of excellence worthy of emulation, not only by their teachers and by their own participation in learning, testing, exhibition, and competition at the highest appropriate levels but also by the finest quality of human endeavor by guests invited to our schools or by visits to lectures, concerts, exhibits at museums or galleries, theatrical productions, and sporting events;

- become inculcated with biblical virtues leading to excellence, taught by example and precept in the living and teaching of those who govern, administer, teach, serve, and support;

- be taught only those cultural values leading to excellence that are compatible with Scripture, such as intellectual integrity or athletic courage, and fostered as corollaries to biblical virtues;

- be urged to recognize the grace of God apparent throughout the whole human race and in every nation and culture;

- be pointed toward every possible adult field of service worthy of God's call and their gifts, fully assured that God is no respecter of the hierarchy, favor, nationality, or gender of persons.

Finally, let it be our covenant together to examine our work daily against the highest standard of our Lord's excellent example of teaching. Let us also follow the injunction of St. Paul, who urges, "Whatever is true, whatever is noble, whatever is right, whatever is pure, whatever is lovely, whatever is admirable—if anything is excellent or praiseworthy—think about such things" (Philippians 4:8).

SIGNED TO AFFIRM MY COVENANT:

_____

SELECTED BIBLIOGRAPHY

Adler, Mortimer J. 1982. *The paideia proposal: An educational manifesto.* New York: Collier.

Blackmer, Alan R., ed. 1952. *General education in school and college.* Cambridge, MA: Harvard Univ. Press.

Blamires, Harry. 1978. *The Christian mind: How should a Christian think?* Ann Arbor, MI: Servant Books.

Eliot, T. S. 1940. *The idea of a Christian society.* New York: Harcourt, Brace.

Gaebelein, Frank E. 1954. *The pattern of God's truth: Problems of integration in Christian education.* New York: Oxford Univ. Press.

———. 1985. *The Christian, the arts, and truth: Regaining the vision of greatness.* D. Bruce Lockerbie, ed. Portland, OR: Multnomah Press.

———. 1995. *Christian education in a democracy.* Colorado Springs, CO: Association of Christian Schools International. [Previously published 1951. New York: Oxford Univ. Press.]

Gangel, Kenneth O., ed. 2002. *Called to lead.* Colorado Springs, CO: Purposeful Design Publications.

Greene, Albert E. 1998. *Reclaiming the future of Christian education.* Colorado Springs, CO: Purposeful Design Publications.

Haile, Peter K. 1978. Why I believe in schools that are as Christian as possible. *Latin America Mission Evangelist* (October–December): 4–5.

Harbison, E. Harris. 1956. *The Christian scholar in the age of the reformation.* New York: Scribner's.

Hauerwas, Stanley, and John H. Westerhoff, eds. 1992. *Schooling Christians: "Holy experiments" in American education.* Grand Rapids, MI: Eerdmans.

Hicks, David V. 1981. *Norms and nobility: A treatise on education.* Westport, CT: Praeger Publishers.

Hoffecker, W. Andrew, ed. 1986. *Building a Christian world view.* Phillipsburg, NJ: Presbyterian and Reformed Publishing Co.

Kienel, Paul A. 1998. *A history of Christian school education.* Colorado Springs, CO: Association of Christian Schools International.

Lockerbie, D. Bruce. 1972. *The way they should go.* New York: Oxford Univ. Press.

———. 1979. *A man under orders: Lieutenant General William K. Harrison, Jr.* New York: HarperCollins.

———. 1981. *Who educates your child? A book for parents.* Grand Rapids, MI: Zondervan. [Previously published 1980. New York: Doubleday.]

———. 1986. *The cosmic center: The supremacy of Christ in a secular wasteland.* Portland, OR: Multnomah Press. [Previously published 1977. Grand Rapids, MI: Eerdmans.]

———. 1994. *A passion for learning: The history of Christian thought on education.* Chicago: Moody Press.

———. 1998. *Dismissing God: Modern writers' struggle against religion.* Ada, MI: Baker Books.

———. 2000. *From candy sales to committed donors: A guide to financing Christian schools.* Stony Brook, NY: PAIDEIA Press. [Previously published 1996. Milwaukee, WI: Christian Stewardship Association.]

———. 2001. *Thinking and acting like a Christian.* Stony Brook, NY: PAIDEIA Press. [Previously published 1989. Portland, OR: Multnomah Press.]

Lowrie, Roy W. Jr. 1985. *Insights for Christian school board members.* Colorado Springs, CO: Association of Christian Schools International.

Malik, Charles Habib. 1980. *The two tasks.* Westchester, IL: Cornerstone Books.

Marsden, George M. 1994. *The soul of the American university: From Protestant establishment to established nonbelief.* New York: Oxford Univ. Press.

———. *The outrageous idea of Christian scholarship.* 1997. New York: Oxford Univ. Press.

Moreland, J. P. 1997. *Love your God with all your mind: The role of reason in the life of the soul.* Colorado Springs, CO: NavPress.

Nash, Ronald H. 1990. *The closing of the American heart: What's really wrong with America's schools.* Richardson, TX: Probe Books.

Neuhaus, Richard John. 1984. *The naked public square: Religion and democracy in America.* Grand Rapids, MI: Eerdmans.

Rian, Edwin H. 1949. *Christianity and American education.* San Antonio, TX: Naylor.

Riesen, Richard A. 2002. *Piety and philosophy: A primer for Christian schools.* Phoenix, AZ: ACW Press.

Sire, James W. 1988. *The universe next door.* Downers Grove, IL: InterVarsity Press.

Vryhof, Steven C., et al. 1989. *Twelve affirmations: Reformed Christian schooling for the twenty-first century.* Grand Rapids, MI: Baker Book House.

———. 2004. *Between memory and vision: The case for faith-based schooling.* Grand Rapids, MI: Eerdmans.

Zylstra, Henry. 1958. *Testament of vision.* Grand Rapids, MI: Eerdmans.